P9-CLN-950

A President in Love

LEE COUNTY LIBRARY
SANFORD, N. C.

A
President in Love

THE COURTSHIP LETTERS

OF WOODROW WILSON

AND EDITH BOLLING GALT

EDITED BY EDWIN TRIBBLE

LEE COUNTY LIBRARY
SANFORD, N. C.

Illustrated with Photographs

HOUGHTON MIFFLIN COMPANY BOSTON

1981

Copyright © 1981 by Edwin Tribble

All rights reserved. No part of this work may
be reproduced or transmitted in any form by any
means, electronic or mechanical, including
photocopying and recording, or by any information
storage or retrieval system, without permission
in writing from the publisher.

Library of Congress Cataloging in Publication Data
Wilson, Woodrow, Pres. U.S., 1856–1924.
A President in love.

Includes index.
1. Wilson, Woodrow, Pres. U.S., 1856–1924.
2. Wilson, Edith Bolling Galt, 1872–1961.
3. Presidents — United States — Correspondence.
4. Presidents — United States — Wives — Correspondence.   I. Wilson, Edith Bolling Galt, 1872–1961.
II. Tribble, Edwin.   III. Title.
E767.W837 1981   973.91'3'0922 [B]   80-22330
ISBN 0-395-29482-7

Printed in the United States of America

P 10 9 8 7 6 5 4 3 2 1

CONTENTS

ILLUSTRATIONS

following page 104

The President and Mrs. Galt at a World Series baseball game between the Phillies and the Boston Red Sox, on October 9, 1915 —two days after their engagement was announced.

President Wilson making a Flag Day address on the steps of the Treasury Department building on June 14, 1915, only a few weeks after he met Mrs. Galt.

A widely circulated newspaper composite picture of the President and Mrs. Galt released at the time of the announcement of their engagement in October 1915.

Helen Woodrow Bones.

Edith Bolling Galt in a photograph taken by Arnold Genthe in 1915, the official picture used in connection with the announcement of her engagement to President Wilson.

The President and Mrs. Wilson leaving a meeting of the Daughters of the American Revolution in Washington a few months after their marriage.

A photograph of President Wilson autographed for the crew of the U.S.S. *George Washington* on which he went to Paris for the peace conference in 1918–1919.

The President and Mrs. Wilson, from a photograph in the Wilson room at the Library of Congress.

The President and Mrs. Wilson and Dr. Cary T. Grayson during a visit to Princeton University.

Harlakenden House at Cornish, New Hampshire — the Summer White House in 1915.

Colonel Edward M. House.

Wilson with Secretary of State William Jennings Bryan in 1913.

A newspaper photograph of Mrs. Galt's house at 1308 Twentieth Street made at the time of its demolition in 1960.

The President and Mrs. Wilson at the opening of the first air mail service, between Washington and New York, on May 15, 1918.

A card enclosed in the President's gift to Mrs. Galt on their wedding day.

INTRODUCTION

In the spring of 1915, when Woodrow Wilson was struggling with the gravest and most far-reaching decisions any American President had ever been called upon to make, he fell deeply, heedlessly, boyishly in love. Public affairs waited while he spent hours writing long letters to the woman he loved and reading and re-reading her replies. This is the story of that romance, based on a correspondence only now made available to the public, letters unique in Presidential history for their passion and zeal.

Wilson was then the most powerful man in the world. A great and widening war was raging in Europe, and the course this nation took would determine who would win it. Winston Churchill, writing many years later in *The World Crisis*, put this into its proper perspective:

> *It seems no exaggeration to pronounce that the action of the United States with its repercussions on the history of the world depended, during the awful period of Armageddon, upon the workings of this man's mind and spirit to the exclusion of almost every other factor; and that he played a part in the fate of nations incomparably more direct and personal than any other man.*

The United States, except for brief hostilities with Spain, had been at peace with all the other great powers for almost a hundred years. Now it was being forced into taking sides in a war. Its elected leader was the man on whom these decisions involving life and honor fell. The country was not directly threatened, it had no treaties to honor, it had not calculated any probable geographical gains or losses; what happened was going to be the direct result of the decisions of its President. And the President, a scholar, politician, and man of principles, received at this time ("a gift from heaven," he said) the friendship and then the love of Edith Bolling Galt.

Mrs. Galt, a beautiful Washington widow, "an unknown person who has led a sheltered existence," suddenly became one of the most famous women in the world. She herself, in one of these remarkably revealing letters, saw her role clearly: "I love the way you put your dear hand on mine while with the other you turn the pages of history."

Both actors in this romance were comparatively new to the world stage. Elected Governor of New Jersey in 1910, Wilson had risen in two years and 170 days from a citizen who had previously never held public office to the Presidency of the United States. Now, only two years later, his New Freedom program had already accomplished the major domestic reforms he had promised. They included some of the widest changes in modern times: a new Federal income tax, tariff reductions giving consumers lower prices on wool products, paper, sugar, and lumber, and innovations in banking and antitrust laws that decreased the power of Big Business and charted a new economic future for the country. All these, however, were eclipsed by the war in Europe that in August 1914 had set the Central Powers — principally Germany and Austria-Hungary — against the Allies — England, France, and Russia. Germany was the dominant military nation in the world, and England the dominant naval power. Germany's objective was nothing less than the subjugation of Europe, and her callous invasion of neutral Belgium was seen as proof of it.

Wilson at first had been able to view the struggle with a certain academic detachment. "No single outstanding fact caused the war," he wrote; "really the grave blame rested upon the whole European system, a concatenation of alliances and treaties, a complicated network of intrigue and espionage which unerringly caught the entire family in its meshes."

Wilson saw himself as a possible mediator for peace, and he tried. After the usual diplomatic moves were rebuffed he turned to special emissaries. In this spring of 1915, his closest friend and adviser, Colonel Edward M. House, was in Europe for private talks with leaders of the countries at war to urge them to make a peaceful settlement (possibly with Wilson as the mediator).

England, with her naval power, determined that her enemies on the Continent would not be supported and strengthened by sea, early in the war set up a blockade against certain contraband to Germany. This naturally interfered with American trade and caused friction between London and Washington. There followed many months of painful, bewilderingly detailed arguments over freedom of the seas, the maritime rights of neutrals, and the legal nature of the varieties of contraband. Meanwhile, Germany said she was being starved by the British blockade and, in retaliation, in February 1915 declared a war zone around the British Isles. Thus began the notorious submarine attacks on maritime commerce that lasted, in their first phase, until September. There were only 21 submarines (called U-boats) in the first fleet that started preying on all Allied shipping, but they made history. It was inevitable that they would sink neutral ships, and when they did the outcry from the rest of the world led, in the end, to the entrance of the United States into the war on the side of the Allies.

The President had declared neutrality as soon as the war started, informing Germany that he would hold her to "strict accountability" for loss of lives and property in submarine sinkings. Whether actual neutrality could be achieved was hard to say. There were many intangible factors. For one thing, at least a third of the more than 100 million people in the United States were foreign born or of foreign-born parentage, and of these nearly nine million had been born in Germany or had parents born there. Time was to prove that real neutrality was indeed impossible. In addition, it was clear from the beginning that Wilson's own leanings were toward the Allies. "Apparently the Germans do not know how to keep faith with anyone and we are walking on quicksand," he wrote to one correspondent early in the war. As the fighting intensified he got pressure from both sides and found little help in conflicting reports from intelligence and diplomatic sources. And — to complicate all this — he was beset by a personal problem.

The President's first wife, Ellen Louise Axson Wilson, had died on August 6, 1914, just as the war was beginning. They had been married for twenty-nine years, happy years of the greatest intimacy; indeed, it was said that he depended more upon her than on any other person. Ray Stannard Baker, his chosen biographer, called her "the woman he loved utterly and trusted utterly." At his side in public life, she advised him on the gravest affairs, and his respect for her opinions was well known. When she died he was devastated: "God has stricken me almost beyond what I can bear," he wrote to a friend.

Ellen Wilson knew that he would feel lost without her, and she felt that he could endure grief but not loneliness and that he could not live without love. The day before she died she asked her doctor to promise to tell him that she wanted him to marry again. When he was inaugurated, only two years before the spring of 1915, there were four women in his immediate family: his wife and three daughters. In the eight months between November 1913 and August 1914 all had left the White House. Two of the daughters were married and the third was living elsewhere. The only woman in his household now was a first cousin, Helen Woodrow Bones. It was she who first noticed the President's loneliness and depression; only two months after Ellen Wilson's death she wrote a friend: "No one can offer Cousin Woodrow any word of comfort, for there is no comfort." Wilson himself wrote of his "intolerable loneliness and isolation since Ellen died."

The President's health was in the care of the White House physician, Cary T. Grayson, a lieutenant in the Medical Corps of the Navy and a man who became an intimate friend. Grayson was a handsome, thirty-five-year-old Virginian, urbane and likable. He had caught the new President's eye on Inauguration Day (he was already in the White House as President Taft's physician) when Wilson's sister, Mrs. George Howe, slipped on a stairway and cut her forehead. Grayson's efficient and tactful handling of the situation impressed the new President, who asked him to remain as his Naval aide and personal doctor. He stayed throughout Wilson's eight years as President, was extremely close to him, went everywhere with him, and became as much a part of the White House scene as the Chief Executive himself. Bernard Baruch, the New York financier and later a Wilson adviser, described Grayson as "the President's intellectually compatible friend who wants nothing, who represents nobody, whom he can trust implicitly."

After Mrs. Wilson's death Helen Bones, who had been acting as her personal secretary, found the White House a lonely place. Margaret Woodrow Wilson, twenty-nine and the President's oldest daughter, cared nothing for official life and now was in New York studying for a singing career that never really succeeded. Jessie, twenty-eight, the second daughter, married Francis B. Sayre on November 25, 1913, and was living in Williamstown, Massachusetts. Eleanor, twenty-six, the youngest, married Secretary of the Treasury William Gibbs McAdoo on May 7, 1914, and had her own house in Washington.

Dr. Grayson decided that Helen Bones needed friends and some diversion. His fiancée, Alice Gertrude Gordon, lived in Washington and knew many people, among them Edith Galt. He considered Mrs. Galt attractive and good company, and when he discovered that she liked to take long walks, he thought of Helen Bones.

Edith Galt was forty-two at this time, sixteen years younger than the President, a woman of beauty and personal charm. She was five feet nine inches tall, gray-eyed, and had luxurious dark hair. "A fine figure of a woman," wrote Colonel Edmund Starling of the White House Secret Service, "somewhat plump by modern American standards." She smiled easily and told delightful stories in a soft Southern accent.

Mrs. Galt was from a notable Virginia family, a direct descendant of Pocahontas. She was brought up in Wytheville, where her father was a judge. One of her sisters, Gertrude, married a Washington man named Alexander Galt, and Edith married his cousin, Norman Galt, in 1896. The Galts were owners of Galt and Bro., the best-known jewelry store in the capital. It was founded in 1802 by James Galt, who in turn left it to his two sons, Matthew W. and William. Matthew Galt was the father of Norman Galt, who, at the time of his death in 1908, was the sole owner of the business. He left it to his widow, who kept it until 1934, when she sold it to a group of employees. It is today the oldest business firm in Washington and the oldest jewelry store in the country.

After Norman Galt's death his widow continued to live in their house at 1308 Twentieth Street, Northwest. It was a three-story row house of red brick, indistinguishable from many others in the neighborhood. The Dupont Circle section was then the most fashionable in town, an area of hundreds of such houses and also of many huge mansions built by millionaires who had come to Washington from all over the country in the late nineteenth century. The Galt house had been built in 1889 by Norman's father at a cost of $10,000. Mrs. Galt sold it after she went to live in the White House, and it was for many years a private residence but later housed a dancing school. It was torn down in 1960 to make room for an apartment building.

Although she lived in the middle of Washington's most social section, Mrs. Galt took no part in that life. "I am not a society person," she wrote. She had even less interest in official life since she had no political connections. She had never been inside the White House. She had seen Woodrow Wilson three times in public, although she did not consider any of them memorable occasions. The first time was in 1909 when, as president of Princeton University, he was making an address to a group of alumni in the Bellevue Stratford Hotel in Philadelphia. She'd peeped into the ballroom out of simple curiosity. The next time was the night of March 5, 1913, the day after his inauguration as President, when she had gone to the National Theater and occupied a seat directly under the new President's box to see Billie Burke in a play by Arthur Wing Pinero called *The "Mind the Paint" Girl,* a play of such mediocrity that anything else happening in the theater that night would be memorable. The third time was when he addressed a joint session of Congress in April 1913 and she had taken her mother to hear him. Unable to get a ticket for herself, she was admitted to the visitors' gallery by a vulnerable doorkeeper whom she had bribed with a piece of candy. Two years passed before Edith Galt saw the President again, and this time she actually met him.

On a day in early March 1915, Dr. Grayson asked Mrs. Galt if he might bring Helen Bones to call. Eleanor McAdoo went along, and the four of them went for a ride in the White House automobile.

Miss Bones, usually referred to in the Wilson family as "dear little Helen Bones," was thirty-six, unmarried, a slim, short woman with blue-black hair and gold-flecked eyes. She was modest and thoughtful. The President himself called her "a perfect companion because glad to think of me and what is best for me and not anxious to talk and have her own way." She came from Rome, Georgia, where many of Ellen Wilson's relatives lived, and thus, knowing the families on both sides, was invaluable in handling the Wilsons' personal obligations to their relatives.

Miss Bones was very pleased to meet Mrs. Galt, and they became friends. At the end of a walk in the park a few weeks later (the date was sometime in March) Miss Bones invited her new friend to the White House for tea. At first Mrs. Galt demurred, saying she had not worn her best walking outfit that day and, besides, her shoes were muddy. Helen Bones assured her that neither mattered, that they would not see anyone. She was wrong. As they left the elevator on the second floor they ran into the President and Dr. Grayson. Miss Bones introduced Mrs. Galt to the President, and he invited both to join him and Grayson for tea. It is hard to believe that such an eventful meeting — as it turned out — was on a date that none of the principals would remember exactly later, but it is true. Dr. Grayson recalled that although they had actually met on that March day, the President had seen Mrs. Galt once before. One afternoon a few weeks earlier, when he and the President were driving on Connecticut Avenue near Dupont Circle, he had seen her and waved to her. "Who is that beautiful woman?" the President asked, but the matter ended there.

Now, the White House tea went well. The President enjoyed Mrs. Galt's conversation and her sense of humor. She was invited for dinner on March 23 with Helen Bones and Grayson, and after dinner the President read poetry to them. Then one day in April when she and Miss Bones started out for another automobile ride, they found the President in the car and ready to go with them. He enjoyed drives around Washington and into the nearby Virginia and Maryland countryside and had mapped out regular routes that he liked to take again and again, enjoying the same scenery. His car, a familiar sight in the streets, was a Pierce Arrow with right-hand drive, Presidential seals on the doors, and a top that could be removed in the summer. His escort, modest by present practice, consisted of a Secret Service car in front and another in the rear, both without the sirens or flashing lights that herald today's approach of a President.

In the spring days that followed, Mrs. Galt was frequently in the President's company, for rides, dinners, and teas. In fact she accompanied him to the opening game of the American League baseball season in Washington on April 14 when the Senators (led by the legendary Walter Johnson) beat the New York Yankees 7 to 0. The President was photographed throwing out the first ball, and seated in his box was Mrs. Galt, identified by sports writers only as "Miss Gault." Then one day — April 28 — he sent her a letter, the first of many he was to write to her in the next eight months, the letters that have survived as the record of their courtship.

Woodrow Wilson was fifty-eight, an impressive man who had assumed naturally the role of leader of 100 million people. Personally, he was lithe and active, described by a friend as "keen, sharp-cut, spare in mind as in feature, deft in his movements, a silent, intense worker, a lover of intellectual athletics, delighting in new and strong ideas." Weighing about 175 pounds, he was five feet eleven inches tall, with gray-blue eyes and hair lightly touched with gray. A severe stroke in 1906 had left him with a slight defect in his left eye, and he wore pince-nez eyeglasses, the style of the time. He had been a lawyer (briefly), a teacher, university president, and governor of New Jersey. A professional writer, he was the author of books of history and political science as widely admired for their literary qualities as for their factual content and philosophy. His style, formal by modern standards, was in the academic tradition of his time.

He was also a tireless letter writer. Hundreds of his letters to Ellen Wilson have survived. Mrs. McAdoo edited a selection of

them in a book called *The Priceless Gift* in 1962, and readers
of these letters to his second wife will naturally wonder if those
to his first wife were of equal ardor. The answer is that they were.
In fact they were so intense that Ellen Wilson once wrote to
him: "I think you have made up your mind to turn my head
entirely. Do you suppose, sir, that any feminine head is strong
enough to stand such deep draughts of mingled love and
praise? These maddening draughts have such an effect that I
am kept in an almost constant state of intoxication."

The letters he wrote to Edith Galt were as ardent. He was
always seeking the perfect way of saying "I love you." The
repetition is impressive, then puzzling, and finally almost numb-
ing. He knew, however, exactly what he was doing. "My heart
seems to need to have its ardor poured out in words," he wrote.
"I think we interpret these things to one another, Sweetheart,
just as a delightful means of making love ... I never tire of
telling you the same thing."

Wilson was obviously a highly sexed man. He referred to "the
riotous element in my blood" and to "my intensely passionate
nature." On one occasion (February 14, 1899) he wrote to
Ellen Wilson: "I am particularly susceptible to feminine beauty
and to all feminine attractions. A pretty girl is my chief pleasure ... girls of all degrees of beauty and grace have a charm
for me which almost amounts to a spell."

As the father of three daughters, his domestic establishment
had always been mainly female. He once joked about being
"submerged in petticoats." But he did not seem to mind. Much
was made of his Presbyterian background. He was called a
Puritan (although he liked an occasional Scotch highball and
enjoyed wine), and there is evidence of strict moral judgments
in his papers, both public and private. He was generally described as complicated, although modern authorities consider
him fundamentally a simple predictable man. However,
analysts from famous professionals to members of his own
family tried to explain what they felt were inner conflicts and
contradictions. Sigmund Freud (in *Thomas Woodrow Wilson:
A Psychological Study*, written with William C. Bullitt) advanced theories as varied as the generally accepted one that
"the rapid turning from his dead wife to Mrs. Galt was proof

rather than disproof of his affection for the former," to his original one of the influence of the President's father upon him.

And there are many far homelier conclusions, tossed off at random by less sophisticated thinkers but containing, perhaps, their own grains of truth about Wilson when he was alive. His sister-in-law, Margaret Axson Elliott, wrote of him in her memoir *My Aunt Louisa and Woodrow Wilson*: "He was too thin-skinned to get out and wrestle with the 'tough guys.'" Edith Gittings Reid, an old friend from Baltimore, aimed for the widest possible explanation in her book *Woodrow Wilson: The Caricature, the Myth and the Man*: "He believed that ideals could be put to practical use and be lived, and on that rock he broke, as all humanitarian idealists who have taken Christ as Exemplar must break." In all his life it is easy to see him moving from simple conscience to moral grandeur.

A biographer might seek in Wilson's excessive admiration for William E. Gladstone some key to his own secret aspirations. He mentioned many times that he found peace of mind in reading and re-reading John Morley's *The Life of William E. Gladstone*. One who looks into that substantial volume today finds, apart from long-forgotten fights over minor British political issues, an almost frantic search for the greatness in the man, in such passages as this one, which must have set an ideal for Wilson:

> His [Gladstone's] brilliancy, charm and power, the endless surprises, his dualism or more than dualism; his vicissitudes of opinion, his subtleties of mental progress, his strange union of qualities never elsewhere found together; his striking unlikeness to other men in whom great and free nations have for long periods placed their trust ...

The incessant search for clues to Wilson's successes and failures runs through all the countless volumes published about him. This book is certainly not the place to try even to summarize adequately the best-informed or the best-guessed opinions of the things that moved him, so this aspect will be left to others. It serves our purpose to keep thinking of him here as simply a man, a very human man, one described by Ellen Axson when — shortly after she became engaged to him — she was asked what he was like. She paused a moment and then, quoting Wordsworth, said, " 'A noticeable man, with large gray eyes.' "

As for the public man, where we are on firmer ground, it is true that to the world he showed perhaps a little too much reserve and aloofness; and this, with his long, rather pale face and severe expression, created an air of formality or remoteness. But nothing could have been further from the truth. No matter where he was, he was always in the midst of a regular, intense correspondence with women friends. He wrote long and affectionate letters to the wives of two professors with whom he had served at Johns Hopkins University (one of them was Edith Reid) long after such friendships usually lapse into brief notes or cards. In later years a fervent correspondence with a woman named Mary Allen Hulbert Peck almost created, as we shall see, a genuine problem in his life.

In the time of his letters to Edith Galt, a theme of loneliness was the dominant one and their constant pleas for companionship might give the impression that the author was writing with all the time in the world and from a quiet and isolated place. Actually, of course, he was writing from one of the busiest places in the world, the White House in wartime. People were competing for his attention every hour of every day on problems so varied, so complex, and so numerous as to test not only his competence as a great leader but also his time and patience, and even his physical well-being. He did not ignore these pressures in his letters, but it is clear that he could put them out of his mind. How he found time to write so frequently and at such length (and always by hand) is one of the mysteries of this correspondence. When he did mention public affairs it was because he wanted to share them with his beloved, and his comments were exceedingly frank, much more than in his letters to others. In one note containing an especially severe judgment on a colleague he wrote to Mrs. Galt: "Everything *will* out when I am talking to you." He sent state papers to her so that she would know what he was doing, frequently attaching comments to them. She usually returned them for the files.

The style of Wilson's letters is one of romantic exuberance, sometimes overdone, and frequently there is an oratorical ring to them; he was, after all, famous as a speaker. The letters are almost entirely devoid of humor. Newspaper reports of his speeches sometimes referred to him as a witty man, but there is little sign of it here. His friends said that he had a light side and that he told stories with a sly sense of the ludicrous. He was especially known for his Southern "darkey" stories, which were perfectly acceptable, even admired, in his day. A typical one, as recalled by one of his friends, was about an old preacher praying, during the 1886 earthquake in Charleston, "Oh, Lord, come and save us. Don't send your son, Lord, come yourself. This ain't no time for chillun." And there is a letter (elsewhere) in which he revealed what he did not like when he mentioned seeing "that terrible play of Oscar Wilde's, *Lady Windermere's Fan.*"

The Wilson-Galt courtship was carried out under awkward, almost impossible, circumstances. The President's moves were watched constantly; Secret Service men and reporters were always nearby. To discourage gossip (there was more than he knew about), he felt that he could not go to Mrs. Galt's house or appear in public with her unless a member of the family was present. Because the first Mrs. Wilson had been dead for only a few months, many people thought it was disrespectful to her memory for him to be courting another woman so soon. His campaign for re-election was coming up in 1916, and many Presidential advisers said, as word of his private infatuation got around, that he was making a serious political mistake. There was much whispering, but no one had the courage to tell him.

For the next five months — until the engagement was announced officially on October 6 — the President and Mrs. Galt wrote often and were together as much as they could be. She was invited to the White House, ostensibly as a guest of Helen Bones, but no one was fooled. Chief Usher Irwin H. (Ike) Hoover wrote that on many evenings Wilson and Mrs. Galt "would retire to the President's study and the rest of the company would find amusement in other parts of the house." Soon everything at the White House revolved around her. She dined there three or four times a week; wherever the President went provision was made for her to go. The long automobile rides became more frequent, sometimes two in one day. In September the President had a direct telephone line installed from his bedroom to Mrs. Galt's house, but even then he continued to write her many letters. He sent her an orchid every day. Hoover wrote: "The President was simply obsessed, he put aside practically everything." Colonel Starling told his mother, "He's hooked hard and fast and acts like a schoolboy in his first love experience."

The letters were exchanged under the most complicated circumstances physically. There was, first, the need for secrecy, and it was not easy to accomplish this. Helen Bones acted as a personal courier when the correspondents were in Washington. Wilson's letters could not simply be dropped into the White House mail system; often they were put in public mail boxes. Mrs. Galt's were usually routed through Chief Usher Hoover, whose discretion in handling them won the gratitude of the President. Sometimes when Mrs. Galt was out of town and the last mail delivery of the day had been made with no letter from her, Hoover went in person to the Washington city post office to look for the one letter Wilson was waiting for.

Often the correspondents wrote every day, especially when they were apart. On some days Wilson wrote three or four times, enclosing several letters in the same envelope. Many were extremely long, proof of the hours the busy President spent in composing them.

The letters in this volume were selected from the eight-month period from April 28 to December 18, the day on which the writers were married. They wrote only a few after their marriage and none was of importance.

The Papers of Woodrow Wilson, including all that have historical importance, are now being published in many volumes by the Princeton University Press. The letters quoted here will be found complete and in their proper chronological order there, along with the President's state papers, correspondence, and various memoranda. In 1939 Mrs. Wilson told in her autobiography, *My Memoir,* how she felt about making her life with Woodrow Wilson a matter of public record: "And if I take the public into my confidence about these matters, it is because the high office which my husband held robs them of a private character and makes me feel happy that they belong to history." But even then she did not publish these love letters. "No one ever wrote such letters as yours," she had written him, "and I feel when I read them that I am cheating the world in keeping them as my sacred own . . . that other people ought to be allowed to know you in such a revelation of your exquisite self and how the words express that which is to most people inexpressible." So, in 1960, only a few months before she died, she solved the problem by deciding that they should be held under lock and key for fifteen years after her death, when they could be made public.

Those years have now passed and here is the correspondence — revealing the "exquisite" side of Woodrow Wilson that Edith Bolling Wilson had felt the world should know.

EDITOR'S NOTE

There were two hundred fifty letters in the entire Wilson-Galt correspondence and the ones here were chosen for two reasons: to form a narrative of the courtship or simply because they were the most interesting. All were love letters, and repetition was no embarrassment to either writer; indeed, often it seemed an objective. I have sacrificed many of these repeated protestations of affection to avoid monotony, but I have left in enough of them to make sure that the reader doesn't forget that this is a love story. I have kept almost everything that pertained to public affairs and personalities of the times. I have felt free to cut within the letters, and thus some inconsequential day-to-day material has been dropped. All omissions — entire paragraphs or even a few words — are indicated by ellipsis points.

Alterations in style and grammar have been kept to a minimum. Since Wilson was a professional writer and Mrs. Galt a well-read and articulate woman, such things as obvious misspellings, unorthodox abbreviations, and wrong dates are few and have been corrected silently. With the exception of one or two by Wilson, all these letters were handwritten. In appearance his were models of elegant clarity. He wrote in a superb copybook penmanship, orderly and legible. (He could write nearly as well with his left hand.) Mrs. Galt's handwriting was more casual; sometimes it sprawled and some words were hard to read. She had certain idiosyncrasies; she almost always used dashes or slanting lines instead of periods and the uncertainty was compounded because her capital letters were little if any different from her lower-case letters. It was hard to know when she really wanted to use a dash, if she ever did. Her spelling was almost perfect, with one or two consistent exceptions: For example, she always wrote "seperate" even in sentences where she spelled the trickiest words correctly. She was not above jotting down a note every now and then in pencil; Wilson almost never did.

In some cases, notably Wilson's, I have taken the liberty of breaking into several paragraphs exceptionally long passages for the sake of making them easier to read.

Salutations and signatures have been left exactly as they were written. In a few cases, it will be noted, perhaps with puzzlement, there were no signatures at all. Since neither principal was writing this kind of letter to anyone else, signatures may have been considered unnecessary. Salutations were omitted occasionally also. Both correspondents were conscientious — if not always consistent — about datelines on their letters, and these too are as they wrote them.

Footnotes have been used where explanations were obviously needed. They mainly concern individuals, including members of Congress, governors, Washington officials, and many others who were well-known in 1915 but are less so now. In a few cases names appear without identity, and this means that I have been unable to find out who they were. On the other hand, I have considered it unnecessary to identify public figures of such lasting fame as Theodore Roosevelt or Herbert Hoover or Henry Ford, for example.

Words in brackets have been inserted in a few cases for clarity, especially in partial quotations.

For permission to make this selection I am deeply indebted to Dr. Arthur S. Link, editor of *The Papers of Woodrow Wilson,* and the Princeton University Press. I am grateful also to Charles P. Corn, editor-in-chief of E. P. Dutton Company, and Robert A. Rutland, editor of *The Papers of James Madison,* for invaluable advice and encouragement. I was given help and scholarly courtesies by Paul T. Heffron, acting chief of the Manuscript Division of the Library of Congress. The sharp eye and expert assistance of Linda L. Glick, my editor at Houghton Mifflin, are much appreciated. And special thanks to Emily, my wife, for moral support and many suggestions.

APRIL 1915

April 28, 1915, was a day like many others in the Wilson White House, perhaps a little gloomier. Colonel House left Paris for London, the last stop on his return trip to Washington after failing to convince the leaders of the belligerent countries that they should stop the war. The President had to write a letter to Secretary of State William Jennings Bryan to turn down an idea the Secretary had advanced that Wilson thought to be impractical. The sad truth was that Bryan was drifting into complete disagreement with the President over our course in the war. Christian idealist and passionate promoter of world peace by international treaties, Bryan seemed to deserve the label "pacifist." He opposed the stern tone of the protests to Germany and could not understand why Wilson did not make equal demands on England. He had little patience with those who sympathized with the Allies.

Now Bryan had come up with the idea that the President should make a public appeal to the belligerents to stop the war. Wilson, thinking such an appeal would be useless and preferring to keep operating behind the scenes in his peace efforts, wrote to Bryan on April 28 to tell him so.

News from the war was not encouraging. In the East the Germans were defeating the Russians in Poland. In the West the French were planning a great drive in the Champagne regions. The British were developing an ill-fated attack upon the Dardanelles to try to knock Turkey out of the war and to open a route for aid to Russia. The Turks, as it turned out, would

LEE COUNTY LIBRARY
SANFORD, N. C.

not be driven away; the campaign was abandoned and Galli-
poli became a British word for defeat. Italy was on the point
of joining the Allies, and both sides were trying to enlist Bul-
garia. Lloyd's of London was setting odds of 17 to 1 for those
who wished to bet that the war would be over by August 31.

Some other foreign matters were on the President's mind —
a revolution in Mexico, where he was trying to bring peace; and
Japan's moves to extend her power in China, which had led to
an ultimatum that Peking considered an infringement on her
sovereignty, causing alarm in both London and Washington.

There was news about our somewhat casual efforts at preparedness. All commanders of coast defenses throughout the
country had been instructed to make a thorough study of the
fortifications under their charge and submit recommendations
for improving and bringing them up to date.

As for local news — should the Recorder of Deeds for the
District of Columbia be a Negro? (Wilson had promised the
Democratic blacks in the Capital that they could keep that job,
or at least they thought he had promised it.) D. W. Griffith's
new moving picture, The Birth of a Nation, was stirring up a
row. Negroes objected to it because they saw it as a cruel slan-
der on their race; Northerners opposed alleged Reconstruction
exaggerations; and liberals worried about the Ku Klux Klan's
being shown in a favorable light. Wilson had been led inno-
cently into the controversy because he was a friend and former
Johns Hopkins University classmate of Thomas Dixon, author
of the novel from which the film was made. He agreed to the
showing of the film in the East Room of the White House in
February, shortly after it was released, and this was seized upon
by the producers as a sign that the President had endorsed it.
Now Wilson was writing a letter to Democratic Representative
Thomas Thatcher of Massachusetts saying that he had not endorsed the movie, that he did not consider its being shown in
the White House as approval of it.

The personal news was pleasant. The Washington Post said
another Wilson grandchild was expected soon (this was Ellen
Wilson McAdoo, born on May 21, 1915, daughter of the Secretary of the Treasury William G. McAdoo and Eleanor Wilson
McAdoo). And there was also a story that the furniture in the

Red Room of the White House had finally been sent out to be repaired, having been chewed up by beetles.

None of these matters required a letter from the President, but another one did: He wrote to Edward W. Bok, editor of the Ladies' Home Journal, telling him that he would be delighted for Mr. Bok to bring in his young son for a short visit with his hero. The next letter in the April 28 sequence, as it has come down to us in the official correspondence, was to Edith Bolling Galt:

The White House
28 April 1915

My dear Mrs. Galt,

I have ordered a copy of Hamerton's *Round My House* through the bookseller, but while we are waiting for it I take the liberty of sending you a copy from the Congressional Library. I hope it will give you pleasure — you have given me so much!

If it rains this evening, would it be any pleasure for you to come around and have a little reading — and if it does *not* rain, are you game for another ride? If you are not in when this gets to you, perhaps you will be gracious enough to telephone Margaret.

Your sincere and grateful friend,
Woodrow Wilson

The complete name of the book was Round My House: Notes of Rural Life in France in Peace and War, *and it was by Philip Gilbert Hamerton. The author, a British essayist and art critic who lived from 1834 to 1894, contrasted British and French social customs in an effort "to make different nations understand each other better." The setting of the book, published in 1876, was Autun, where the author had a country house, and the time was the 1870s, when France and Germany were at war. Wilson had admired Hamerton's gentle, wordy, somewhat banal prose from the time he first read this book in 1879, the year he was graduated from Princeton. He had sent another book of Hamerton's, The Graphic Arts, as a gift to his first wife when they became engaged.*

Mrs. Galt's reply to the President was quick — it was dated the same day — and it violated a rule of Washington social etiquette: One did not decline invitations to the White House.

1308 Twentieth Street
April 28, 1915

My dear Mr. President,

How very good of you to remember my desire to read *Round My House,* and take the trouble to send to the Congressional Library to gratify me.

Your wish to give me pleasure has been so abundantly fulfilled already that for you to take time to send a personal note is only generous good measure with which you fill my goblet of happiness — Thank you.

I am very tired tonight, and can think of nothing more restful than to come and have you read to us — or — in case it clears, blow away the cobwebs in another way, by another lifegiving ride. *But* — (that word that so often destroys my pleasure) I have promised my dear mother to spend this evening with her. So I must not yield to the impulse to come.

Just a word more to tell you how deeply I value the assurance with which you send your note. Such a pledge of friendship blots out the shadows that have chased me today, and makes April twenty-eighth a red letter day on my calendar.

Faithfully and proudly your friend,
Edith Bolling Galt

Two days later the President wrote Mrs. Galt another letter about Round My House, *a hastily scrawled note written after he had put in a full day at his desk with routine matters, including signing an act creating Naval Oil Reserve No. 3 near Casper, Wyoming, a tract which became better known as Teapot Dome.*

W.W. TO E.B.G.

The White House
April 30, 1915

Dear friend,

I am sorry I could not find a fresh copy of this book but this copy is in fairly good condition. I hope it will give you some of the same pleasure it gave me years ago when I first read it.

It is a great privilege to be permitted to share any part of your thought and confidence. It puts me in spirits again and makes me feel as if my *private* life had been recreated. But, better than that, it makes me hope that I may be of some use to you, to lighten the days with whole-hearted sympathy and complete understanding. That will be a happiness indeed.

Your sincere and grateful friend
Woodrow Wilson

Don't trouble to acknowledge this.

MAY 1915

May was a month of crisis. On the first day Germany took bold and "insolent" action. The British Cunard liner Lusitania was sailing from New York, and this advertisement appeared in the city's newspapers beside the announcement of the sailing: "Travellers sailing in the war zones on ships of Great Britain and her allies do so at their own risk." It was signed by the German Embassy in Washington. This — and the acts that quickly followed — proved to be a turning point in the swing of public opinion in this country toward the Allies, the beginning of the road to our declaration of war two years later.

The situation was complicated by differences of opinion within the State Department over allowing United States citizens to travel on British ships. Secretary Bryan believed strongly that travelers had no right to risk involving their country in war by sailing on ships of belligerents, but his opinion did not prevail and our outrage over the advertisement was stated by Robert Lansing, counselor of the department. Rumors grew that Bryan would resign.

The President's role was a difficult one indeed. His personal sympathy was with the Allies and Lansing's position, but he still admired Bryan's sincerity and felt that it was important to have the Secretary's viewpoint represented in the government. Things could drift along — but not indefinitely.

And there was more trouble on May 1. On that day the German submarine war involved the United States directly for the first time, when an American ship, the oil tanker Gul-

flight, *en route to Rouen from Port Arthur, Texas, was hit by a torpedo off the Scilly Isles. It was not sunk, but two sailors were drowned and the captain of the ship died of a heart attack the next morning. The United States protested at once. The Germans explained that their submarine crew thought the Gulflight was a British ship; they offered to make reparations for another of "those unfortunate accidents."*

The next day — Sunday, May 2 — the President had a short respite from Washington alarms when he went to Williamstown, Massachusetts, for the christening of his first grandchild, Francis B. Sayre, Jr., son of Jessie Wilson Sayre, whose husband was teaching at Williams College. Francis Sayre, Jr., later became an Episcopal minister and served for many years as dean of the Washington Cathedral.

The Williamstown trip was soon over, and Wilson was back in Washington conferring with Secretary Bryan, who had come up with a new idea for handling the submarine crisis: The United States would continue to make strong representations to Germany but would postpone final reckoning until after the was was over. The President thought little of this and turned it down. Bryan was losing every move.

On Tuesday, May 4, the newspapers reported that the Russians were being driven even farther back along a 60-mile line in Western Galacia and that the Germans had resumed their offensive at Ypres and were using asphyxiating gas. And on the evening of that day, Mrs. Galt dined at the White House. Putting aside the news of torpedoed ships, the nuances of neutrality, divisions in his Cabinet, and news of Allied losses in Europe, the President took her out onto the south portico overlooking the Washington Monument, which was bright in the moonlight of the chilly May night. It was exactly six days after he had written to her for the first time, only a few weeks after he had met her, and nine months almost to the day after the death of his first wife.

It was then that President Wilson asked Mrs. Galt to marry him.

Edith Galt's reaction, she wrote later, was surprise. She told him she thought that they had not known each other long enough and that she was not sure in her own mind. He agreed to wait. After she returned to her house that night she wrote him this letter:

E.B.G. TO W.W.

1308 Twentieth Street
May 4, 1915

Your dear love fills me with a bliss untold.
　　Perfect, divine.
I did not know the human heart could hold
　　such joy as mine.
But it does more for me, it makes
　　the whole world new.
Dreams and desire within my soul
　　it wakes more high and true
Than ought I have ever known.
For I do see, with sad surprise,
　　how far I am beneath your thought of me
For, lover wise, you've crowned me queen
　　of grace and truth and light
All pure and good.
In utter faith have set me on the height of womanhood
Since you exalt me thus, I must
　　not prove your wisdom vain.
Unto these mighty heights, oh help me
　　wondrous love I must attain!
Since love invests me with such
　　royal dower
The marvel sweet, shall in my
　　own life, by the same power
Be made — complete.

　　This little poem I learned years ago — little thinking how perfectly it would express what is in my heart tonight. It is long past midnight. I have been sitting in the big chair by the window, looking out into the night, ever since you went away my whole being is awake and vibrant.
　　I wish you were here so I could talk to you — for then I

know you would understand, and a written word is so cold, so capable of conveying more or less than we can express in speech. But I will try to tell you — How I want to help! What unspeakable pleasure and privilege I deem it to be allowed to share these tense, terrible days of responsibility, how I thrill to my very finger tips when I remember the tremendous thing you said to me tonight, and how pitifully poor I am to have nothing to offer you in return. Nothing — I mean — in proportion to your own great gift!

I am a woman — and the thought that you have need of me is sweet!

But, dear kindred spirit, can you not trust me and let me lead you from the thought that you have forfeited anything by your fearless honesty to the conviction that, with such frankness between us, there is nothing to fear. We will help and hearten each other. There will be no subterfuges.

You have been honest with me, and, perhaps, I was too frank with you — but if so, forgive me! And know that here on this white page I pledge you all that is best in me — to help, to sustain, to comfort — and that into the space that separates us I send my spirit to seek yours.

Make it a welcome guest.

E.B.G.

The President's reply — written the same night but before he had read her letter — began with these poems:

> When to the sessions of sweet silent thought
> I summon up remembrance of things past,
> I sigh the lack of many a thing I sought,
> And with old woes new wail my dear time's waste:
> Then can I drown an eye, unused to flow,
> For precious friends hid in death's dateless night,
> And weep afresh love's long-since-cancelled woe,
> And moan th' expense of many a vanish'd sight.
> Then can I grieve at grievances foregone,
> And heavily from woe to woe tell o'er
> The sad account of fore-bemoaned moan,

Which I new pay as if not paid before.
But if the while I think on thee, dear friend,
All losses are restored and sorrows end.[1]

I lay awake and listened, ere the light
Began to whiten at the window pane.
The world was all asleep; earth was a fane
Emptied of worshippers; its dome of night,
Its silent aisles, were awful in their gloom.
Suddenly from the tower the bell struck four,
Solemn and slow, how slow and solemn! o'er
Those death-like slumberers, each within his room.
The last reverberations pulsed so long
It seemed no tone of earthly mould at all.
But the bell woke a thrush; and with a call
He roused his mate, then poured a tide of song;
"Morning is coming, fresh, and clear, and blue."
Said that bright song; and then I thought of you.[2]

I did my best to do your bidding, for it is in pleasing you; but grief and dismay are terrible companions in the still night, with hope lying dead and I could not endure them beyond the dawn. I will do better. They shall not conquer me. I shall get used to them, as I have to many others like them, and be by degrees stronger than they are, — and with God's help, and yours! I wonder what God intends to do with me, having cast me off?

Please promise *not* to go to the Orient. Don't put *every* burden on me.

Your devoted friend, and your dependent friend,
W.W.

After he wrote this letter the President received Mrs. Galt's pledge of her friendship, and he wrote another, happier one:

---

1 Shakespeare's Sonnet XXX.
2 Unidentified.

W.W. TO E.B.G.   The White House
                                                     5 May 1915

Dear, dear friend,

I am infinitely tired tonight — in brain and body and spirit — for it is still, for me, practically the same day on which I put my happiness to the test, — and I do not know that I can say anything as I would say it; but there are some things I must *try* to say before the still watches come again in which the things unsaid hurt so and cry out in the heart to be uttered.

It was this morning — while I lay awake thinking of you in all your wonderful loveliness and of my pitiful inability to satisfy and win you, to show you the true heart of my need, and of my nature, — that you wrote that wonderful note Helen brought me today, with its fresh revelation of your wonderful gifts of heart and mind, — the most moving and altogether beautiful note I ever read, whose possession makes me rich; and I must thank you for that before I try to sleep, — thank you from the bottom of a heart that your words touch as if they knew every key of it. I am proud beyond words that you should have thought of me in such terms and put the thoughts into such exquisite, comprehending words.

God had indeed been good to me to bring such a creature as you into my life. Every glimpse I am permitted to get of the secret depths of you I find them deeper and purer and more beautiful than I knew or had dreamed of. If you cannot give me *all* that I want — what my heart now finds it hard to breathe without — it is because I am not worthy. I know instinctively you *could* give it if I were — and if you understood, — understood the boy's heart that is in me and the simplicity of my need, which you could fill so that all my days could be radiant.

Browning speaks somewhere of a man having two sides, one that he turns to the world, another that he shows a woman when he loves her.[1] I think you have not opened your eyes to see that other side yet, though I laid it bare to you without

---

[1] God be thanked, the meanest of his creatures
   Boasts two soul-sides, one to face the world with,
   One to show a woman when he loves her!
   From "One Word More" by Robert Browning

reserve and I must have a chance to show it to you. These are the supreme years of my life. Minutes count with me now more than days will some time, — and my *need* is supreme. I know you can fill it because you do fill it every moment I am with you. Every power in me is happily free when you are by, with the light in your eyes I love so.

You have not stopped thinking of me as the public man! You have not yet looked with full comprehension on your friend and lover, Woodrow Wilson, whose heart must be satisfied if his life is to tell for all it might tell for and who would want you — oh with *such* a longing whether he had even been heard of or not. What you have given me is inestimable, precious to me beyond words, beautiful and a very fountain of happiness. Perhaps the rest will come when you see how simple, how natural, how inevitable an addition it is — always provided you think me worthy of love and of all a woman can give. You will not *forbid* the thought to come, will you? Here stands your friend, a longing man, in the midst of a world's affairs — a world that knows nothing of the heart he has shown you and which would as lief break it as not, but which he cannot face with his full strength or with the full zest of keen endeavors unless you come into that heart and take possession, not because he is exposed but because, simply and only because, you love him. *Can* you love him? You have given him all but that — in what wonderful measure and with what exquisite insight — and he has all but the utmost of what he needs (this precious note and the sweet words you spoke, the sweet touch of your hand last night prove that). Will you come to him some time, without reserve and make his strength complete?

Forgive all errors in what I have said, — read it with your heart, as I know you can, and will, and know that, whatever happens, you will have the companionship, the gratitude, the loyalty and the devoted, romantic love of

Your devoted friend
Woodrow Wilson

What would I not give for words that would really make you see and feel what is in my heart! You *could* not shrink!

W.W.

How much of my life has gone into this note you will never know, unless, some day —

Do not misunderstand. What I have now at your generous hands is infinitely precious to me. It would kill me to part with it, — I could not and I hope you could not. And I will be patient, patient without end, to see what, if anything, the future may have in store for me.

During the evening when Wilson was proposing to Edith Galt something that was troubling him came into the conversation. In her next letter, written at midnight the next day, Mrs. Galt referred to the subject, one which gave the President so much pain that he did not wish to discuss it: the threatened resignation of his Secretary of State.

William Jennings Bryan was then fifty-five, a Democratic politician who attracted many ardent followers. He was called "the Great Commoner," and a man in sharper contrast to the patrician President could not be imagined. He had come the long, hard way from county politics in Nebraska to national leadership by way of the House of Representatives, countless thousands of crowd-stirring speeches (he was noted as an orator), innumerable precinct meetings, and an unsuccessful campaign for the United States Senate. Three times — in 1896, 1900, and 1908 — he had won his party's nomination for the Presidency and three times he had been defeated. What he won was a following that took pride in backing a gallant campaigner, a fighter for lost causes. His influence in the party was still great in the 1912 convention. He made a shrewd move, disavowing personal ambition and throwing his strength to Wilson, who then won the nomination. The grateful new President made him his Secretary of State although Bryan's inclinations were mainly toward domestic affairs. (The decision is easier to understand when it is recalled that Wilson had not even mentioned foreign affairs in his inaugural address.)

It was not long before Wilson's administration was dealing almost exclusively with foreign matters, and Bryan quickly found himself in trouble over a long-held and sincere belief that war was only sanctioned murder. Before the beginning of the war of 1914 he had told Wilson that he wanted to make

achievement of international treaties the center of his adminis-
tration of the State Department. A very practical man in the
turmoil of national politics, he wanted to operate on a higher
plane in his conduct of foreign relations. His high-mindedness
was admired — if not emulated — by many. "He was too good
a Christian to run a naughty world," said a Cabinet colleague,
Franklin K. Lane, Secretary of the Interior.

Thus, in the spring of 1915, while events in Europe were put-
ting pressures on the United States, its peace-loving Secretary of
State was being pushed into the middle of a war. None of the
belligerents wanted to antagonize the most powerful neutral
nation in the world, but they were openly violating neutral
rights, balancing their needs against the displeasures and pos-
sible actions of the United States. England, moving to bring all
neutral trade and shipping under her control, extended her
blockade of the German ports, and the contraband list grew to
cover cotton, wool, leather, rubber, copper, and chemicals —
all vital to an economy trying to fight a war — and even food
was included. England seized cargoes bound for the neutral
nations of Europe on the ground that their ultimate destination
was the Central Powers. United States parcels were seized in
the mails by Britain, and Washington's protests took on a tone
of anger. The United States made frequent objections, but
England refused to change the system; her only concession was
a promise of fair settlements for legitimate losses.

Sentiment in this country was on the side of the Allies, but
Bryan kept pointing to British violations of international law.
He branded the British blockade a move to starve women and
children in Germany. He was particularly outraged that Amer-
ican citizens were still allowed to sail on British vessels. He
could not accept the inconsistency of the American government
in warning its citizens to flee from trouble in a revolution in
Mexico but failing to discourage travel on ships liable to be tor-
pedoed in the Atlantic. Why should the United States be asked
to risk war in behalf of an individual whose action in sailing on
the ship might be considered reckless in the first place? He was
opposed to American firms' lending money to belligerents and
made a moral issue over claims for loss of merchandise in sub-
marine sinkings: "We cannot afford to make merchandise a

cause for use of force . . . any dispute about merchandise can be settled after the war."

Bryan fought the double standards of our neutrality policy, but it was a losing battle. Sympathy for the British ran deep in this country. The plight of Belgium's invasion by Germany in violation of earlier promises and admiration for France's fight against invasion had an enormous effect on the way Americans felt. There also was the fact that England's violations of our neutral rights were concerned chiefly with property whereas Germany's violations involved loss of lives. Bryan was blind to these things; he could see only a literal neutrality. Against his obstinacy stood the President's determination not to sacrifice or even to debate any American rights. In all his notes to Germany he had merely stated these rights; he considered them not open to debate.

E.B.G. TO W.W.

May 5–6, 1915

My Precious One,

. . . I did want to ask you more about the resignation of "W.J.B." but saw the subject troubled you so would not let myself discuss it. I think it will be a blessing to get rid of him and might as well frankly say I would like to be appointed in his place — then I should have to have daily conferences with you — and I faithfully promise not to interfere in any way with your continuing to do all the work!

I know how you feel about being loyal to this person, but if he deserts you now he is entitled to small courtesy or consideration and I would not hesitate to put myself on record if he does so scurvy a thing.

Remember when you are sitting silent and with Presidential Presbyterian air in church tomorrow that just a few squares away there is someone who loves you, who says a fervent prayer for "all in authority" and who longs to have you with her where she can turn to find, in your dear eyes, the answer to so much that is in her heart . . .

Always,
Edith

Wilson's reply on May 6 contained an implication — not otherwise brought out here or elsewhere — that Mrs. Galt may have been unhappy in her first marriage:

W.W. TO E.B.G.

The White House
May 6, 1915

. . . That note you wrote me yesterday before the dawn ("before the dawn!") lies before me, my little charter of liberty! and I realize that I have not answered it — except in my heart. I can hardly see to write for the tears as I lift my eyes from it, — the tears of joy and sweet yearning. Yes, dear loving friend, "we will help and hearten each other." My heart sends you back your words — oh, with what gladness and pride, — "I pledge you all that is best in me — to help, to sustain, to comfort." "Into the space that separates us I send my spirit to seek yours. Make it a welcome guest!" How welcome a guest your spirit is, my dear, I hope God will give me the grace to show you — without selfishness of any sort. And how proud I am to be its host — and its haven of welcome — how proud and how happy! For there never was a more beautiful spirit, a spirit more altogether lovely. I will be its knight — serve it, not myself, and feel myself grow a better, purer man in the service! . . .

It grieves me that you should have been unhappy, that clouds should ever have shadowed you who are by nature and every sweet gift so radiant and full of the perfect light that shines in the heart of a completely gifted woman. If I can never have the privilege of shielding you from all the world, I can at least shield you from anything that is selfish in me and let no shadow darken your thoughts that may gather in my sky. It will be my study and my joy to make you *glad* that you met me.

My love shall never stand in your way. You have had too little joy in your life; I shall try to add to its stock, not take away from it! I would rather see light — the light of joy and complete happiness — in those eyes than have anything I can think of for myself. I seem to have been put into the world to serve, not to take, and serve I will to the utmost and demand nothing in return. It is so a man may show himself worthy, perhaps, to call himself

Your devoted friend,
Woodrow Wilson

After the President left a Cabinet meeting on Friday, May 7, and before he could start a planned golf game, Rudolf Forster, his executive secretary, handed him a cablegram containing news that was to dominate his thoughts and actions for months to come.

A German submarine had sunk the Lusitania without warning about fifteen miles off the southwestern coast of Ireland, and 1198 lives were lost, including 128 Americans. Since the Germans had issued a warning to passengers sailing on the liner it was widely believed that the sinking was premeditated.

This shocking act stunned the country, and it was plain to many that it would be only a matter of time until we were at war. The sinking was also one of the world's great disasters: The 32,000-ton luxury Cunard liner was the queen of the Atlantic fleet, the fastest of its kind, making the crossing in four and a half days. It was the ship of the rich and the famous: On this trip were Alfred Gwynne Vanderbilt, the financier; Charles Frohman, the famous play producer; and Elbert Hubbard, probably the most widely read writer of his time.

Wilson's first wish was to isolate himself from the unbelievably enormous public outcry that arose. Upon hearing the news, he went immediately to his private study on the second floor of the White House and at first did not allow himself to hear all the dramatic details; he wanted to think over the full implications of the gravest crisis of his Presidency as dispassionately as possible. Something had to be done soon, however, and the next day, Saturday, May 8, this statement was released by the White House:

"Of course the President feels the gravity of the situation to the utmost, and is considering very earnestly, but very calmly, the right course of action to pursue. He knows that the people of the country wish and expect him to act with deliberation as well as with firmness."

*The President's calmness was not shared by everyone. News-
paper headlines were the largest ever and editorials the strong-
est. The White House received 2000 telegrams in the first two
days, almost all demanding action against Germany. Colonel
House cabled from London urging that the President demand
that Germany stop making war on noncombatants. "WE CAN NO
LONGER REMAIN NEUTRAL SPECTATORS," he said. Walter Hines
Page, our Ambassador in London, had felt from the beginning
that we should give greater support to Great Britain, and now
his letters became more ardent than ever.*

*Five days later a report was published in London that further
aroused public opinion in this country against Germany. It
detailed alleged atrocities in Belgium and pictured the Huns as
a hated race. The fact that the chairman of the committee making the report, Lord Bryce, was well known as a former ambassador in Washington, gave it further credence here.*

*The President began drafting the formal protest over the
Lusitania on his typewriter, correcting it in his own handwriting. From the first, he handled the entire matter personally.
Three days later, on May 10, he went to Philadelphia to fill a
long-planned engagement, an address to 4000 newly natural-
ized citizens. It was in this speech that he used a phrase that
was to haunt him:*

> The example of America must be the example not merely of
> peace because it will not fight, but of peace because peace is the
> elevating and healing influence in the world and strife is not.
> There is such a thing as a man being too proud to fight. There
> is such a thing as a nation being so right that it does not have to
> convince others by force that it is right.

*The phrase "too proud to fight" aroused the hopes of pacifists
to such an extent that Wilson had to explain that it was not a
declaration of policy on the Lusitania but merely an expression
of "a personal attitude." Events that followed immediately after-
ward proved that the words were indeed ill-chosen. The remark
was sufficiently disavowed, but it was not quickly forgotten.*

*The day after this speech the German Ambassador, Count
Johann von Bernstorff, expressed regrets over the loss of the
American lives, but his words did not impress Wilson. The*

wording of the first Lusitania *protest, dated May 13, was reviewed carefully at a Cabinet meeting, with Secretary Bryan urging that the language be toned down. The advocates of strong words, led by Wilson himself, won, however, and the note went to Berlin condemning the submarine warfare and upholding the right of American citizens to travel anywhere they wished. It was a virtual demand that the Germans abandon submarine warfare on unarmed merchantmen. Bryan persuaded the President to issue a statement suggesting arbitration of the issue at the same time the note was sent. The statement was drafted, but under stronger pressure from Lansing and others, Wilson decided not to send it. Bryan had lost again.*

The public demands for action were growing into an almost irresistible force, but there were also those who understood the enormity and complexity of the President's problem. Alton B. Parker, the Democratic Presidential nominee in 1904, said: "The attempt to persuade the public what action the Lusitania *requires the President to take is unfair to him . . . he alone must bear the heavy burden of responsibility."*

Wilson certainly made no effort to evade his responsibility, but he tried to make his life as bearable — even as pleasant — as he could under the circumstances. He sought, first, the company of Edith Bolling Galt. The Lusitania *crisis had come only three days after he had asked her to marry him. They were seeing each other now almost daily and were writing as often. How much they talked about the war will never be known, but the letters they exchanged were far from dominated by it. The* Lusitania, *for example, was not mentioned until two days after the sinking:*

W.W. TO E.B.G.

The White House
Sunday P.M.
May 9, 1915

. . . You may take as long a time as you need to accept in your heart the fact of my love, "holding it in tender hands," as you so sweetly phrase it, but you must accept it *as a fact.* The only question is, may I have your love in return, to treasure and live upon? Why should the fact of my deep love for you be even for a moment strange or incredible to you? You are altogether lovely. You are such a woman as any man would bless God to have known and been allowed to love who had any touch of the same nobility in him. You "warm" my heart, whether you will or not; but you cannot "ease" it until some day you come to me with faith and utter acceptance in your eyes.

And why should you thank me for speaking to you the other day of the great problems I am facing these terrible days (when I can think of nothing bright but you)? If I could but have you at my side to pour my thoughts out to about them, I would thank God and take courage, and bless you that you cared and comprehended and gave me leave to make you my confidante! Everything about you is a blessing and a help to me and seems to deliver me from all weakness and discouragement, — from worry and even from thought of fatigue. Ah, how shall I ever open my heart to you in *words?* I can do it only in life and act. My love for you passes present expression.

I *need* you. I need you as a boy needs his sweetheart and a strong man his helpmate and heart's comrade. Do not *doubt* the blessed fact. And when you have accepted that, God grant you may see your way to my side. I am not seeking to hurry you, my precious friend, or to take you by storm or put any, even the least, pressure on you, — but only make you understand to the utmost. For I *love* you, with a love as pure as it is irresistible, which exists for your sake. I love *you*, not myself!

You must be conscious that your mind and spirit are the perfect mates of mine, that our thoughts and instincts and affection for one another suit and complete one another as the light and the flame. Do you think that it is an accident that we found one another at this time of my special need and that it meant nothing that we recognized one another so immediately and so joyously? And think what the last year has been for me, the days counting for more than weeks of ordinary life (even an ordinary life here in this great office), and its months as if they were years — and I struggling through dark days alone — *no* one understanding altogether, with the heart as well as the mind. Do not these extraordinary circumstances alone and of themselves explain a great many things for you which you did not understand at first?

I hope that you will think of me tonight. I shall be working on my speech of tomorrow evening [in Philadelphia] and on our note to Germany. Every sentence of both would be freighted with greater force and meaning if I could feel that your mind and heart were keeping me company.

W.W.

Mrs. Galt tried to tell her suitor where her mind and heart were in this short but sad letter he received just before he left for Philadelphia:

E.B.G. TO W.W.

1308 Twentieth Street
12:15 P.M.
May 10, 1915

In just ten minutes I am leaving the house to come and have a minute alone with you and I am going to try so hard to make you understand and not be disheartened or hurt. You will try to understand, dear kindred spirit, won't you? and I know that I would not add one feather's weight to the burden you are carrying. Still I must tell you the truth. And together we will trust the future.

We both deserve the right to try and if you, with your wonderful love, can quicken that which has lain dead so long within me, I promise not to shut it out of my heart but to bid it welcome — and come to you with the joy of it in my eyes.

On the other hand, if I am dead (as I believe) you will not blame me for seeking to live even if it means pain in your own tender heart when my pulse refuses to be in unison with yours. Goodby and know that you carry away with you all that brings me happiness.

Edith

On his return to Washington from Philadelphia, Wilson started putting final touches on the protest to Germany over the Lusitania *and held a three-hour-long Cabinet meeting on Tuesday, May 11; but he also found time to write to Mrs. Galt, who was still struggling in her indecision, and to think of Matthew Arnold:*

The White House
May 11, [1915]
Tuesday 7 A.M.

I do not know just what I said at Philadelphia (as I rode along the street in the dusk I found myself a little confused as to whether I was in Philadelphia or New York!) because my heart was in such a whirl from that wonderful interview of yesterday and the poignant appeal and sweetness [of] the little note you left with me; but many other things have grown clear in my mind.

You have seen me from the top of your tower, on one of your visits to the sweet air and the life about you, where men and women are free and you have stretched out your hands to me and called to me to rescue you — *and I will;* unless there is some secret passage in which you will hide yourself in sudden panic when I have made my way into that tower. Even that I am sure I could find! I might be better equipped for the fight — I would to God I were!

It may be that if the Knight were younger and had beauty of person that matched his love and courage, you would save him the agony of the siege and come out with shining eyes to deliver him the keys with your own hands. And yet the very fact that he looks gray and grim and yet has the indomitable spirit of the Knight in him and loves without limit and without thought of being said nay may stand him in sufficient stead. Nay it must. He has been permitted a sacred enterprise: there is a heart to be rescued from itself, — which has never known that final divine act of self-surrender which is a woman's way to love and happiness. If she cannot be taken — taken away from herself by siege, she must be taken by storm — and she shall be!

Please read Arnold's "The Buried Life," dear, that I read you once, and let the meaning of it grow very clear to you.

Was it not interesting that the very day I spoke of it — and before I had actually spoken of it — you changed your signature, first to "E" and then to "Edith?" Is it not thrillingly interesting to see how our hearts draw together whenever you come to the top of your tower! I dream that some day you will take down the rusty keys and come out to me, as sweetly and

naturally as a child, with utter faith in your shining eyes and no
quiver of doubt or dismay — coming, of course, because I am
waiting and am already your own

W.W.

*Wilson wrote twice on May 11. It was an anniversary — one
week! — of the day on which he declared his love:*

W.W. TO E.B.G.

The White House
Tuesday evening 9 P.M.
11 May 1915

. . . It has been a week of self-revelation for both of us, since
I poured my love out to you in the half-light there where we
sat in the still evening, and I found the sweet lady I spoke to
a prisoner in her own thoughts; and now you are awake and
free! The little god is blind himself, but he has made us see.
And, oh, how happy he has made me! My heart echoes every
syllable of what you have written and knows what was un-
spoken. I felt that I was at home again this morning because I
was where you were.

If I said what was worth saying to that great audience in
Philadelphia last night it must have been because love had
complete possession of me. I did not know before I got up very
clearly what I was going to say, nor remember what I had said
when I sat down; but I knew I had left the speech in your
hands and that you needed me as I needed you.

And, oh, I have needed you tonight, my sweet Edith! What a
touch of your hand and a look into your eyes would have meant
to me of strength and steadfastness as I made the final decision as
to what I should say to Germany. You must have felt it. You must
have heard the cry of my heart to you and known in every fibre of
you that I needed you. And I know that you would have come
if you could and would have given me the full solace of all that
is in your woman's heart, and I have been happy in spite of my
loneliness — you *have* helped me.

I did not need to be told of your love, my heart only asked
because I could not feel your touch and see you. I have looked
into your eyes, dear, while the veil was over them, until I was

fairly faint with thirst. The veil is not over them now, for you are awake and I love you beyond measure. God bless you! We shall help each other henceforth whether we can touch hands or not.

W.W.

At about the same time Wilson was writing his letter on the Philadelphia speech Mrs. Galt was thinking about the same subject:

E.B.G. TO W.W.

11 May 1915
Midnight

I cannot go to sleep until I tell you how completely you have been with me all day and what fun it has been to hear everyone talking of you.

It began at 8 o'clock this morning when I went to market and heard this greeting from my butcher:

"Well, Mrs. Galt have you read the President's speech made in Philadelphia? He is the greatest man this country has ever produced and he is going to stay right where he is another four years."

Then groups of people standing near me, all discussing your speech, and all filled with admiration.

Then I came home and Helen brought me something which made the thing I call a heart, for lack of a better word, beat to words that thrill and burn — when I read that you did "not know just what I said in Philadelphia because my heart was in such a whirl from that wonderful interview of yesterday." Well, I didn't *want* to be a worm, I *was* a worm with no head to lift from the dust at your feet. You — in a whirl from an interview with me! The very thought is presumptuous.

But, I must go on with my story. At noon I had an interview with my lawyer, whose opinion I value as much as anyone I know, and he could talk to me of nothing but you and what you had said.[1] Lifting the paper from my desk where I had been

_____
[1] The man Mrs. Galt was talking about was Nathaniel Wilson, a leading lawyer in Washington. He had come from Zanesville, Ohio, in 1868, and was an assistant United States Attorney in the trial of John H. Surratt for complicity in the assassination of Abraham Lincoln. He was later in private

reading, he said: "This is the finest utterance I have ever read. The English is so clear, so simple, and yet so magnificent in its principles, in the man's conviction to do right at any personal cost and in his profound comprehension of the greatest burden that has ever come to any President that it seems inspired."

He waited a long minute and then he turned and took my hand and said: "Child, I don't know why, but I feel you are destined to hold in this woman's hand a great power — perhaps the weal or woe of a country. You can be an inspiration and a force if you do not wilfully shut your eyes to opportunity. In order to fit yourself for this thing that I feel will come to you, you must work, read, study, think! Don't shut yourself up in this house alone because you are afraid to go into the larger life, for fear of failure."

Doesn't this seem almost uncanny? And I tried so hard to keep pride out of my eyes and voice when he praised you and yet he seemed to be looking through and through me.

Don't think from this that he can imagine the wonderful thing you have given into my keeping. I know he could not do that, but it is a possibility of the future to his mind because he knows and trusts me. It would not be fair not to tell you that he has said very much the same thing to me for four or five years and it is only because of what was singing in my heart that it is freighted with such meaning . . .

Edith

The President's reply revealed his relief in getting away for a little while from the work on the Lusitania *protest and his pleasure in hearing praise for his Philadelphia speech:*

W.W. TO E.B.G.

The White House
Wednesday evening
12 May 1915

I have just put the first touches on our note to Germany and now turn — with what joy! — to talk to you. I am sure you

---

practice, representing many large corporations and many wealthy individuals. He was a close personal friend of Mrs. Galt's, and she referred to him in this correspondence as "the old Mr. Wilson." He was seventy-nine at the time and died in 1922 at the age of eighty-six.

have been by my side all evening, for a strange sense of peace and love has been on me as I worked — maybe brought by that note you wrote last night (you are a bad girl to sit up so late!) with its story of the day.

I cannot put into words the happiness with which that dear note filled me! To have brought you out of darkness into light, my sweetheart, seems to me the crowning privilege of my life; and to have your day filled with me, — how that makes my heart sing and all work grow easy!

And your lawyer — hurrah for him! I am glad a man of such insight and vision should bear the name of Wilson. This was truly one of the most interesting and thrilling incidents I ever heard of. How true every word he said, — how full of wisdom and comprehending affection for you, — except the advice "Work, read, study, think!" Heaven forbid you should *prepare* as for a business! . . .

W.W.

On the same day, the President received a long letter from Secretary Bryan saying that he had signed the first Lusitania protest (it was sent on May 13) but "with a heavy heart." He could not believe that the United States would give up its role as friend to both sides in the war and the possibility that it might be able to act as a peacemaker. Nor could he understand why the protests to Germany were so much stronger than those to England, a country that was also violating international law in stopping and searching our ships.

On the day after the protest was sent, Bryan addressed another letter to the President, this one suggesting a "compensatory" protest to England against her continuing the blockade and asking her to take some action to keep Americans from traveling on her ships. The President replied patiently (he had gone over all this with Bryan before), that he felt it would do no good to send another letter, because people would not comply with any effort to keep Americans off British ships.

Wearily Wilson turned to a short respite. He was planning a trip to New York on May 14 to review the Atlantic fleet, which was in harbor there after exercises on the east coast. He had asked Mrs. Galt to be a member of the party for the trip.

[27]

This letter that she wrote him on May 12 refers to a "disappointment," which is not explained elsewhere in the correspondence:

E.B.G. TO W.W.

1308 Twentieth Street
May 12, 1915
7:30 P.M.

"I could not love thee dear so much
Loved I not honour more"

This must be my excuse for the shock and disappointment I gave you this afternoon. I wonder now how I had the courage to tear down my own image you had made in your thoughts of me and shatter it in the dust at your feet but it is done and I feel like poor Humpty Dumpty — "all the king's horses and all the king's men can never put me together again!"

The only real harm though is for you and the shock of readjusting your thoughts. Tell me frankly if you would rather I did not go on the trip. Whatever is best for you will be my happiness and I will always trust and understand you. Don't say I am morbid and love darkness better than light . . .

Edith

The President and his party — Mrs. Galt was included — left Washington on Friday, May 14, going to Hampton Roads, Virginia, and sailing from there for New York that night. Aboard the Mayflower, *he wrote her this short note:*

W.W. TO E.B.G.

USS *Mayflower* at Sea
Saturday 6:40 P.M.
May 15, 1915

Dearest, what a delight, what a solace, what a tonic to everything that is best and a source of happiness in me it has been to be near you all day! It has made me feel that the boat was *home* and full of the sweet influences that guide a man and make him sure of his anchorage and of the meaning of life for him. And the more I see you, the more the feeling grows, the feeling of identification, and of being somehow made complete by your presence. Has it been fun for you too, dear? Do you feel that I am your natural comrade and understand at every turn, catch your thoughts by a mere exchange of glances and respond without word or hint of what is in your heart? . . .

The Mayflower arrived in New York on Sunday night, May 16, and the President and his party remained aboard until the next morning, when he went to a stand in front of the New York Public Library at Forty-second Street and Fifth Avenue and reviewed a marching parade of 5000 sailors and Marines chosen from the 25,000 in the fleet force there. After a luncheon attended by city officials at the Biltmore Hotel, he again boarded the Mayflower and rode by the ships at anchor in the Hudson river. Almost 800 guns were fired in salute as the Commander-in-Chief passed the battleships, destroyers, submarines, and auxiliaries. Secretary of the Navy Josephus Daniels was at the President's side during the review, and aboard the dispatch boat Dolphin was Assistant Secretary Franklin D. Roosevelt. Hundreds of thousands of spectators lined the banks of the Hudson for the show, and Wilson was clearly the hero of the day. The review turned out to be of unexpected importance to Wilson: It was his first appearance before large crowds in the streets since the Lusitania sinking, and the welcome he received was considered an endorsement of his handling of the crisis.

The next day (Tuesday, May 18) the Mayflower went to lower Manhattan and anchored in the harbor near the Statue of Liberty while the President watched the fleet steam out to sea for maneuvers. The Mayflower then left for its return trip to Washington by way of Hampton Roads.

On the way up the Potomac the next day the President and his guests stopped at two historic places: Westmoreland, the birthplace of George Washington; and Stratford Hall, the birthplace of Robert E. Lee. At Stratford, then still in private hands, the surprised owners (a family named Stewart) were told that the President of the United States was approaching from the water in a rowboat for an early afternoon call.

The Mayflower reached the Washington Navy Yard early in

*the morning of May 20, and Mrs. Galt sent the President this
letter of appreciation for the trip:*

E.B.G. TO W.W.

1308 Twentieth Street
May 20, 1915

Oh! to be with you tonight my precious one, to put my arms
around you and hold you close and tell you how long the day
has been without you.

I have been back in prison. Instead of golden sunlight and
silver waters there has been rain — and wet streets. And my
heart has been seeking you — and leaving me in a strange unfamiliar world with nothing at 1308 Twentieth Street the
same as when I left it a week ago.

You have been so vitally before me that I lose the sense of
being alone and find myself turning to welcome your coming
if there is noise or motion in the house.

Do you remember William James' Essay "On a Certain
Blindness in Human Beings"? I don't know what led me to
read it again tonight but, even with one eye still asleep, I found
things in it that I never *really* read before because I was blind
myself. I mean the fable of the monk who heard the bird in the
wood break into song and then "all life that is not merely mechanical is spun out of two strands — *seeking* for that bird, and
hearing him."

Dear heart I have been seeking for so long for that bird and
now I am hearing him — clearer and sweeter in his call each
time and if you will kiss the other eye into life I believe I will
see him.

Edith

*The fable referred to here is actually quoted by James from
an essay by Robert Louis Stevenson, "The Lantern-Bearers":*

*There is one fable that touches very near the quick of life —
the fable of the monk who passed into the woods, heard a bird
break into song, hearkened for a trill or two, and found himself
at his return a stranger at his convent gates; for he had been
absent fifty years, and of all his comrades there survived but one*

to recognize him. It is not only in the woods that this enchanter carols, though perhaps he is native there. He sings in the most doleful places. The miser hears him and chuckles, and his days are moments. With no more apparatus than an evil-smelling lantern, I have evoked him on the naked links. All life that is not merely mechanical is spun out of two strands, — seeking for that bird and hearing him. And it is just this that makes life so hard to value, and the delight of each so incommunicable. And it is just a knowledge of this, and a remembrance of those fortunate hours in which the bird has sung to us, that fills us with such wonder when we turn to the pages of the realist. There, to be sure, we find a picture of life in so far as it consists of mud and old iron, cheap desires and cheap fears, that which we are ashamed to remember and that which we are careless whether we forget; but of the note of that time-devouring nightingale we hear no news ...

Wilson took great pleasure in sending flowers to Mrs. Galt. Orchids were her favorite. "You are the only woman I know who can wear an orchid," he wrote her once, "on everybody else the orchid wears the woman." On May 23 she thanked him for a box:

E.B.G. TO W.W.

1308 Twentieth Street
May 24, 1915
Monday night

Dearest one,

... This is not at all the way I meant to begin my talk with you tonight, my Lord, it was to specially tell you how wonderful these exquisite orchids are. I never before had an *entire box* of these lovely things and I feel indeed like a princess, so rich am I in prodigal loveliness.

I wish you could see my room as I write. You would forget it is a prison and mistake it for "my lady's bower." Shall I tell you a little bit about it since it cannot be blessed with your dear presence? Well, I have my piano up here and that is open, with some tiny golden-hearted roses in a vase on the side. Then there is a big square window with a broad window seat and lots of cushions and by this stands my big chair where I curl up to

think. There is a table by this with a light and some books —
and, tonight, there is a wonderful pale mauve orchid there
looking like a spirit that had stayed its flight and paused there
for a moment. Beyond this there is a long couch on which I
imagine you resting while I am at my big businesslike desk
opposite, where I have orchids on either side of me to gladden
my eyes when I have to turn away from you. Besides these
things, the room is made livable by a wood fire and more books
and a few household goods that I love. It pleases me to feel
you are here and I find it hard to stay at my desk instead of
coming over and kneeling beside you and whispering something
you already know . . .

Goodnight,

Edith

*In a letter from Mrs. Galt on May 27 there is a mention of
"Colonel House," the introduction into the correspondence of
the man who was Wilson's closest friend and adviser.*

*Edward Mandell House was a Texan, fifty-seven years old
(about two years younger than Wilson), a genial man of political experience and sagacity. Having suffered a head injury
when he was twelve years old, he was in frail health for the
rest of his life. House had never sought office himself, but he
worked long and hard for others. No Democratic activity —
large or small, important or unimportant — was complete without him. A wealthy man by inheritance, he was able to give not
only unlimited time but also material support to his candidates
and causes. Taking part in public affairs became his obsession
and joy. He remained in the background but was known by
everyone.*

*The Colonel (a grateful Texas Governor had put House on
his staff with the honorary title, and it stuck) first met Wilson
in the fall of 1911. By that time House decided that he should
move onto the national stage politically, and he was looking
around for a man to back for the Presidential nomination in
1912. He found him in the New Jersey Governor, whose can-
didacy was just getting started. Impressed by the reform program Wilson had been able to get enacted into legislation in his
own state, House saw in him a man of principle and integrity,*

learned but not arrogant, and, moreover, a man who could be elected. The last prospect particularly pleased House, who was a very practical man. He formed an immediate and lasting friendship with the Governor, and the two were seldom apart after that. There was a rapport that has intrigued historians.

House was everywhere in the 1912 campaign, making new friends, calling on old ones, always preaching Woodrow Wilson. After Wilson was elected, House was more in demand than ever: recruiting for the new Administration, keeping the Democratic machinery functioning in the smallest precincts, looking over legislation that the Administration was going to support. Wilson extended to him a confidence he gave to no other friend or adviser. He felt that House's mental processes were so close to his own that it was uncanny. "Talking to him is like talking to myself," he said. And the conversations went on. House was a constant visitor to the White House. The word soon went out in politically cynical Washington that House was the man to see in the new regime. He made a full-time career of being "personal friend to the President." The newspapers referred to him as "Assistant President" or "The Silent Partner." There was no indication that he disliked any of this. But he was very quiet about it; he had a great gift for working unobtrusively. It was said of him that he could "walk on dead leaves and make no more noise than a tiger."

Of all the President's intimates, House lasted longest. He was there through all the war years, and he was a member of the Peace Conference delegation to Paris after the war was over. His role at the conference finally led to the coolness and later all-but-open break between the two men over compromises House was willing to accept in the Versailles Treaty. But all this was long in the future. Now, in the spring of 1915, he was still in Europe on the latest of several peace missions for Wilson but was reporting little hope of success. He believed it was inevitable that we would enter the war. Having been told by British statesmen that our entry would shorten the war and save lives, he was advancing an idea that appealed to Wilson: It was that after an Allied victory "we would be in a strong position to aid the other great democracies in turning the world into the right paths. It is something that we have to face with fortitude,

*being consoled by the thought that no matter what sacrifices
we make, the end will justify them." Thus, the Colonel's
powerful voice was added to those urging Wilson to lead the
country into war.*

*This was Mrs. Galt's first mention of Colonel House — a
very casual one:*

E.B.G. TO W.W.

1308 Twentieth Street
May 27, 1915

. . . It was so nice to talk to you but you sounded weary and
discouraged and I knew this other old ship business was resting its great weight on you.[1] So that I wanted to come and see
if love was stronger than any other thing, to put my arms about
you and whisper all the tenderness and sympathy that was in
my heart. I do hope you went right to bed and to sleep some
way. Somehow, Dearest, I must help when you need me, it
breaks my heart not to. Just five minutes after I talked to you
Dr. Grayson called me and said he had been riding with you,
that he thought you were blue and awfully worried over the
new situation and that he wished you had Col. House or someone to talk things over with — that would be a relief and help.

He, Dr. G., is certainly absolutely devoted to you and would
give up anything to serve you. One thing he said pleased me for
it relieved a fear that he might know more than we believed. It
was this: "Well, Mrs. Galt, you seem to understand the President and do him more good than anyone else. You don't *worry*
him and I *wish you would go* whenever they ask you for he
really needs all the diversion he can get." . . .

Edith

*Revealing as they are, these letters are, of course, by no
means a complete chronicle of the intimacy between the President and Mrs. Galt, but their relationship by late May had
reached a point where the President would write:*

---

[1] The United States steamer *The Nebraskan* had been hit by a mine or
submarine off the coast of Ireland.

The White House
Thursday morning
27 May 1915

All the household is asleep, the study door is closed, and here I am alone with my darling, free to talk to her and think only of her, the tasks of the day unable yet to exercise their tyranny over me, and my heart full of what she said to me yesterday, that with me she was perfectly happy and that my prediction had come true, that love *had* cast out all fear that, with me by her, nothing could ever crush or really hurt her, — so that I can turn to her here in this quiet room as to my own sweet comrade and lover, no barrier any longer between us, my heart thrilling with pride and fairly melting with tenderness, dream that her dear, beautiful form is close beside me and that I have only to stretch out my arms to have her come to them for comfort and happiness and peace, my kisses on her lips and eyelids, my *thoughts* of *her* and of all the incomparable wealth of beautiful things now released in her, to bless everyone with whom she comes in contact.

I venture to say, my Lady, my Queen, that never in your life have you looked so wonderfully beautiful as I have seen you look when the love tide was running in your heart without check, since you came to understand yourself and me. I have seen a transfiguration, and it has filled me with as much awe as ecstasy! — I can't think this morning, — I can only *feel* and only realize the exquisite thing that happened to me, the beautiful love I have won, the ineffable charm of the sweet woman who has given it to me, the added value and joy that have come into life for me because of her, her spirit all about me, adding to the brightness and freshness and life-giving airs of the morning . . .

Your own
Woodrow

From the exhilaration of this letter there was a sudden change into doubt and fear. The cause for this remains a mystery; the only logical presumption is that there was a misunder-

standing between the two when they went for an automobile ride the night before the following exchange of letters:

E.B.G. TO W.W.

1308 Twentieth Street
May 28, 1915
Friday morning

My dearest one,

I would not try to write you last night although my heart longed to pour itself out to you and try to ease the pain I caused your own big, tender heart. I thought it was wiser to wait until this morning and now it is hard to put into words just what I mean. But you are always so splendidly honest with me that I am going to try once and forever, to let you look straight into the depths of me — and then never again refer to this *more* than painful subject.

I know you are right in every word you said last night, and I am asking something that is childish and impossible. But, try as hard as I can, *now* it seems the only way. If this can be changed it will be because you are master of my heart and life — (and oh! you don't know how I long to make you so) — but you must conquer! I have promised not to raise burnings and not to think defeat possible. I will valiantly keep these promises — for I love you, and your love for me has made the whole world new and when I am there with you there is no fear — only happiness.

Edith

W.W. TO E.B.G.

The White House
May 28, 1915
Friday

Dearest Edith,

I simply cannot write today. An almost sleepless night of agonizing doubts and fears is no proper preparation for the only kind of letter my tender love for you will ever let me write — a letter to comfort you and make you happy. My only message is this:

For God's sake try to find out whether you really love me or not. You owe it to yourself and you owe it to the great love I have given you without stint or measure. Do not be afraid of what I am thinking, but remember that I need strength and certainty for the daily task and that I cannot walk upon quicksand. I love you with all my heart.

Woodrow

E.B.G. TO W.W.

1308 Twentieth Street
May 29, 1915
Saturday

Dear, weary heart —

I have thought of you so tenderly these last hours, since I knew you were in pain, mental and physical and felt so ashamed that I should add to the burden.

If only I could brighten this dreary day for you but my love seems inadequate.

I have given it to you and found such happiness in the giving — and instead of bringing joy to you — your note yesterday tells me it is only a "quicksand."

I am waiting for Helen to come and see if you still want me to come to dinner tonight.

I long to talk to you — but perhaps I would only add to your burden.

I trust you to tell me if this is so? My tenderest thoughts fly to you, seeking like birds to find a sheltered nest, and I long to know that you are happier and better today.

Edith

Friday, May 28, had been one of the darkest days in the courtship. Depressed, the President canceled his Cabinet meeting and all his appointments (including one with the newly elected Senator Warren G. Harding, Republican of Ohio, who was to call to pay his respects) and spent the day in his room. By Saturday morning the President had found a way out of his depression and sent Mrs. Galt this triumphant letter:

W.W. TO E.B.G.

The White House
29 May 1915
Saturday morning 7

My darling,

After many, many hours of deep depression and exquisite suffering, which brought on a sort of illness which I could not explain to the doctor and for which he could do nothing, the light has again dawned for me and a new certitude and confidence has come to me.

I have been blind as well as you. I have *said* that love was supreme and have feared that it was not! I have told you the truth and yet have myself acted as if *I* did not believe it. That weakness is gone. I not only believe that love is supreme but that it is *creative,* and that belief shall inform everything that I do or say henceforth. You love me — I *know* that you do — so much more than your words tell me so — your very presence is radiant with it when we are together and every touch of your dear hand has in it the sense of identification and loving intimacy: and you have invited me to make myself the master of your life and heart. The rest is now as certain as that God made us and gave us the sweet knowledge of each other — and *I shall win,* by a power not my own, a power which has never been defeated, against which no doors can be locked, least of all the doors of the heart.

Henceforth, we are not going to *discuss* our love, but live upon it, and grow in it...We are natural comrades. Our minds and spirits go out to meet one another with a perfect understanding and an enjoyment that makes our hearts young and light and free...

Woodrow

The satisfaction the President had found in his private life was not matched by any lessening of his worries over affairs of state. Reports had already reached him that the German reply to the May 13 Lusitania protest was highly unacceptable. It ignored Wilson's demands that Germany disavow the sinking and deferred all direct questions on the matter.

On the twenty-eighth Colonel House sent a cable urging that the President not contribute further to Great Britain's troubles by sending any more protests over her neutrality violations. Not surprisingly, Secretary Bryan continued to urge that he do so.

On the thirty-first the President went to Arlington National Cemetery to speak at the unveiling of a memorial to the men who had died in the sinking of the battleship Maine *in Havana in 1898, his mind on the men he might have to send into battle. As Wilson was leaving the White House he passed a demonstration of thousands of women, members of the Women's Peace Party, urging him to stay out of the war in Europe. Coincidentally, he had just written a letter to the woman he loved saying that what he really wanted to do on this May morning of growing problems was to find some way to immortalize her:*

W.W. TO E.B.G.

The White House
31 May 1915
Monday morning

My sweet darling,

A day when I neither see you nor get a message from you is blank on the calendar!

I went to bed early feeling very lonely indeed last night. You have become indispensable to me, my sweet one, and it is *so* far from here to 1308 [Twentieth Street]. My thoughts run back and forth across the distance every minute of the day and my heart knows nothing of it; it is always with you, never here while you are away; but I miss your *presence* so, my Love! You are so vivid. You have such a wonderful personal charm, you carry such an atmosphere of sweetness and intelligence and power to comprehend and sympathize and love, if you will, that you make any place in which you are radiant with your presence, *full* of the sweet charm and dominance of you! I wonder if you can possibly realize how your whole personality suggests love and the very impersonation of all that is loveliest in womanhood? Not that you wear love on your sleeve. I do not mean that. On the contrary there is an extraordinary suggestion of dignity and reserve about you at *all* times. One knows instinctively that you *give* the sweet things in you only when you think the gift is worthily bestowed. But one cannot look at you without feeling that he is in the presence of a noble woman to whom belong all the greatest gifts of tenderness and love.

And these noble qualities are so nobly housed! You are so beautiful! Your beauty is of the noblest type. You might pose for any one of the great women the world has loved and been ennobled by and everyone would wonder where the artist found a mate for his original. My Love, my Lady, I love to lay these tributes of my praise at your feet. I love to try to put into words, no matter how imperfectly I succeed, my unbounded admiration of you. I would be happy if I could somehow immortalize you. I will not cheat my heart by holding anything back. You are entitled to know the place you hold in my mind and heart. Throughout years to come I shall let you know by something better and greater than words.

Woodrow

JUNE 1915

June was a wonderful month in the Wilson-Galt courtship. The two had reached an understanding that their romance, despite its many obstacles, was going to last; their letters were filled with satisfaction and new hope. "There is nothing worthwhile but love," wrote the President on the first day of the month. There was an outside world — the front pages of all the newspapers were filled with war news, but it was almost ignored in this correspondence of two happy people, one of whom was a man who had the lives, welfare, and destiny of 100 million people in his hands.

Fighting on the Western front in Europe had reached a stalemate. Thousands were dying but nothing was settled. Specifically, the French were in a battle at Souchez, an attack on the western flank of the bulge between Neuve-Chapelle and Arras in northwest France. Although they failed to capture Vimy Ridge, they did punch a hole in the German lines. Before the month was many days old the Germans had outraged the world by shelling the famous cathedral at Rheims. They had also released poison gas in the trenches on the Western front, a breach of the Hague convention of 1899 and a move that further branded them as cruel and inhuman. On the Eastern front, where Germany was attacking, thousands of Russians were dead or wounded or captured. The attack was considered a success.

A zeppelin air fleet had made a raid over London suburbs, and though the censors suppressed the details, it was reported

*that ninety bombs were dropped, resulting in four persons killed
and many fires started.*

*After two more ships were sunk in the Atlantic in submarine
warfare, the Admiralty said that since the war had begun, only
ten months earlier, fifty-six British merchant ships had been
sunk by German cruisers, twelve by mines, and sixty-two by
submarines.*

An editorial in the Washington Post *urging quick expan-
sion of our Army and Navy mentioned, casually, the possibility
of war "in case Germany fails to meet demands that have been
made on her."*

*The President turned more and more to letters to the one
person who could make him forget the outside world:*

w.w. to e.b.g.

The White House
1 June 1915
Tuesday morning, 7 o'clock.

My lovely sweetheart,

I find I am getting to look forward to these quiet morning
hours alone with my darling, when I can sit here and, without fear of interruption or thought of the outside world, say
to her what I would whisper into her ear could I but hold
her close in my arms and forget everything but our love. There
is no one else in the world for me now — there is nothing
worthwhile but love. Nothing else gives life, or confidence, or
joy in action. A man is not sufficient by himself, whatever his
strength and courage. He is maimed and incomplete without
his mate, his heart's companion, the dear one to whom he is
lover and comrade. Oh, it was sweet of you to come to me in
my need! I love to think how you walked out of the great
world into my little circle here, almost as if by chance, but
really by gracious beckoning of Providence, and met me face
to face with those dear frank eyes of yours and that wonderful
smile of friendly greeting, giving me a thrill at the very first
touch of your hand, and how immediately, when we had the
chance, we found one another, found that we were meant for
comrades, that it gave our spirits a happy pleasure to be together and walk the same path of intimate intercourse together.

And then, — oh, it was inevitable, Sweetheart! I could but love you when once I had found you, — I could but tell you (we could keep nothing from one another) that never-to-be-forgotten night only four weeks ago! And now — oh, what joy it gives me to write it! *you love me!* And tonight we shall say it all over again to one another, with nothing *but* joy and hope and confidence in the sweet repetition. You have brought me into the light, my darling. God bless you!

The day's very solemn duties will probably invade this quiet place where I sit now with no thoughts but thoughts of you. The German note must be answered and answered very soon. But when I see your eyes alert tonight with the sweetest, holiest thing in all the world, and hold you close in my arms and kiss you, with pledges as deep as my soul, I shall be made fit for that and more.

Woodrow

E.B.G. TO W.W.

June 1, 1915
11:30 P.M.

My best Beloved —

I am so happy that I cannot go to sleep until I tell you — What a sort of dream-evening this has been — so radiant were the hours, and how completely you filled them.

This first June day has been so crowded with joy that my heart can have no more — and I must talk to you, and make you feel how splendidly I love you. Each time we are together, dearest, you seem more completely to fill my need and to stimulate and awaken every emotion.

While I write there is a gleam of the magic circle on my finger that warms my heart with its more than precious message from you. At night I usually take off my rings but this one will stay where I can feel it, even in my dreams. And it brings me the most exquisite pleasure . . .

Edith

The Germans' reply to our Lusitania *protest on May 28 was now at hand. It claimed that the* Lusitania *was armed*

*and carried Canadian troops. Later it was found out that the
ship was not armed and carried no troops but that the cargo
did include 4200 cases of small arms cartridges and 1250 shell
cases, this being allowed by American law. The tone of the
reply was unsatisfactory to Wilson, and he went to work immediately on his second note. As it was being drafted, he received a request from the German Ambassador, Count von
Bernstorff, for a meeting with the President, and when Mrs.
Galt heard this, she wrote at once:*

E.B.G TO W.W.

June 2, 1915
Wednesday morning

My precious one —
Please don't think me silly or afraid. I admit I am a coward
when I think any harm might come to you. So please don't
see von Bernstorff *alone.* I have just read in the *Post* that he
is coming to see you today and it gave me a sudden panic. I
never realized so fully before how I love you. The world would
be a blank without you.

Edith

*The President was amused by Mrs. Galt's fears over his
safety during his meeting with the Ambassador. Bernstorff
was considered an able, if wily, diplomat. He had been in
Washington since 1908, and after the beginning of the war
in 1914 his job had been to put the German case before the
American people. This was increasingly difficult, but no one
denied that he went at it with vigor. He realized from the beginning that if America came into the war it meant the defeat
of Germany. Wilson and Lansing kept him at arm's length,
but Colonel House appreciated him more. "If it had not been
for his patience, good sense, and untiring effort," the Colonel
wrote in October 1915, "we should now be at war with Germany."*

*Wilson's reply to Mrs. Galt's note of concern, dated the next
day, June 3, described the encounter but did not go into the
substance of the meeting, in which he told von Bernstorff that*

he was willing to negotiate but did not give any hint of a compromise. He made it clear that if Germany would give up her inhumane tactics in sinking ships, he would try to get the British to relax the Atlantic blockade.

W.W. TO E.B.G.

3 June 1915
Thursday, 7 A.M.

My precious Darling,

. . . I smiled, my darling Sweetheart, at your little panic about Bernstorff yesterday, but it was a very, very tender smile and a very happy smile, and how my heart leaped at the revelation of that sweet little penciled postscript! God bless you!

As a matter of fact the poor distressed man came to ask how he could assist to bring his crass government to its senses, for he sees the blunders it is making. I liked him for the first time. He dropped the Prussian and became the man.

The weather of course kept me indoors, and I did a jolly lot of work. Now that my heart is at ease I can do my work again and much better than before — and yet not for a moment lose touch of you and the inspiration your sweet, wonderful love gives me. Margaret and Helen and I went over to see Nell and the baby (and incidentally Mac) after lunch and when we came back to the house I indulged myself in a two-hour nap (necessary before seeing Miss Boardman for half an hour about Red Cross relief in Mexico!);[1] but for the rest, it was work, work, work, till bed time, including getting all the things straight in my head which I must include, either explicitly or by implication, in the note to Germany which I am going to try to draft today. It is a different thing working here at this desk now that you preside over it. While I sit in my chair I am all the time conscious of the sweet lady who has stood there bending over me. I feel her gentle caresses and the precious kisses she gave me, and everything is made easy — I am strong and happy because I am her own

Woodrow

---

[1] Mabel Thorp Boardman of Washington was for many years Secretary of the American Red Cross.

The President allowed Mrs. Galt to read the draft of the new note on the Lusitania, *and she refers to it in the next letter:*

E.B.G. TO W.W.

June 3, 1915
Thursday night

My precious one —

I have read Washington's "Farewell Address" and your note to Germany and it is now so awfully late that I can only talk to you for a minute.

I was so genuinely pleased when you said you wanted to read me your answer to Germany. And it was the greatest delight to be in your chair surrounded by all the work-a-day things that come in such daily touch with you — and have you there opposite me, reading what is to be such pregnant history, and letting me share the vital things that are making you famous. My darling I am not quite clear as to what I said . . . but I think to me, there was nothing of *you,* yourself, in it and therefore it seemed flat and lacking color. I know how hard it is to *answer* anything, in comparison to the freedom of choosing what you feel to write — and therefore I am conscious how much you are circumscribed and it is because of my love for you that I am hard to satisfy.

The [first] note to Germany — as I have just re-read it — is so splendid that it will go ringing down the ages. And this new one must be an echo, only in reiteration of principles and you must put some little of your *splendid* self in it.

Good night, or rather good morning, my beloved one — and always remember that I love you.

Edith

W.W. TO E.B.G.

4 June 1915
Friday 7 A.M.

My darling Sweetheart,

No, indeed, it is no dream! It *was* a dream, my dream, but it came true, — and how completely and gloriously! It is a calendar month today since I told you of my love for you, — told you because it had taken complete possession of me and

I *could* not hold it back, — and now! It *is* almost incredible that such a wonderful and ideal thing could happen in a single month, — but it was the lovers' month, the happy month of May, when many wonders come to pass and everything is re-created. Now you love me and are all the world to me! I lack nothing but to be with you always. Ah, my sweet One, it is more delicious and satisfying to be together such time that I see you than it ever was before — and more exquisitely painful to part; and yet happiness is more possible than ever, too, while we are separated, — indeed I cannot be really *un*happy even when you are away from me because of the deep, the blessed realization of your wonderful love that remains with me and makes every day bright and full of strength.

Oh, it was sweet to hear my darling whisper last night that she could not be happy away from me, and my heart knows to the full what the pain is she was thinking of. But there is something wonderfully sweet that sustains me and that shines also in her letters when we are apart, — certitude of love, the glory of it, the sustaining power of it, and confident hope of fulfillment! I dread to have June end and have you go away from Washington (I have no love for the place and when you are out of it it will be empty of *all* that redeems it!) but, oh, it will be delightful my precious one, my own darling, to think, to know that you are *at my home* and that when I go there I shall find *you!* Wherever you are will henceforth be my only real home, the only home of my heart, the only place where I can be really happy and at ease. Ah, Sweetheart, as I dream here in this quiet room you seem still to be in my arms and I seem still to feel on my lips those sweet kisses by which you gave me leave to seal myself.

Your own
Woodrow

My love is so much greater than anything I can write.

E.B.G. TO W.W.

June 4, 1915

My precious One —

You are a perfect wonder! Never have I seen so finished an actor, and you have charmed my small sister so that she can

talk of nothing else.[1] All the way home after we left you she
plied me with questions such as these —

"Hasn't he the most wonderful eyes you ever saw? and such
an exquisitely modulated voice — did you notice how beautifully he expressed himself — and yet so simply and naturally?
And, I hope you don't think I am too absorbed in him, and
did not pay enough attention to Miss Wilson — but he is so
fascinating I could not help it," etc etc until I almost forgot
my own part and answered just the way I felt — but caught
myself in time to be mildly enthusiastic about you and do a
lot of raving over Helen and Margaret . . .

Oh! I want to talk to you — I can't write. Did you — as the
paper tonight says — finish the reply to Germany today, and
will it go forward tomorrow? I hope for your dear sake, it is
over for you will then have a freer weekend holiday with that,
at least temporarily, off your mind . . .

There is just room on this page for a long goodnight. I hope
you are already in the land of dreams — and that the morrow
will bring you happiness.

Edith

W.W. TO E.B.G.

5 June 1915
Saturday, 6:55 A.M.

My Darling, My Darling,

If ever again I have to be with you for an hour and a half
with only two stolen glances to express my all but irresistible
desire to take you in my arms and smother you with kisses,

---

[1] Mrs. Galt was a member of a family of nine children. She had five
brothers and three sisters, one of whom, referred to here, was Bertha Bolling.
Unmarried and two years older than Edith Galt, Bertha Bolling lived in Washington with their mother, Mrs. William H. Bolling. Their father was dead.
In one of her letters to Wilson, Mrs. Galt described Bertha Bolling in this
way: "I meant last night to tell you a little regarding this small sister of
mine for whose benefit you are willing to test your histrionic ability. Please
be very tender in your judgment of her. She is so devoted to me that she is
apt to be jealous of anyone I care for — but it is only because her own empty
little heart has been cheated and starved of that which she deserves — and
the lack has made her narrow and terribly sensitive. Out of the abundance
of the glory of your love, I can see the pitifulness of her deprivation . . ."

I am sure I shall crack an artery! I schooled myself beforehand
for the task with this poem of one of the old Elizabethans
"Eyes, hide my love, and do not show
To any but to her my notes,
Who only doth that cipher know
Wherewith we pass our secret thoughts:
Belie your looks in others' sight,
And wrong yourselves to do her right." [1]
It was fun, in a way, while it lasted, and done with zest
because you had bidden it, but, oh, after it was over, your
lover was very sad to have missed all the sweet talk he might
have had with the lady he adores, — who was dressed bewitch-
ingly, looking her very best, and too tempting for words. Phew!
Please do not exact it again! — I liked your sister so much, my
Darling. She is good fun; she knows how to talk and she can
talk about interesting things and not be dull. I am sure that,
if she gives me a chance, we shall be good friends. I hope she
liked me as much as I liked her. We shall find a great deal in
common, — And I worked for you all last evening, too, till late
bedtime, — revising the reply to Germany. I have simplified
it and, I believe, strengthened it in many ways, and hope that
I have brought it nearer to the standard my precious Sweetheart, out of her great love, exacts of me. Bless your heart.
How fine you are and how deeply I admire you, — and my
love surpasses words, — as I shall try to tell you this blessed
night when I shall be happy again with you. Your own
Woodrow

The new note to the Germans on the Lusitania *aggravated
the very delicate matter of Wilson's relationship with his Secretary of State. Bryan had urged more strongly than ever that
this note be moderate and that efforts be made to find some
compromise. When the President read his draft to the Cabinet,
however, the Secretary realized that it was even stronger than
the first. Still fighting, he suggested again that the President
also send a protest to England over the blockade. This led to
a caustic exchange with Wilson, who resented Bryan's con-*

---

[1] Samuel Daniel (1562–1619) "Hymen's Triumph."

tinued opposition. At the end of the session the Secretary told the President that his conscience would not allow him to sign the note and that it was unfair for him to remain in the Cabinet. The note was the immediate cause, but in fact Bryan had been unhappy about other things. He had long felt that, with Wilson writing the important State Department documents on the war, with Counselor Lansing dealing with the President directly, and with Colonel House abroad talking to the heads of states about United States foreign policy, he was only a figurehead. So, after several more conferences with Wilson (who kept thinking he might be making a political mistake in letting the Secretary go), Bryan finally submitted his resignation on June 8. On the next day the Lusitania note that he could not bring himself to sign was sent to Berlin, signed by Robert Lansing, Secretary of State ad interim.

In this second protest Wilson brushed aside a German claim that the Lusitania was armed. He said again he expected observance of fair play and neutral rights, principles which "lifted the case out of the class of ordinary subjects of diplomatic discussion or of international controversy ... The government of the United States is contending for something much greater than mere rights of property or privilege of commerce. It is contending for nothing less high and sacred than the rights of humanity." He intimated again that an ultimatum might follow if Germany did not give assurances that such occurrences would not be repeated.

Bryan's resignation had been on the minds of both the President and Mrs. Galt even before he submitted it formally on June 8, and it figured in several of their letters before that date:

E.B.G. TO W.W.

1308 Twentieth Street
June 7, 1915
3 A.M.

Dearest —

I cannot write tonight, or rather this morning — for I have a very heavy heart — but I know you will be disappointed not to have a word. So this is just to tell you that my thoughts will be with you, and I hope "W.J.B." will prove himself worthy of your trust and confidence and you can get him to do the wise thing.

Don't worry over my sadness — it is nothing about you — and your love seems all the more a haven. I will tell you of it when I see you and in the meantime I must think out what is my duty. Perhaps it will mean a shorter stay at Cornish — but, at least, we will have your first visit there over the 4th. Then I may have to join my mother and sister.

God keep and bless you always,

Edith

W.W. TO E.B.G.

7 June, 1915
Monday, 6:35 A.M.

My precious Darling,

I waked up earlier than usual this morning — came suddenly *wide* awake — and for a few moments could not think what was the matter with me. Then I knew. It was that you had thought of letting Miss Gordon live with you next winter and monopolise you to the inevitable exclusion of the man who loves you as, I believe, few women were ever loved before! [1] That danger is gone now, I know, but the keen pang it had cost me last night had left its touch on my heart and I waked as I do only when something has disturbed me.

For that disturbed me much more than has the circumstance of W.J.B.'s threatened resignation. You cannot criticize me for any lack of loyalty after this, my Quixotic Darling! Remember, Sweetheart, that what I told you Friday night is literally true: you have my happiness in your keeping. Please as you love me, include me in all your future plans — as I do you in all of mine! — Oh, but it was sweet to be with you last night! That pretty little gesture you made towards me when you saw me yesterday in the motor at the Circle was my undoing. I could not bear to end the day without even a touch of your hand!

The way you let your hand rest in mine, my bewitching

---

[1] Alice Gertrude Gordon, fiancée of Dr. Grayson. She was generally called Altrude by her family and friends. She was the daughter of Mr. and Mrs. James J. Gordon of Washington, family friends of Mrs. Galt. She and Dr. Grayson were married in 1916.

Sweetheart, fills me with happiness. It is the perfection of confiding love. Everything you do, the little unconscious instinctive things in particular, charms me and increases my sense of nearness to you, identification with you, till my heart is full to overflowing. It is such a *pleasure* to love you, — such *fun* to love you! It so *lightens* my heart. It fills me with a sort of buoyancy that is life itself. In brief, my whole heart and my life itself — everything that is of the present or future — are wrapped up in you. And your love for me, my Darling! It seems to me the expression of everything that is adorable in a woman. You love as prettily, as charmingly, as you do everything else, and with an appealing sweetness that brings tears of joy to my eyes when I think of it, and when I *see* it makes me the happiest man in the world. How I love to make love to you! It is the delight of trying to express everything that is fine and true in me to the one woman who seems worthy of it all. My Sweetheart, my delectable comrade, — dear chum of my mind and my heart, please remember this sacred partnership when you plan, and prefer no one to

Your own
Woodrow

E.B.G. TO W.W.

1308 Twentieth Street
June 7, 1915

Thank you dearest one for calling me up to tell me of your ready and tender sympathy which I knew I could always claim.

I am quite content with the paper as it now stands — and reading it myself I am able better to follow the things that sounded involved before — you don't know how much I treasure your confidence in me, and your splendid acceptance of what was really ignorant criticism.

As regards "W.J.B." — of course I am not glad if it puts any additional burden on you, but I believe it will work out for your ultimate good — and your own loyalty is unmatched by his. Forgive this hurried line — I could not read the paper until now as Altrude came immediately after it did and I had to wait.

Don't worry over next winter — I am sorry if I caused you pain. I never want to do that. Goodby until tonight when I will answer your dear notes.

Edith

W.W. TO E.B.G.

8 June 1915
Tuesday morning, 7 o'clock

My precious Darling,

Yesterday was a day of intense anxiety for me, but one blessed thing came out of it, — a fuller consciousness than ever before of what your sweet love means to me. All day long, back of the deep perplexities, lay the joy of what you have given me, of what you have become to me. In the midst of it all my heart could hum a little song of happiness, and, but for the ache there was there *for* you, because *you* were sad and anxious about your own dear ones, and I could not help except dumbly, the comfort and deep content of it would have conquered everything else in my thoughts.

I am afraid, my dear one, that many consequences will spring out of Mr. B's [Bryan's] action which will be very serious to the country and to the administration, — for the newspapers do not express the real feeling of the country for that strange man, and he is evidently going to make a determined effort to direct public opinion in this German matter. He suffers from a singular sort of moral blindness and is as passionate in error as in the right causes he has taken. There are deeper waters than ever ahead of us.

To me personally it is, of course, a matter of indifference, but it may mean serious things for the country, and the country I love with a deep passion. But with your hand in mine, your life linked with mine, my incomparable Darling, *nothing* will hurt me *too* deeply . . . You *fill* my heart. Your sweet love awakens in me everything that is sweet like life itself, and everything that is strong. How many people you comfort and sustain and give joy to, my Darling, ministering to them the sympathy and help that gives life; and to me you have given all, — that *royal* heart of yours! What can *hurt* me now, what dismay me or turn me aside? When I take you in my arms tonight nothing but sheer joy can come near me. I am safe and happy because I am

Your own
Woodrow

News of Bryan's actual departure from the Cabinet was a sensation in the newspapers of June 9, and Wilson refers to that in his next letter. The banner headlines and endless columns of news and discussion would indicate that the resignation was a shocking surprise; as a matter of fact, of course, it had been long expected. The departing Secretary did nothing to dampen the discussion, and two days later he issued a 4000-word "Appeal to the American People" in which he asked that they understand his position that he could not sign the new Lusitania *note without violating his obligation to his country to prevent war. "I ask you to sit in judgment upon my decision to resign," he wrote. The long document also contained a sharp criticism of the* Lusitania *note.*

The Secretary's departure — putting the divided opinion in this country over the war into focus and generating public discussion — was a further strain on Wilson. He did not want to alienate the Bryan followers, a hugely vocal, pacifist group, but neither did he want to retreat from his strong stand on the German submarine warfare. He held to his course but the toll was beginning to show. A dispatch from its Washington correspondent to the New York Herald *on the day of the crisis said:*

"President Wilson is very tired. There are lines in his face; he has no smile; his shoulders drooped a little today. The worry he has experienced in the last few days is telling on him. He is a trifle irritable."

w.w. to e.b.g.

The White House
9 June, 1915
Wednesday

My precious Darling,

I suppose the papers will be very interesting reading this morning, but I think I shall allow myself the usual indulgence of not reading them.[1] I know so well what they are going to say that I could almost write their editorials for them. What a bore that would be! Comment does not help when difficult things are to be *done*. I always prefer to skip the buzz of the first week or two after a striking or really important thing has happened and be guided by the later opinions, the second thought, of the country, the permanent after-impression — and to wait for my own second thought, too.

The impression upon my mind of Mr. Bryan's retirement is a very painful one *now*. It is always painful to feel that any thinking man of disinterested motive, who has been your comrade and confidant, has turned away from you and set his hand against you; and it is hard to be fair and not think that the motive is something sinister. But I shall *wait* to think about *him* and put things to be done in the foreground. I have been deserted before. The wound does not heal, with me, but neither does it cripple.

My thought this morning, therefore, is that there is now a chance to do a great deal of *constructive* work in the State Department for which Mr. Bryan had no gift or aptitude, — if only I can find the right man for the place, or, rather, if only I am free to *take* the best man for the place. Fortunately the chief characteristic of my mind is that it always at once moves on *to the next thing*.

All this, dear heart, just to relieve any anxious thoughts you might have about me this morning, — any fear that I was at all touched with discouragement. Mr. B. can do a lot of mischief, but he cannot alter anything essential, and my personal fortunes are neither here nor there.

This is not a tube-rose letter, my strange, lovely Sweetheart. Tube-roses do not grow in my garden. I abominate them. But blood-red roses grow there, whose perfume ought to make any heart seem full of the very spirit of life; and this is a bunch of blood-red roses which I hope that you will wear at your heart to warm you with the devoted love of

Your own
Woodrow

---

[1] Chief Usher Hoover said Wilson read only the *Christian Science Monitor*, which he considered "the only paper in the country which tells the truth."

E.B.G. TO W.W.

1308 Twentieth Street
June 9, 1915
Wednesday A.M.

Hurrah! Old Bryan is out! This editorial in the *Post* does my heart good and I know it is going to be the greatest possible relief to you to be rid of him.[1] Your letter [to Bryan] is *much* too nice — and I see why *I* was not allowed to see it before publication.

I could shout and sing that at last the world will know just what he is . . .

Please let me see the editorials, if there are any possible ones, in *favor* of "W.J.B." — and I shouldn't *mind* reading others about an *adorable* person if they are interesting.

Your *penitent* and worshipping
Edith

E.B.G. TO W.W.

1308 Twentieth Street
June 9, 1915
2:15 P.M.

You are a very subtle, and a very adorable person — I hate to admit that the "blood-red roses" not only glow with color, and warm my heart with their sweetness but also prick with a tiny thorn — which to be perfectly honest, is exquisite pleasure.

You are a fencer so worthy of anyone's steel that fencing becomes a delight — and I just glow when you beat me at my own game.

I don't know how many times I will try to parry your thrust before you get entirely under my guard — (and, I warn you that I am a good fighter, and stubborn beyond measure) but you have my heart on your side — which is a tremendous

---

[1] The *Washington Post's* editorial on Bryan, typical of many in other newspapers, said: "The people will support the President as against Mr. Bryan or any other man who proposes an ineffectual method of enforcing American rights. It is to the President's credit that he stood firm against what must have been insistent pressures from Mr. Bryan for the enfeebling of American policy."

handicap to me — and I promise to be a good sport and acknowledge it if I am beaten.

I have just had another call from Mr. [Nathaniel] Wilson and I think that, in spite of his imaginings, I have convinced him *you* are above suspicion as far as falling in love with me goes. He talked on and on about you, and the *crisis* in my life coming out of your friendship for me — that by September he expected to hear that I had come to some fixed and definite plan for my future — that no responsive person with such quick sympathies as mine could come in touch with such a personality as yours without having the deepest emotions awakened and stirred to the depths, etc. etc. When I said "Please be more direct in what you expect of me — you give me the impression that you are warning me against something — and I can't quite determine what." At last he said, "Well, to sum it all up, I don't mean it as a warning, that is not the word — but I might say as a prophecy — He is a man and you are a woman — each most attractive — why shouldn't you attract each other, or at least one attract the other?" You should have heard me laugh — as I answered, "Oh, I see. You know the President's charm and what you term the *glamour* of the White House and you are afraid I will get my silly little head turned by their charming hospitalities to me as Miss Bones's friend, — and end by falling in love with the President — I, who pride myself on my coldness and unresponsiveness."

Whereupon the old gentleman said — "No, I don't mean that exactly but we could not expect him, as burdened as he is, to have time or thought for such things himself — although he may rest in your sympathy and companionship — which would be the foundations for stronger emotions, if he were circumstanced as private individuals are — and which in the future, with more leisure, might develop into love — but with you it is different. You have lived apart from the world so long that to be thrown suddenly so immediately into the strong light that beats upon the throne and come in touch with a man who holds the center of the stage, not only by position, but attainments — is enough to create any sort of intense feeling in you who were made for warmth and life in its deepest fulfillment." So, my Lord, *I* am the suspicious person — and you, wrapped in the

robes of state and serious meditation, could never be thought
of as a lover — or a person in whose garden grow deep red
roses — Roses that bring sweetness, and light to the heart that
beats under their fragrant petals when they are sent, fresh cut,
from this living stem.

I am so happy that you are not letting Mr. B's act really de-
press or trouble you — it must come right — and cannot add
to your burden, save for the moment until things and people
readjust.

How I want you this afternoon! It is a great punishment that
now I must wait for days before I can see you. The sands of
the priceless hours we were together last night ran low before
I *found myself* — and your dear note tells me you can "turn
to the next thing" and not even bend gracefully that rod of
iron inside. Well! I can't. I am *homesick* for you — and want
your arms about me.

Edith

W.W. TO E.B.G.

The White House
10 June 1915
Thursday morning

My adorable Sweetheart,

... The great deeps in you, my Edith, are breaking up and
when their great tides begin to run without let or hindrance
you will be the happiest woman in the world and I the happiest man! You will be more than happy: you will be one of
the noblest women in the world, for utter allegiance to Love
will have transformed you.

Ah, Dearest, I have tried to grow bigger and truer and better
as the years have gone by, have tried myself to learn the
lesson I speak so inadequately in that little essay about how a
man comes to himself and I can testify that the only power
that has ever helped me in the least is Love. And my love for
you has come to me in these days, when I seem to be put to
the supreme tests of my life, like a new youth, its enthusiasm
and romance seeming to make duty itself clearer and easier
and more worthy of the best that is in me. Your love for me
has given me life not only but has also brought me back gaiety

and elasticity and ease of action. I love you with an infinite tenderness, my own Darling, but with something also that goes much deeper and stirs me more than mere tenderness, — with a sort of fierce devotion compounded of every masculine force in me and drawn out by your own strength. You have never realized the splendid strength that is in you because you have never before given it the right direction; but you are finding it now. You are, oh, so *fit* for a mate for a strong man! Love has come to you now like a challenge, — and all that is loveliest in you is coming out like a new glory. And I adore you. My heart is full of light and joy because of you. It is such a delight to love you! You do not yet know the force or depth of it; but you shall know to the utmost what I mean when I say that I am

Your own
Woodrow

E.B.G. TO W.W.

1308 Twentieth Street
June 10, 1915
11:45 P.M.

It just broke my heart, my precious one, to hear you say how lonely and unaided you feel in this great work you are doing so splendidly.

Of course I knew that it was so, but fondly hoped you were unconscious of the way you carry all the burden on your own dear shoulders and what figureheads most people are! Oh, how I longed to put both my arms 'round your neck, and beg you to let me take part of the weariness, part of the responsibility and try to make you forget everything else in the assurance of the love and loyalty that fills my heart.

Please try to feel it enfolding you, My Beloved One. Wrapping you up as a garment — a shield, and a very present help. Only thus can I be worthy of the great love you have given to my keeping — and only thus can I feel I am serving my Lord and Master.

This has been such a happy evening together and I did not once catch sight of the rod of iron inside — so flexible and easy to adjust does it seem.

Tomorrow is another old Cabinet meeting day which means you will be tired out. I am so sorry!

Goodnight and may morning bring you new strength and comfort.

Edith

W.W. TO E.B.G.

11 June 1915
Friday morning hour. I won't say what.

My own Darling,

That ride last night was a very searching experience to me. From beginning to end it seemed to me like an epitome of my own life, — as I was trying to tell you in broken sentences, — a ride through the night, clinging to love, personal love the one thing a man's heart cannot live without, — and all the while your face only half disclosed in the changing light, and yet at last, as we neared home (you and I who live apart and yet have the same home) wholly revealed to me, in the full light, radiant with tender love, too deep for words. It seems to me that this is the way I see you always: first through a half light full of shadows in which you elude me, and then with a final revelation full of perfect solace and hope and joy. And above us all the while, staring day, but heavens full of stars, immense, calm, eternal, filled with peace and certainty and the reassurance that there is no chance but fixed laws of God to which all the world moves obedient, not least the fortunes and hearts of men. I started out on the ride disturbed and unhappy, but I came back, though very solemn and a bit sad, yet sustained by a new sense of strength and a new confidence that God's in his Heaven and all's well. Days like these certainly try men's souls, — when loyalty and devotion and the things that spring from the very heart are being tried out, and the real standards by which we are to be judged made clear.

How instantly the country hit upon the heart of the matter in condemning Mr. Bryan; how quick and clear it was in saying that that is not loyalty or true fealty that is given *upon terms*. How instinctively the larger things are seen, and true self-forgetfulness demanded of those who serve and profess to serve, not for themselves, but for love! Sadness *will* creep in when the test fails. I have to admit (to the dear one I love most in all the world) that the defection touched me to the quick and the week has been one of the hardest in these hard years which have exacted such a tribute of sorrow; but I have not for a moment lost hold of myself and love has been my sufficient salvation — the love that *will* not fail and that will not stop to count the cost.

Your own
Woodrow

E.B.G. TO W.W.

1308 Twentieth Street
June 11, 1915
10:40 P.M.

Dearest and Best —

I have just read over again your sad little note written this morning at an unknown hour and my heart yearns to tell you again of all the love and tenderness that wells up in it. I have been very near you today, and tried to compel your spirit to feel mine near and to bring you abiding assurance of "the one thing that a man's heart cannot live without." Did you feel it and were you happier because of it?

Helen and I had such a good time together today, and I hope you did not miss her too much — How I wished you could have been with us.

After we got back — at 2:30 — I went out to Cleveland Park to play auction bridge with eight very nice people. (I should say seven, since I was the other fellow) and there I heard an interesting history of General Lee's birthplace — where we had such a happy time! — or rather the history is more of the present owners and who they are. I will tell you about it when I see you. I stayed there until 6 when I took one of the guests home. She lives in a quaint old house in Georgetown and the grounds are filled with splendid old forest trees in and out of whose friendly branches darted red birds like tongues of flame — and over all the fences ran a riot of Dorothy Perkins roses. It is a restful, sweet old place and I felt refreshed by lingering a minute while she cut sprays of roses for me, which I took to Mother because someone else, who had a garden, had sent me a great box of "lovesome" blossoms which make my room fragrant while I write.

You see you asked me to tell you of what I do — so this is a history of a day. I took dinner with Mother, after which I took Randolph, my brother, for a ride.[1] We went down by the Potomac, but the call of Virginia was strong, so I crossed the bridge and went to Arlington. We were caught in a shower so I came home at 9:30 and am going to bed as soon as I finish this.

Always yours,
Edith

W.W. TO E.B.G.

12 June 1915
Saturday morning

My own Darling,

I turned in at half past nine last night, as tired a chap as ever you saw, and got about nine hours sleep — and am still sleepy! But, though I am even yet not quite awake, I feel greatly rested and know that I shall feel very differently today. Yesterday I was pretty well played out. And how I did miss that sweet ally of ours, that darling cousin of mine, dear Helen. She went out at eleven in the forenoon to be with you and did not turn up again until seven! I envied her with all my heart when I found that she had been with you for lunch. For my need of you, my precious sweetheart, seems to increase with each day, — each day that I know you better and that we are drawn closer to one another by some common experience.

I feel, and rejoice to feel, that this desertion of Mr. B's was an experience we went through together and which has bound us together by a new and more intimate sympathy and sense of identification. How little the public knows of *all* it has meant to me, and of the sweet *solace* it has brought me, in my dear Love's sympathy and loyalty!

And, speaking of how little others know of the joy that has

---

[1] John Randolph Bolling lived in Washington. He held various jobs in business and became secretary to his sister after President Wilson's death. He died in 1951.

come to *us* in these trying days, I am reminded of your last conversation with Mr. [Nathaniel] Wilson (I was reading your account of it over again last night just before I went to sleep) and my half *ashamed* feeling that *I* should *not* be suspected! He knows what an adorable person you are. He must know that, unless I am something less than human, I *must* fall in love with you! Indeed he does know that I will some day when I begin to take notice. With the feeling about you that I have, and that he evidently has in a different way, I hate to have him think that I have not already rendered you my homage, my Queen. I am not so slow as he thinks and you are irresistible. Above all, I do not *like* to have him think that you would fall in love with me before you know that I had fallen in love with you. Why not tell him, and set him right about both of us? I am so proud and happy about it all that I would love to tell it to everybody who really knows either of us, for it is the best part of my life now that I am

Your own
Woodrow

W.W. TO E.B.G.

13 June, 1915
Sunday morning

My adorable Sweetheart,

The delight of last evening is still upon me so strongly that it is almost as if I were still looking deep into your eyes and reading there the whole sweet secret of my happiness. I think you do not know how much of yourself you unconsciously reveal, — you certainly do not know what a heart full of beauty you show and of a tenderness that surpasses beauty, even surpasses the charm that makes you always irresistible.

Little as Mr. Wilson knows about *Woodrow* Wilson he knows you, for he describes exactly what has been pent up and hoarded in you and what will happen when you wake and find yourself. He does not know that it *has* happened. He only suspects it. He sees a great change in you and is seeking to understand it, and, knowing and affectionately admiring you, as he does, he is so afraid that what he suspects has *not* happened to you — that you have not heard the call of supreme love and responded — to become the perfect woman he knows it would make you and I know it has made you, often as you try to draw back into your smaller, your prison self and deny the miracle and mystery.

Seeing you as I saw you last night, my radiant, wonderful Darling, is like witnessing some deep and glorious mystery, like being present while life is created. There are moments when I feel the *awe* of it and wonder why *I* was permitted to be the instrument of it. And the beauty and joy of it is unspeakable. I love you with an intensity that *hurts* me because it can have no adequate expression. And, oh, my precious Queen, how empty the house is without you — how empty my arms are, and my lips can speak nothing worthwhile all day long for lack of your kisses. I am infinitely homesick for my Darling — and shall always be when she is not with me, to share every experience and every thought and every turn of life and fill it with the love without which it can contain neither happiness nor inspiration . . .

Your own
Woodrow

E.B.G. TO W.W.

1308 Twentieth Street
June 13, 1915

Dearest One —

It seems so natural a thing to be with you now instead of anyone else that I find myself always expecting you — and yet I was *so* surprised to find you at my threshold when I opened the door tonight. I wonder if it pleased you as much as it does me that the first time you *asked* for admission to my home I myself answered your call and threw the door wide to bid you welcome. Of course you did not come in, only took my hand in yours for a moment, and gave me one of your deep looks from those wonderful eyes and I followed you into the night!

Does it not mean something that at first it was dark — with rain falling softly, like happy tears, and then the sky cleared and thousands of stars came out to smile down on us. And we went on and on over old roads that seemed new because we were together! I like to think it does mean something, and to follow it out still further is to believe that as soon as we *parted* the clouds gathered, and the pouring rain that beats against the windows as I write, came down in torrents and the house seems lonely and empty without you.

I wish I could have helped you with tomorrow's speech [at the Treasury Department on Flag Day] — but I can never quite believe you when you say you don't know *what* to say. I know you will say something that no one else could ever say, and it will be something I shall glory in. Wish I could hear it as you utter it — but I will read it in the papers — and try to picture how you look when you say it . . .

Thank you for all the lovely, sweet things you said to me in your note today that had to be hidden for so many hours before I could know them.

Goodnight, always yours,
Edith

W.W. TO E.B.G.

16 June, 1915
Wednesday morning

My precious Darling,

Last evening brought me a new and exquisite happiness, the happiness of taking care of you and comforting you. When I was trying to soothe and relieve your dear head my heart was too full for words with the job of rendering you a little tender service, with love in every touch of my fingers, and when the tears came and you came into my arms as to a home and haven, I could have wept with you for the sheer joy of it. And your simplicity and sweetness in it all were beyond measure touching and beautiful, my adorable Sweetheart. I hope some tithe at least of the happiness it gave me came to you also.

I wandered about my room for a good while after you left, trying to quiet the pain of parting with you, and then, when I could not do that, went to bed to lie awake whispering endearments to you until the comfort and joy came back and I slept like one to whom hope has pledged fulfillment by bonds that cannot be forfeited. I think your dear heart must have come back to me and touched me with some sweet embrace, for I somehow knew that you were near me. And this morning the joy and deep abiding happiness of your exquisite love is still like a glory about me and I seem to have a new life. I could not long be still and murmur sweet names to my Love, I just had to hurry here to the study and write a message that would a bit take the strain off my heart that I must always feel until we are separated no more. My wonderful Sweetheart! Your sweetness last night, and your utter loveliness in it all, filled me with unutterable longings and delights, — longings to satisfy you, and delights that I should be the object of it. And the singular *dignity* of it! Not a touch of weakness, — just the self-revelation of a tender and noble woman whose heart has been pent up and kept proudly aloof, and who now turns to her lover and throws the gates wide, — no, not quite wide yet, but wide enough to show him the sweet and holy places where her true spirit lives. And he *knows* they are holy, takes the shoes off his feet, and stands with worshipping eyes to see his sovereign lady in all her perfect purity and beauty, knowing that he is blessed beyond all other men and has seen his own happiness in the sweet revelation! With my whole heart and spirit.

Your own
Woodrow

The next letter is the first in which Wilson mentions another international problem that was plaguing him: the "delicate and ticklish" situation in Mexico. That country had been in a state of revolution for four years. Wilson did not hesitate to intervene to see established there a government dedicated to long-overdue social and economic reforms. First, he refused to recognize a regime that had come into power as the result of an unlawful, bloody overthrow of a constitutional and popular government.

The cast of characters was a large and volatile one. The 35-year-old dictatorship of Porfirio Díaz had ended in his resignation in 1911. He was succeeded by a reformer named Francisco Madero, who tried to introduce economic changes that would bring land and liberty to Mexico's masses and who was in turn overthrown in a bloody coup by a military usurper, Victoriano Huerta, just before Wilson became President. Most of the countries of Europe recognized Huerta as the only effective force in Mexico, and United States business interests urged Wilson to do the same. He refused. He wanted a regime based on law, not force, and one that would reflect the needs of "the 85 per cent of the people who are struggling toward liberty."

Soon a counterrevolution broke out, led by Venustiano Carranza, an old Madero supporter, and Wilson backed him. Huerta abdicated and Carranza took over. But this was Mexico, and the fighting kept going on; nobody knew what to expect. Carranza became unhappy with Wilson's support, and things were getting into a very tangled state indeed. To complicate things further, Washington got involved in an unnecessary military confrontation over a supposed insult to the flag, and our Navy occupied the port of Veracruz. This further strained relations with Carranza.

Three Latin American countries — Argentina, Brazil, and Chile — offered to try to compose the differences between the warring Mexican factions, and Wilson eagerly joined in their mediation efforts. Meetings began on May 20 at Niagara Falls, meetings popularly called (as in these letters) "the A.B.C. conference." The three were in time joined by Bolivia, Uruguay, and Guatemala. The meetings of these well-intending powers were going on as these letters were written, and there are frequent short references to them in the next few months. In October Wilson officially recognized Carranza.

The Mexican troubles of this time are remembered by Americans chiefly now because they involved — in 1916 — a general named Francisco ("Pancho") Villa, who broke away from Carranza and started a war of his own to exterminate Americans in the northern part of Mexico and almost caused a war between the two countries.

W.W. TO E.B.G.

18 June, 1915
Friday morning

My beloved Sweetheart,

. . . I shall turn to my duties today with a new zest, for I am renewed every time I am with you. There is not only a great deal to do but this is the time to do it when (and while) the country is back of me with enthusiasm and something like unanimity — while it believes implicitly in my judgment and is ready to think me right in everything I do — for there's no telling how long it will last, and some of the things waiting to be done are very delicate and ticklish. For example, there is not only the Mexican situation which has to be handled with velvet gloves, and in which I am dealing with an incredibly volatile people, but also some intimate political matters like the chairmanship of the National Democratic Committee and the outlining of plans (including getting money) for next year's campaign. McCombs, the present chairman, has turned out to be the most unconscionably jealous and faithless and generally impossible person, and nobody is any longer willing to work with him — and he ascribes his failures to me! [1] But all these things have grown easy because I am

Your own
Woodrow

W.W. TO E.B.G.

19 June 1915
Saturday morning

My beloved Sweetheart,

How perfectly bewitching you looked yesterday in that lovely pink hat as you sat on the South portico, laughing gaily at something I could not hear, — something, I think that your sister was saying. I had not been invited to the tea, indeed I had been carefully kept in ignorance of who was coming not only but of the fact that anybody was coming, and I know (occasionally) how to take a hint; but I had not been forbidden to *peep* at the lady I adore. I slipped quietly into the Green Room and there, from behind the lace curtains, feasted my eyes on the loveliest person in the world, — with, oh, such a longing to go to her and take her in my arms and cover her

---

[1] William F. McCombs (1875–1921), a New York lawyer who had studied under Wilson at Princeton, became an early supporter and worker for him, and managed his campaign for the Presidency in 1912. He then became chairman of the Democratic National Committee, but a difficult personality and illness soon made him a problem to Wilson's advisers, who were urging that he be replaced before the campaign of 1916.

with kisses, whispering in her ear every sweet secret of deepest love! And then I forced myself to turn away and go off for a ride through alternate rain and sunshine. It was sweet of you to choose the seat you did. You must have known that only there could your lover manage to see you without being seen. I wonder if you will chide me for what I did yesterday afternoon, — for calling on W.J.B. to say goodbye? The only thing that made me feel uneasy about it was that I could not do it with genuine cordiality; but I did it on the best political advice! If we treat him with perfect generosity (and in the midst of it all he is praising me, you know, very generously indeed) the least bit of reaction against us on the part of his friends (whose name is legion) is prevented and absolutely all his guns are spiked. He looked amazingly well and refreshed! No stranger man has lived, and his naïveté takes my breath away. I will tell you about our conversation (or rather about what he said, for I let him do all the talking) this evening. Mrs. Bryan, I thought, was constrained and uneasy, but not he! He was full of enthusiasm about what he was doing for peace and about what he was going to do, and perfectly at his ease. I made the excuse of a clap of thunder to get away . . .

Your own
Woodrow

There was certainly no relaxation in public affairs, but June was vacation time in Washington. The President had no hesitancy in leaving town for several weeks and he did so. For the previous two years he had established a Summer White House at Cornish, in the mountains of New Hampshire, and he did again this year. He was to leave Washington in the last week in June, and the good news to him was that Mrs. Galt had agreed to go too. She was ostensibly to be the guest of Helen Bones, but few in the Presidential entourage were fooled. Few in Washington were fooled either, for that matter; the gossip had already started when it became known that the attractive, lively widow was such a frequent guest at the White House.

Mrs. Galt always maintained that her circle of friends was not large, that she had no interest in "society" as such, but the number of people who claimed to know her was growing. The

*social columns of the Washington newspapers duly recorded
that she was going to Cornish to visit Margaret Wilson and
Helen Bones, but everybody knew that newspapers never told
the real story anyway.*

*Mrs. Galt left by automobile on June 20 and the President
followed her by train two days later.*

E.B.G. TO W.W.

June 20, 1915
Sunday morning
Very early

My precious One —

When this is in your dear hands I will have started on the
broad highway that will lead to your home! and how much
more than a tiny piece of paper I am leaving with you.

Can you feel it throb and beat as you hold it, and will you
let it whisper, all these intervening days before you come, I
love you? Will you let it nestle close next to your own heart
and leave no room between for loneliness or sadness?

When the house seems empty will you go to your window
and look out to the great out-of-doors and feel that I am there,
calling back to you, signalling to you to hurry and come — that
you, and only you make my world complete?

You will not be alone my loved Lord for you will feel my
spirit so near that you have bent to whisper to summon it and
I will come and fold you in my arms . . .

Your own
Edith

W.W. TO E.B.G.

The White House
20 June 1915
Sunday evening

My precious darling,

Good-bye! It breaks my heart to write the words, — and you
would understand so much more perfectly what they mean to
me if I could hold you close in my arms and whisper them to
you between kisses. But you *will* know what they mean: your

own dear heart will echo the meaning, — of our first parting since our hearts came together in perfect understanding.

Perhaps, as you say, this is the close of the first chapter of our happy, happy romance, my Sweetheart, but there will be no break in the lovely story and the meaning of it will grow deeper and sweet and more wonderful to the end, — a story of deepening comprehension of the wonderful and beautiful thing that has happened to us, of a love daily made more true and serene and perfect. Its most wonderful and inspiring passages are yet to come. I look forward to them with such eagerness and such happy confidence and with such unspeakable joy — to the constant and unbroken companionship and intimate partnership of a life made bright by love, — a love which has come to us with the slow and steady revelation as of a thing predestined and inevitable and which will go on from revelation to revelation until we stand in the full light of a perfect joy.

In this very moment of sadness (more poignant than I had dreamed possible) I feel the elation of a man who is moving steadily towards the most rewarding and the sweetest experiences of his life. My discovery of you has *moved* me so, my adorable Sweetheart, and it is pure joy without touch of either fear or misgiving. Let us both think of the future and plan to make this second chapter more wonderful than the first. It is only an imaginary division in the story. Every morning I am going to write to my Darling as before. What are time and space to us more than mere teasing inconveniences? They are only for a little while and we shall win a victory over them . . .

Your own
Woodrow

W.W. TO E.B.G.

[Addressed to Hotel Wolcott, New York
Thirty-first Street by Fifth Avenue]
The White House
21 June 1915
Monday morning

My Beloved, My Beloved!

What shall I say to you this morning? Here I sit at my desk; the hour is the same that finds me every morning pouring my heart out to you, — but, oh, the difference! The house is empty. The town is empty! My Sweetheart, my darling is gone, and I sit here with a longing at my heart which I can hardly endure. But I have just read that tender, that wonderful good-bye letter you handed me last night and my eyes are still dim with the tears it brought into them, tears of deep and exquisite happiness because of your love. The letter is a vision of yourself, my lovely Darling, and it has brought me what you always bring me — what you brought me last night. I loved your gayety then, Sweetheart. I understood it. I felt the keen charm of it. I struggled to free myself and share it. And then, seeing, as you always do, what I was suffering, what I needed, you turned to me with a tenderness and love which are surely the most winning and adorable any man was ever permitted to see, and the weight was lifted from my heart, I lived again, and was inexpressibly happy. And I am happy this morning, my sweet one, in spite of the lump in my throat. For this wonderful love you have given me fills all the world with peace for me, fills the otherwise empty house with your presence, fills my heart and all my thoughts and makes me proof against weakness, proof against real sadness, even now. I am complete in you, and nothing can really hurt me while you love me. I know, to use your own dear words, that I am *not* alone, that your spirit is near me all the while, and that I have but to whisper to summon it. My heart will turn to you every minute for that sweet comfort. I wonder if the people about me here will realize that I am not really here at all — that my thoughts are away? For they will be. Where you are will always henceforth be where I am, in heart and thought and spirit. And being with you will be life and joy to me always. Don't think, dearest, that you did nothing to help me when I talked of the chairmanship — you did everything. You comprehended and sympathized and were the true comrade of all my thoughts. You were my own incomparable mate, who have completed my strength by your love and brought every perfect blessing to your own

Woodrow

When you are shopping, buy for Helen something she wants — for me — please.

E.B.G. TO W.W.

The Wolcott
New York
June 21, 1915
10:29 P.M.

Dearest One:

I do hope the day has not seemed very long — and that you got the telegram we sent from Philadelphia when you got back from golf. Helen sent you another from here and we thought of calling you on the phone but decided it was better not, though the man at the desk has just told us the White House called to know if we had arrived and that has worried our blessed little chaperone lest her message seem long in reaching you — bless her heart! What do you suppose she bought and put on my dressing table? Your picture — such a lovely one that I have only to lift my eyes to find yours — and oh! it is such a comfort . . .

We got off in five minutes after I penned Mr. Hoover and had a beautiful run over the most perfect roads. The only thing to mar the happiness was that you were not there to share it — and we missed you so.

We got to Philadelphia about 2 and as White wanted gas for the car we went to Wanamaker's where we sent you the telegram.[1] We started again at 2:30 and went through Trenton where we saw the State House and thought of the many hours you had spent there — and caught a glimpse of your old colored messenger. Then we went direct to Princeton which I think is perfectly charming.

Helen and I got out and walked through the grounds and she told me so many interesting landmarks. Of course my chief interest was you — and where you had been — had lived — had worked — all of which this dear little guide anticipated and told me all she knew. Then we went to see your portrait, which I think is perfectly awful! If you looked like that I could

---

[1] Edward White, a White House employee.

not love you — but it serves to emphasize your splendid interest and strength which is so lacking in the picture that it makes it a burlesque. Only the hands are good — not so much as replicas of yours — as that they express vigor and purpose and individuality. We left Princeton, after having tea at the Inn, about 6:30 and had to make two detours before coming to Jersey City but the roads all the way were fine and almost no dust.

The lights in the water reflected from the thousands in the city were exquisitely lovely as we neared the ferry — and we are not one bit tired. Mr. Jervis and White took such splendid care of us that we did not have to think for ourselves.[2]

All this is but a sketch of the day to tell you how completely I realize that these more than delightful things have all come to me through you and your dear love. Never for a moment can I forget your thought and tender solicitude — and be happy because of its eloquent assurance of your love.

This time last night we were together, but any Tuesday, Wednesday, Thursday — and we will be together again — and I will whisper all I want you to know. Helen and I laughed so at the way the telegraph operator read her writing in the message she sent you from Philadelphia. It was "The Pres — the White House" but he read it *Wm* President — the White House — and could not read the last word at all. It was *love*. Poor man! Perhaps he does not know the meaning of it. Now I must stop. Thank you for your blessed note of last night. I am going to have a fine time directly reading it all over again. My tender love — always yours

Edith

P.S. This is literally the longest day in the year.

---

2 Richard Jervis, a Secret Service man attached to the White House. There are frequent references to Secret Service men since they went everywhere with the President and members of his family. They were discreetly intrigued by the President's romance with Mrs. Galt and liked her. One of them, Colonel Edmund W. Starling, wrote his reminiscences, *Starling of the White House,* in which he recalled that Mrs. Galt's Secret Service code name was "Grandma."

W.W. TO E.B.G.

[Addressed to Hotel Kimball, Springfield, Mass.]
22 June 1915
Tuesday morning,
7 o'clock

My precious Darling,

Now I *know* that the twenty-first of June is the longest day in the year! I did everything I could think of to fill it up, but it remained hopelessly empty and quite interminable. There did not seem (for once) to be work enough to fill the morning till noon when I had an engagement to see McAdoo and "our Virginia Glass" about rural credits legislation at the next session of Congress; and when they came they actually did not stay their full half hour (I never knew such a thing to happen before!)[1]

At 12:30 I shook hands with several hundred veterans of Something, but they would not string out till 1, — so I came upstairs and threw myself on the lounge in my bedroom for a few minutes, and then a very lovely thing happened, which put me in spirits for the day! As I lay between sleeping and waking you came and nestled close to me. I could feel your breath on my cheek, our lips touched, and there was all about me the sweet atmosphere that my Darling always carries with her. I dared not open my eyes. I lay there like one entranced and blessed and rose more than rested, — refreshed, renewed, and happy. My Darling had come to me and the day was redeemed! Grayson came in to lunch and — another. Tell Helen that she just missed her favorite cousin. She had hardly gone before in walked Fitz William Woodrow,* come back to seek a job for the summer which he thought he could get.[2] And so I sat down to lunch with the two men, not thinking of them at all, but of two lovely ladies speeding over highways, and wondered if my face showed the sweet vision I had had as I

---

1 Representative Carter Glass, Democrat of Virginia, and chairman of the House Banking and Currency Committee. He was later a United States Senator from Virginia.

2 Fitz William Woodrow, twenty-four-year-old son of the President's first cousin, James Hamilton Woodrow of Columbia, S.C. He had been a student at Princeton while Wilson was there.

rested in the room overhead. At two I had another interview, with the editor of a St. Louis newspaper whom I have known for a long time. At half past 2 I went to the dentist's (you see I had planned the day to suit my humor and provide abundant diversion) and let him stand with both feet on a nerve or two for the space of an hour or so. After that I took a ride and there were not rides enough to last till Margaret's train time. When her train time came she did not — her train was an hour late. There were the same gentlemen for dinner. I worked until I was so sleepy I could not see, waiting to hear that the dear lady who had taken her departure that morning and taken my heart with her was safe, with "our blessed little Helen," in New York. You should have seen me walking fiercely up and down the hallway upstairs here while the office was trying to get the Hotel Wolcott and quiet me. No message had come except the one of the afternoon which relieved my anxiety about Helen's neck!** And so at last the day ended. I knew my precious one was safe and my heart was quiet enough to let me go to bed.

Ah, my Beloved, each day some new turn of experience makes me realize more fully than ever how deeply I love you. I dare not try to write you a love letter this morning. It *hurts* too much, because you are away. I know I could not see the page before me through the tears of happiness and loneliness that would blind me are blinding me now. Suffice it to say I love you with the whole passion of my life and am altogether

Your own
Woodrow

Dearest love to Helen.

* He is to lodge here for the present.
** The telegram from New York did not reach me till this moment. Bless you both. 9:15 A.M.

On June 23 — the date of the next letter to Mrs. Galt — the President officially designated Robert Lansing as Secretary of State. He had been Acting Secretary since Bryan's departure two weeks earlier. Lansing, a specialist in international law, was fifty-one, a suave, urbane New York lawyer, the perfect

administrator for a President who wanted to be his own Sec-
retary of State. His father-in-law, John W. Foster, had been
Secretary in the Harrison administration.

The war news was particularly bad: On the Eastern front the
Russians had lost Lemberg in Russian Poland to the German-
Austrian forces and were retreating on a 250-mile front.

W.W. TO E.B.G.

Wednesday morning,
23 June 1915

My precious darling,

I am sure you must feel, without my telling you, how constantly and lovingly my thoughts have followed you ever since
you left; and you came to me again last night, bless your heart,
just as I was falling asleep, — came with infinite tenderness and
charm. You are never so bewitching as when you make love! I
shall be tempted, till I come to you, to be always dozing. I love
you beyond all words, my adorable Sweetheart, and your love
is my life. With what delight did I seize and devour your dear
letter . . . I am so glad you saw Princeton, after all (though I
coveted being your guide there myself) and thought it attractive. We must go back there some day and really see all of its
charms. It is too various for a mere casual visit. What you said
so sweetly in that letter, my Darling, about my thought for your
comfort and pleasure made me more keenly conscious than I
have been before of the deep longing in me for the privilege of constantly taking thought for you. The sweetest part
of my love for you is that I may devote myself to your happiness. It is so delightful to think of taking thought for you all
the day long.

The chronicle of yesterday was very simple with us: just
desk work, a short Cabinet meeting; a talk with Mac in which
he benevolently and with the best intentions sought to render
assistance in Mexican and other foreign matters which are
none of his business; golf, and a long ride with dear Margaret.
Margaret is the only member of the family who had any adventure. She went riding with a young Princeton man who is
one of [Interstate Commerce] Commissioner [Winthrop More]

Daniels' assistants and, to her keen mortification, was thrown from her horse by his sudden shying. She rolled directly under him, but he stepped carefully over her. Young Woodward sprang from his horse to her assistance and, in his haste and excitement, released his horse entirely. Both horses ran away and the two bored riders had to hunt until they found them at a nearby farm where fortunately they had run into a paddock and could be cornered and caught. Margaret was of course bruised and a little strained but I think not hurt, except in her pride. She went for a long drive with me last night and said she was not even tired — only a little stiff. Horseback riding is certainly the sport for adventure.

Tonight I get away, and, though I shall stop all day tomorrow with Mr. House at Roslyn it will be at least *starting* for Cornish and the sweet, incomparable lady who is all the world to me. And this is my last letter till I see her. This will reach you tomorrow, and the next day I shall come in person to say what no letter can say — what a lover whose love goes too deep for words, is too tender to express in anything but acts of devotion, can say only with his eyes, with the tones of his voice, with kisses and caresses, and the sweet syllables he can whisper into his Sweetheart's ears. Ah, my Love, my Love, how unspeakably eager I am to see you, to be close beside you, to hold you in my arms and feel myself full of the life and joy of existence which only you can give me. And how, after once having had you in my home, shall I ever have the strength to give you up again, again for a little while!

Goodbye, my Darling. How it will brighten all the world to see you again.

Your own

As planned, the President left Washington by train for Cornish. He went first to Roslyn, Long Island, for a short stay with House to hear the Colonel's report on his European trip, where he went to talk to the heads of the warring countries on any possible way for the United States to intervene for peace. The talks had been fruitless. Wilson went from Roslyn to Cornish on June 25.

*The house at Cornish he occupied for the vacation was called
Harlakenden, built in 1898 by Winston Churchill, the American novelist. He had leased it after being favorably impressed
with it from photographs he had seen. It was a Georgian brick
house with large gardens and a superb view overlooking the
broad valley of the Connecticut River.*

*Cornish was a summer settlement that attracted many artists
and writers. The sculptor Augustus Saint-Gaudens had gone
there in 1885 and started the colony. Thomas W. Dewing followed and, in time, other artists, such as Maxfield Parrish, Ken-
yon Cox, and George de Forest Brush. And there were sculptors
Paul Manship and Herbert Adams, writers Percy MacKaye,
Hamlin Garland, Langdon Mitchell, and Norman Hapgood,
Scribners editor Maxwell Perkins, and the famous judge,
Learned Hand. Many other prominent figures in American
culture of the time were regular visitors.*

*The Parrishes — the father, Stephen Parrish, who was an
artist too, and his more famous son, Maxfield — were bulwarks
of the community. Maxfield Parrish became America's best
known artist, for his popular romantic paintings, illustrations for
books and magazines and for advertisements. He lived in Cornish from the time he built a house there in 1889 until his
death in 1966 at the age of 95. He and his family were friends
of the Wilson family, and these letters mention frequent visits
to "the Parrish house." It is not always entirely clear which
house they refer to, since both Stephen and Maxfield Parrish
had places there.*

*Only two brief notes remain to indicate how the President
and the woman he was courting spent their time at Harlakenden:*

E.B.G. TO W.W.

The President's Cottage
Cornish, New Hampshire
June 29

Good morning — do you feel like taking a walk with me this
glorious day, my dearest one or are you afraid of the damp? If
you want to go, I will be ready by 10:30.

E.

w.w. to e.b.g. (on reverse side of card)
Of course, I do, my precious Little Girl. It will be jolly. I
love you with all my heart. I will be ready.

Woodrow

And from the Cornish stay there came — saved in the en-
velope along with the notes about taking a walk — a three-line
document, dated but without comment, perhaps the most im-
portant of all these papers:

Cornish
June 29
A Pledge:
I promise with all my heart absolutely to trust and accept my
loved Lord, and unite my life with his without doubts or mis-
givings.

Edith

JULY 1915

The July days at Cornish were leisurely. The President went 20 miles to Hanover each day to play golf. There were walks in the hills around Harlakenden and long hours with members of his family: Jessie and Frank Sayre and Helen Bones, and with Dr. Grayson, of course. And there was the most important person of all — Mrs. Galt. Newspaper accounts of the Presidential activities did not mention her until July 3, when they reported that the President had taken "the most dangerous automobile ride of his present trip" across a mountain for a distance of 100 miles. With him were Helen Bones and Dr. Grayson "and Mrs. Norman Galt of Washington."

On another day the President and his party were "lost" for five hours as they tried to drive from Cornish to Woodstock, Vermont, over back and unfamiliar roads along dangerous ravines with mountain waterfalls all around. The President's near-obsession with motor trips was being put to the test.

The stay at Harlakenden — the President was there until July 18 — was described as a working vacation, and certain hours every day were devoted to dispatches from Washington. Most of the work was caused by the Lusitania protests to Germany. The Summer White House was receiving hundreds of letters and telegrams every day on the subject. Wilson was so anxious that the public should not get the impression that he was neglecting his work that on July 13 he issued an unusual statement (through the White House in Washington) that he was "keeping constantly in touch with the Secretary of State and every source that could throw light on the situation."

The atmosphere at Harlakenden was wartime tense. Threats and scares had led to increased protection by the Secret Service. Automatic time clocks appeared on the trees around the house for the use of watchmen and guards, and visitors were subject to close scrutiny.

The European fighting continued but with little decisive action. The first reported loss of United States lives since the Lusitania came on July 1 when the British freighter Armenian carrying mules to England from Newport News, Virginia, was torpedoed by a German submarine off the coast of Cornwall and 20 American muleteers were believed lost. Later investigation revealed that the ship had refused to stop after warnings by the submarine, so the sinking was considered justified even though noncombatants were aboard. Thus a crisis for the United States was avoided.

Mobs kept up their steady rioting and looting in Mexico City, and the danger was that the United States, preoccupied with the war in Europe, would become indifferent to the fires raging on its southern border. Another problem — but one no less irritating — was resolved on the twenty-eighth when the President ordered a military occupation of Haiti, which had also been in a state of revolution for several years. Marines landed on the island on this date and order was restored by August 1. On September 16 a ten-year treaty was signed that made Haiti a semi-protectorate of the United States. It was renewed several times in the following years, always to protests and dissatisfaction on the part of the Haitian public and critics in this country, and finally, in 1934, the last of the United States forces were withdrawn.

The Germans' reply to our second Lusitania note arrived in Washington on July 9, and Wilson, deciding to return to the capital to draft his answer, left Cornish on the eighteenth. Mrs. Galt saw him off from the porch at Harlakenden and went immediately inside and penned this slightly anguished farewell note:

E.B.G. TO W.W.

The President's Cottage
Cornish, New Hampshire
July 18, 1915
Sunday, 1:30 P.M.

My precious Sweetheart —

There are so many things I want to say first that I can't decide where to begin — but as a preliminary I will ease my heart by saying that which is dearest in all the world — and it is — I love you — love you — and am utterly lonely without you. Just this time last night the history readers got sleepy and dispersed and you and I were together and I felt your tenderness enfolding me — and we knew the world held only each other.[1] Now you seem far away — but in reality I know you are here — and I can still feel the warmth of your dear arms and rest in the protection of your love.

Oh! how hard it was to let you get in the car and drive off alone this afternoon. All the love in me cried out that you needed me — and I wanted to go — to stay with you — and say to the world how proud I am that that is my place.

But one look at Mr. Murphy recalled me to my humbler self — and I smiled at you through the old wire door (that carried out the idea of my *cage* where I cannot reach you) and tried to look conventional and disinterested.[2] I loved you taking off your hat, and the last showed me your dear head bared, as though you were on holy ground — and indeed this, your home is, and always will be, *holy ground* to me and I *felt* the thought that prompted your uncovering.

When you had gone Helen and I went out on the porch again and tried to talk. At 3 your train went by — and so we knew you were still waiting in Windsor. Then Gertrude Gordon called me on the phone. I had just talked to her when Frank [Sayre] got back — and Helen went to see about her housekeeping and I sat in the hammock and *thought*. A tiny little humming bird darted in and out of those same blue

---

[1] It was the custom at Cornish for the members of the President's family to gather after dinner and read aloud from his *A History of the American People*.
[2] Joseph E. Murphy was chief of the White House Secret Service detail.

flowers that attracted him yesterday when you were in the hammock — and it made me sick to think that these self same flowers and silly little bird were permitted to stay and *you* were gone! . . .

Monday 9:30

You are just due in Washington, and I am welcoming you home Sweetheart, before I run to join Helen. Don't work too hard and try to take rides. It is raining a little here but Frank thinks it will stop so we are going.

Always your

E.

When the President reached the White House on the morning of July 19 he could have read these headlines in his morning Washington Post:

VON HINDENBERG BREAKS RUSSIAN LINES

IN NORTH; VON BUELOW NEAR RIGA

or

AUSTRO-HUNGARIAN ULTIMATUM TO

RUMANIA BEING PREPARED

or

3865 BRITISH OFFICERS KILLED SINCE

THE WAR BEGAN, 700 WOUNDED

The note Wilson had rushed back to Washington to answer said the Germans still intended "to protect and save lives of German subjects" and that this took precedence over obligations to the interests of neutrals. The note repeated complaints against the British blockade and protested bitterly what it called England's aim to starve the German people. It said it would not allow American citizens to protect British ships by being passengers on them. The German position had not changed in any material way, and Wilson was not satisfied with it. He warned his Ambassador to Berlin, James W. Gerard, that he considered a matter of principle was involved, one that would not admit of compromise. He started work at once on his reply — the third Lusitania *protest.*

This third note was designed to put an end to the exchanges, which were already overextended and inconclusive. It called the second note from Germany "very unsatisfactory" and claimed that Berlin regarded itself as exempt from the principles of international law to which it had subscribed. It added that this country would feel impelled to insist on the observance of neutral rights and that any further sinkings "must be regarded, when they affect American citizens, as deliberately unfriendly." Secretary Lansing supplemented this with an oral warning to the German Ambassador that war could not be avoided if American lives were lost in another torpedoing of a merchant ship.

The protest itself was not sent off until July 21, and Wilson refers to it as a work in progress in his next letter, one that contained a dismal picture of life in the White House at the moment:

W.W. TO E.B.G.

The White House
20 July 1915
Tuesday morning.

My precious Darling,

You should see this house, — at least the upper story of it. Downstairs it looks pretty much as it always does, — because visitors look at it all the year round, I suppose; but upstairs! All the hangings are down, everything "stripped to the buff," and all the furniture is in white pajamas. When I arrived there was not a flower in the house, — only empty jars and vases standing about and looking as if they had always been empty and had been left where they were only because no one had thought or cared to put them away. It looked like a house not only vacant but vacated and left unfriended. And yet, as I told you in my note scribbled just after getting here — the very moment I reached the study table — I was not chilled by it all. You were not actually here, or everything would have looked and breathed of home, but your thought and love were here to greet me, not to take care of the house, but to comfort and reassure me and tell me of happy things which make loneliness impossible except in the stillness and vacant rooms about me. How happy it made me to realize it!

I did not take a long breath until after 4 o'clock in the afternoon, but went from one piece of business to another without pause. First I ciphered a dispatch to House about a matter I want him to try to help us handle in England (the matter of making cotton contraband which I mentioned to you the other day). Then I spent an hour with Lansing, catching up with many pieces of business but chiefly discussing, of course, the reply we should make to Germany, our regular correspondent! He had drafted a reply which was all right as far as it went, but which omitted some of the strong points of our case and stated those it did state too dryly. We agreed, therefore after I had made clear my own views of how it should be handled, each of us to try our hand at another draft. Then I went to work at the office (12:30) and, with a brief interval for lunch, worked until half past four, clearing up routine matters there. At 5 the doctor and I took a ride. It had been cooled off enough to sit in, for very soon after lunch a storm came up, a slow, sullen thunder storm with a torrent of rain, and it did not clear until we had been out for half an hour. We had dinner on the terrace, the doctor, Fitz William and I (Tumulty dining out) and after dinner I went at the note to Germany.[1] By half-past ten it was sufficiently in shape to discuss in language and detail with Lansing when I see him this morning at eleven (how I wish I could go over it and discuss it with my sweet partner!) and I ready to *fall* into bed, as you will readily imagine. But I was *too* tired. I am *very* well, immensely braced and invigorated by my three weeks with my Darling, it was only a sort of *satisfied* fatigue after something accomplished. Mac turned up last night and is lodging with us, and Colonel Brown is expected today, so you may think of us as six men condemned to see no one but each other and endure it as best we can![2]

Inasmuch as Tumulty and McAdoo *know* nothing to talk about but business and there is not likely to be silence when we are together, you can easily see how full a week of work your

---

[1] Joseph P. Tumulty, the President's Secretary, was also a political adviser and a personal friend. A Jersey City lawyer, he had been a member of the state legislature in 1907–1910 and then secretary to Wilson when he became governor of the state. He was one of the earliest and most active workers in Wilson's campaign for the Presidency. He was intimately associated with the President throughout both the Wilson terms. He was thirty-six in 1915.

[2] Col. Edward T. Brown, a lawyer from Atlanta and a first cousin of Ellen Axson Wilson's. He and the President were close friends.

lover is to have. But there seems no reason to doubt (Heaven be praised) that I can get off on Friday at midnight and be with my precious sweetheart on Saturday at one, for another week of uninterrupted happiness, and, that being the case, I don't care what happens to me in the meantime. The weather is quite endurable — and I am a salamander.

I *write* of the occupation of the day, My Darling, but my thought is all the while of you. The first chapter was full of happiness and sweetness and the wonder and delight of discovery and love, and my sweet one dreaded to see it end; but the second chapter has been sweeter than the first . . . It has filled my heart with a joy unspeakable. I feel myself united to my Love by bonds which nothing can make sweet or more intimate except *constant* companionship, and I know that she is incomparable and altogether lovely. Ah, my Sweetheart, my precious Sweetheart, you have made me so happy; I love you so deeply and tenderly; I am in every breath of me

Your own
Woodrow

There are a score of things I have not had time to say.

E.B.G. TO W.W.

The President's Cottage
Cornish, New Hampshire
July 20, 1915
9:30 A.M.

My own dearest One —

. . . I followed you all the weary way — and do so hope it was cool and comfortable in Washington. Did you come to the sofa at ten minutes to 1 and rest before lunch? I was in my room by the window in the big chair — and tried so hard to find you — but you seemed remote and as though you were thinking of me — but not able to follow out our program . . .

Well, the dinner party last night was very nice. I was interested to meet Mr. Churchill and found him interesting in some respects, but a subtle comparison always comes up in my mind when I meet men, to a very wonderful person whom I love — and the rest of humanity seems commonplace. This is absolutely true, Sweetheart, I have been so interested these past

few months trying it — and it has never failed — how different
the evening would have been had you been there.

Tonight the elder Mr. [Stephen] Parrish came to dinner —
and tomorrow five ladies to lunch. Then, as you remember, we
go to dinner with Mr. and Mrs. Fitch — and Thursday Miss
Parker has asked Helen and me to lunch with her but if we go
for the long walk with Jessie and Frank of course we will
not go.[1]

I saw in the papers that you were greeted all along the line
by crowds — so, I am afraid you had a tiresome trip . . .

Helen is ready, so goodbye Dearest until tomorrow. Take care
of my Sweetheart and know that I am always yours — Edith

*The next Wilson letter refers to the third Lusitania note sent
by Washington on July 21, the note containing the blunt reference to our regarding any further sinkings as "deliberately unfriendly." At the same time Berlin was informed through diplomatic channels that no reply to the third note was expected.
None was sent, although the matter dragged on for many
months; indeed it was still technically an open question when
we finally entered the war.*

w.w. to e.b.g.

The White House
20 July 1915
Tuesday 5 p.m.

My adorable Sweetheart,

. . . It was cruelly hard to drive away from the house on Sunday and leave you standing there in the doorway as if you were
not a part of me and I were not leaving my inspiration and real
life behind me. I did not lift my hat to my home: I lifted it to
you and did not cover my head again until the turn of the drive
hid you from sight and I was no longer in the presence of the
sweet, the incomparable lady without whose presence no place
can be my home. You are everything to me. Without you I

---

[1] Dr. Albert Parker Fitch (1877–1944), minister and educator, was president of the Andover Theological Seminary at this time. Later he was pastor
of the Park Avenue Presbyterian Church in New York. Marie Parker was
proprietor of the tea house near Harlakenden called the Tea Tray.

am maimed and imperfect. For I have learned what you are and my heart is wholly enthralled. You are my ideal companion, the close and delightful *chum of my mind*. You are my perfect playmate, with whom everything that is gay and mirthful and imaginative in me is at its best. You are the sweetest *lover* in the world, full of delicacy and charm and tenderness and all the wonders of self-revelation which only makes you the more lovely the more complete it is. You match and satisfy every part of me, grave or gay, of the mind or of the heart, — the man of letters, the man of affairs, the boy, the poet, the lover. When you are mine for every day I shall be complete and strong and happy indeed.

Do you wonder what I am doing in the study at 5 o'clock in the afternoon, writing to you? I simply *must* write to you every minute I am free to. It is just as instinctive with me, and just as necessary to me, as if you were here in the house and I were free for a little while to go and hold you in my arms and pour out to you everything that was in my mind or heart. We went out to play golf in Virginia, the Colonel, the doctor and I but it rained before we reached the third hole and we were driven home again. A hard morning went before — an hour with Lansing and two hours with the Cabinet; and, after lunch, I had to see a Senator and an M.C. to hear plaint and dire prophecy of what war was doing and was going to do to the cotton interests in the South.[1] It would have been fine if I could have had a couple of hours of golf, to clear the fatigue out of my

---

[1] The two were Senator John H. Bankhead of Alabama and Representative Samuel J. Tribble of Georgia, both Democrats. They protested the British enforcement of the blockade in the Atlantic, which had succeeded in suppressing the cotton trade of the United States with Central Europe. This was a matter of the gravest concern to Southern states cotton growers, who feared they would have no market for a large part of their crop. Great Britain had bought the part of the 1914 crop that normally would have gone to Germany, but as time for the picking of the 1915 crop neared, the Southern Congressmen were alarmed over the prospect that there would be no place to sell the crop in Europe. Wilson was afraid they might persuade Congress to pass legislation to put an end to arms sales to the Allies as a retaliation. Agreement was reached, however, that England would buy enough cotton from the 1915 crop to stabilize the price at 10¢ a pound. The pact was secret, and England went ahead and put cotton on the absolute contraband list and the pressure from Southerners for a retaliatory move grew even greater, but then the price rose as the British began buying and the crisis was passed.

brain. But a talk with you is infinitely better. That makes me *whole.* I am glad the rain sent me back to you. These sweet intervals when I can give my thoughts altogether to you and pour out my heart to you without restraint or interruption are, next to your own wonderful letters, the means of my salvation when I cannot literally have you, your own sweet self! Lansing and I have virtually agreed upon a note along substantially the lines you and I talked over — but we did not attempt to put the tentative text of it before the Cabinet today. We submitted only an outline of the argument; and the discussion went all ways at once, as usual, Garrison doing, as always, most of the talking.[2] He had brought with him *the complete draft of a note of his own writing* which he read to us. He seems to feel that he owes us this guidance. He does not expect us to see or think clearly enough to accept what he offers, but he feels bound in conscience to at least afford us the chance to be rightly and intelligently led! Dear fellow! It is hard that we cannot always follow him. On the whole I think most of the men approved of the answer Lansing and I outlined, I am glad to say, and I hope they will entirely when they read the completed text. We hope to have it complete by tomorrow and to get it off by Thursday or Friday. Friday at the latest, — and then back to my Darling.

What thoughts of you fill and gladden my heart, my Sweetheart! How deep I have drunk of the sweet fountains of love that are you — and how pure and wholesome and refreshing they are, how full of life and every sweet perfection! I have seen so many lovely things that make me feel as if I had been in a sanctuary, and yet in a place where there was welcome for everything that was human and natural and unaffected and intimate; and I have learned to love you, my Sweetheart, more and more and more, with each day and hour, with each experience and revelation of your very heart. It seems to me now as if you were indeed a very part of me. Those wonderful mornings when our minds grew to be intimate friends; those conferences in which our affairs and interests seemed to draw

---

2 Lindley M. Garrison, Secretary of War. He had been vice chancellor of New Jersey's highest court at the time of Wilson's election.

together and become merged; those afternoons of mere irresponsible companionship in the simple pleasures of a drive or a game of pool; those never-to-be-forgotten evenings when our hearts were opened to one another without reserve and with the joy of young lovers and when, as you say in this precious letter that came to me today, there was no one else in the world for us, — they have made me feel, not only that you were mine and I was yours as it has seldom been given to two lovers to be united but also that I had come into a world of joy and intimate happiness wholly created by one lovely, one incomparably lovely woman to whom my heart must always bow down with a new sense of privilege, a new knowledge of love. My love for you is deeper than all words, my precious One; and I *enjoy* you so! Everything in me enjoys you so, — and misses you so intolerably when you are away from me! Thank God for work! I do not know how I could endure the longing if I were not *obliged* to keep my brains busy all the while. Ah, how I need you! How empty the hours are without you! I can make shift while the working hours last; but when they are over, when there is time and opportunity for a touch of *home,* — when bedtime comes and you are not here to crown the day with your sweet sympathy and tenderness and comprehension of my need, how I get by these crises I do not know — how often, how long I shall be able to get by them I dare not try to think or reckon.

****

Wed. 21 July 7:15 A.M.

I was interrupted — and then had to go to dinner with the boys (!), and after dinner had a long conference with the Secretary of the Interior about the Alaska railways, ending with a discussion of life and religion! And then, being desperately sleepy, I went to my room at 9:30, elaborately anointed my head with hair tonic, a la Mrs. Coon and went to bed — with your picture on the little stand beside me, — so that, after I had read your dear letter again, it was the last thing my eyes rested on before I put out the light and turned over to go to sleep — with, oh, such a longing at my heart, but a sweet longing because I knew that you really and tenderly love me, as only such a woman as you are can, and that some blessed day not far away you would come to me and the longing would be fulfilled. That is what sustains me in the midst of all this terribly responsible work, when the world is gone mad and depends in part on *me* to steady it and bring it back to sanity and peace. I should be in danger of losing my own poise and coolness of judgment if I had not found you and won your precious love. I feel that more and more. You are not only the Darling of my heart but the source of all serenity in me and of the happiness that frees the faculties of a man for action. *I love you with all my heart.*

Your brother Randolph is coming in to take dinner with us tonight. Isn't that fine? I am looking forward with such pleasure to having a chance to really know him; — and perhaps, if the evening is hot, he would like to take a drive with us after dinner. I have not been able to get off any other evening. Grayson had a long talk with Mr. Clapham[3] yesterday which was *most* satisfactory about Rolfe if he will only stay in Panama.[4] It would be folly, and embarrass all his friends besides, for him to come away. — Is my Darling happy? Does she *feel* how her lover's thoughts follow her, and with what infinite tenderness and love? My Darling, my Darling, I am always and altogether

Your own
Woodrow

It was during this five-day stay in Washington that Wilson made an important move in a controversy that had arisen over whether the country should embark upon a huge military preparedness program because of the war in Europe. At first he had opposed a virtual crusade launched by certain political leaders — particularly former President Theodore Roosevelt — and interventionist societies to draw attention to the weakness of the Army and the Navy. It was only gradually, and after the submarine crisis and the Lusitania *sinking, that Wilson*

---

3 Mr. Clapham is not further identified.
4 Rolfe Bolling, Mrs. Galt's oldest brother, was manager of the Commercial Bank of Panama.

reversed his position and became a convert to preparedness. On July 21 he asked Secretary of War Garrison and Secretary of the Navy Daniels to investigate the adequacy of their services and to make recommendations. As a matter of fact, the generals and the admirals had already been at work on such plans, and in November the President was able to present a program to the country. Peace groups, who opposed any use of military power as an instrument of diplomacy, kept up their fight and the continuing dispute consumed much of Wilson's time until an increased armaments program was finally enacted by Congress in 1916.

W.W. TO E.B.G.

The White House
21 July, 1915
Wednesday, 6:50 P.M.

My precious Sweetheart,

My pen will hardly obey me at all because I am tired and a good deal out of spirits, but I simply *must* talk to you a little, my heart needs you so. I am tired, not because of the *amount* of work I have done today, but because of the kind. The German note is complete and will probably go off tonight or early tomorrow morning: today we made all the final decisions of phrase and subject matter. It is so direct and emphatic and uncompromising (I did not see how in the circumstances, to make it anything else) that it brings us to the final parting of the ways, unless Germany yields — which, I fear, is unlikely. That is why, besides being very tired, I am out of spirits and so desperately need my darling, — the touch of her hand, the love light in her eyes, the consciousness of her sweet sympathy and comprehension! And so I must speak *to* her, at least. —

10 P.M.

I was interrupted by the coming of the Secretary of State for a last word or two about the note. He stayed until 7:30 when your brother [John Randolph Bolling] came in for dinner, and since I have had the pleasure of talking with *him*. We have just come back from a ride in the park and he has gone home in the car. I thoroughly enjoyed being with him — and shall try to get him to come again some time. I did not tell

Robinson what route to follow but he took us through the ford beyond the Miller cottage, and I had the thrill of one of the sweetest memories a lover could have.[1] My adorable Sweetheart! How it would have interested your brother if he could have known what my thoughts were at that moment! Lansing left me a copy of the note, my darling, and I am enclosing it. It will not be given to the public till Saturday morning, but of course you may privately read it to the little circle of students of American history whose departure for bed used to be our introduction to paradise!

Tonight you are dining with the Fitches and will meet a man much more vital and interesting than "the wonderful person" whom you love and to whom you generously ascribe such perfections. I am glad your heart is engaged. He is very wonderful!

22 July
Thursday 7 A.M.

I broke off here last night because I was so sleepy that I could not quite see the paper and could not go on rationally, sheer reaction from the strain of the day. The ride had soothed me without resting me. It was a heavenly night, the air a little heavy with moisture but cool and refreshing, the moon prevailing over all and shining with a sort of calm lustre that seemed a sort of rebuke to disturbed and anxious thoughts. And yet it could not cure the ache at my heart because you were not there, but rather increased it with its calm beauty, which made me feel nature unsympathetic and my need for another kind of beauty, the beauty of human love and comradeship all the greater. I talked freely, and enjoyed talking, with your brother and hope that he did not see that I was out of sorts, but *you* would have noticed the difference, for it was an effort and I did not wholly overcome the mood before the ride was over. This morning nothing is left of it except a very solemn sense of the momentous decision I have made and of all the consequences which may be involved for this great country we love and for the millions of people in it who so generously trust me and so confidently depend on me to keep

---

[1] Francis Robinson, a White House driver.

them out of the horrors of this war. Cannot my Darling pray for *me*, that I may be guided and all things overruled for the good of the world? I would be willing to sacrifice myself at any time, but how can any man think with even tolerable composure about sacrificing millions of his fellow men to his own individual, almost unaided judgment? In the midst of all these anxieties and perplexities, my precious Darling, only one light burns steadily for me, and that is the light of your dear love. In the midst of the whole confused scene stands your dear noble figure. Your starry eyes and that wonderful smile of yours, full of love and reassurance and light, seem to me to be my beacons and to show me how to steer. I never needed you more — needed you close in my arms, to whisper into my lips the sweet love that gives me life — than I did last night — than I do at this moment!

I know that your dear spirit is with me — I feel it every hour of the day; but, alas! things do so crowd and distract! You ask whether I came to the sofa for a few moments' rest in your arms before lunch on Monday. No, Sweetheart, your instinct was right. I was thinking of you intensely, but things press hardest and most insistently just at 1 o'clock, just at the culmination of the forenoon's work, and would not *let* me come. The connections *were* imperfect: I could not speak to you or hear you speak. But the wires were not *crossed* and there was no obstacle or impediment between your heart and mine. Business may be imperious and *command* my attention, but my heart is with you every minute of the twenty-four hours. And how deeply, with what eagerness and joy do I love you and claim you for my own! These days of heart-breaking responsibility, on which each twenty-four hours seem to count more than a decade of an ordinary lifetime, are binding us so closely together by every kind of tie that someday we shall be grateful for them and look back to them as the days when we really read one another's souls and *knew* that love and sympathy and comprehension had grown perfect between us, — the time when the real marriage of our hearts was consummated and we were made sure of all that was to follow in the sweet days when we were to be constantly together and always and in everything united. It is my strength that you love me, my precious, my incomparable Darling! How deep do the foundations of our happiness go!

Your own
Woodrow

E.B.G. TO W.W.

The President's Cottage
Cornish, New Hampshire
July 22, 1915
10 A.M.

My precious One —

It seems almost too good to be true that tomorrow night you will be starting back again — and that this is the last letter before you come.

Your dear letter of Tuesday came yesterday while we had four guests to lunch so, again, I had to wait before I could read it — but, at last, they departed and I took it out in the hammock (where we have spent so many happy hours) and read it. You sounded so busy and so content that it did my heart good.

Your description of the house was so forlorn that I almost got blue picturing how dreary a homecoming it made for you — and then a great wave of happiness came over me — that — in spite of such surroundings, you still feel my love and that its very warmth cheered bare rooms . . .

Then at 7 we went to dine with Dr. Fitch and his wife and had a very stimulating evening. As soon as I saw him I recognized that I had heard him preach at New Haven last February . . .

Always your
Edith

Wilson left Washington for Cornish on July 23 and stayed there this time until August 11. Mrs. Galt was there until August 2.

The White House
23 July 1915
Friday 7:15 A.M.

My precious Darling,

It seems absurd to write you a letter that will get to you at the same time I will myself, but somehow it is necessary to ease the impatience of my heart; and, besides, I never believe in my good fortune till it actually comes. I have my travelling clothes on this minute and know of nothing that *can* prevent my start for Cornish this afternoon — possibly on the very train that will carry this letter — but I know that *something* might turn up any moment to stop me — and you will not *have* to read this if I come myself! There will be nothing new or novel in it. The necessity that is on me this morning is laid upon me by my heart *every* morning, and will be until I die, — the necessity to pour out my love to you. In spite of myself I have been sad the past two days, or, rather, oppressed with the consciousness of many things in whose presence I *cannot* be gay or light-hearted, and never before have I felt the need of you, of your care and love and companionship, so poignantly, so as if to be without it were a constant handicap, a momentary loss of force. I cannot work at my best (it has been so all my life) unless my heart is satisfied and at ease. It is not that the work I do is inferior — I could not prove that — but it is done at infinitely greater cost to me, and I cannot doubt that it lacks the spontaneity and color of life that it would otherwise have. My eagerness to get back to you is simply the crying out of every part of me for added life; my mind, which finds yours its satisfying partner, my heart, which feels at every turn of the day and of our sweet intercourse the exquisite response in kind of your own, — the boy that is in me and who has found a perfect playmate, the lover in me who has found love like his own, only more subtle and pervasive, like the perfume of a flower, and the man of affairs, who finds in you a woman fit to be a man's counsellor, "to warm, to comfort, and command" — and yet "not too bright or good for human nature's daily food; for transient sorrows, simple wiles, praise, blame, love, kisses, tears and smiles." You satisfy, delight, *and complete me,* and I cannot for a moment be wholly happy while separate from you! And this is the love message that goes before me. I shall have the exquisite pleasure of *saying* all this to you, — but that will be tomorrow, and my heart must have ease today — as much as I can give it. Your own

Woodrow

I am perfectly well.

W.W. You don't know her! That's the very time she *wants* to comfort and help. She is the sweetest lover in the world. But I have, I hope, at last learned a lesson, — live less selfishly, and particularly to guard myself when I am tired and forlorn — wounded, as at Princeton, worn to a frazzle as yesterday at Washington.

Curtain: 5 A.M.

Correct report. Attest

Woodrow Wilson

My precious Darling,

My heart is yours, — to do with what you will. I have no wish but your happiness.

Your own

Woodrow

Wilson returned to Harlakenden on July 24, the day the content of the third note to Germany was made public. On that date Alfred G. Gardiner, editor, wrote in the London Daily News:

President Wilson is not merely the first citizen of the United States but the first citizen of the world. In refusing to yield an inch on the rights of American citizens he is defending the sacred ark of freedom.

AUGUST 1915

The letters grew in number, and especially in length, in August as the correspondents were separated for almost the entire month. It was a time of travel for Mrs. Galt. Two old friends, Mr. and Mrs. Hugh Lawson Rose, went to Cornish on August 2, and she went with them for a motor trip and visit to their home at 10 Park Place, Geneva, New York. Mr. Rose, described as a retired farmer, and his wife spent much time in travel and led an active social life. On August 20 the Roses and Mrs. Galt went by automobile for the long journey to Ocean City, New Jersey, a trip marked by many tire punctures and other inconveniences of motor travel in 1915. At Ocean City Mrs. Galt met her mother and her sister Bertha for a visit at the Hotel Normandie. On August 30 she went to New York with the Roses and then returned to Washington on September 1.

The President, meanwhile, was at the Summer White House until August 11, when he went back to Washington.

In the first part of the month there was a lull in German-American problems. The war was now a year old and the end was not in sight. Twenty-eight million men were under arms. No one would have been rash enough to guess the outcome, but both sides were predicting victory. A high French official said that the Allies were fit to continue fighting "and will do so until victory is theirs." The Secretary of the Imperial Treasury of Germany said: "The British starvation war has failed . . . Work, skill, discipline, organization and economy . . . and the

*categorical imperative of patriotism . . . will help us further to
win the war."*

*Military analysts chose the anniversary to put the fighting
into perspective.* The Washington Post's *expert wrote:*

> The astounding development of the airplane both for scouting
> purposes and as an offensive weapon is one of the most striking
> features of the first year of the great war. Military men as a
> result of the year's lessons consider an army not equipped with
> airplanes as absolutely at the mercy of a similar force using air
> scouts. It is a blind man fighting a man who can see.

The problems the President faced upon his return to Washington were still centered on the frightening but increasingly likely event of our involvement in the war. There had been another ship sinking, this time the British Iberian, in the warzone off the coast of southern Ireland. It was a merchantman in service carrying horses and mules from America to England, and when it was hit it was going from Liverpool to Boston with a cargo of general merchandise. The principles were the same as in the earlier sinkings, and the President did not mention it when he wrote Mrs. Galt four days later, "nothing new of consequence has turned up."

The President's last days at Cornish were filled with golf and automobile rides and routine business, punctuated by the receipt of such bad news as word that the Republicans were increasing their opposition to his preparedness program and threatening to make it an issue in the 1916 political campaign.

The good news of the day came from Mrs. Galt, who wrote on the first stop after her sad departure from Harlakenden:

E.B.G. TO W.W.

Manchester, Vt.
Hotel Equinox
August 2, 1915
10 P.M.

My precious Sweetheart —

It does not seem possible that only *twelve* hours ago we were on the porch together. I did not know a day could be so long! Tonight when I heard your dear voice on the telephone I wanted to cry out all my love and longing for you — and, instead, I had to be conventional and say only the things neither of us wanted . . .

I have thought of you every minute all along these roads that seemed almost ugly because you were not there. Every foot of the way to Springfield [Vermont] was familiar ground and yet how strange and empty and unfriendly it seemed. It was a positive relief to me when we got beyond Springfield and the constant reminder of our rides together was left behind, for there was such an ache in my heart. I felt I could not look on things that spoke of you. We went to the Adna Crown hotel for lunch and Mr. and Mrs. Rose said the food was good, but as it was not spiritual food I could not eat it and talked to cover my lack of appreciation. Just after leaving there we ran into a heavy storm and the going was bad until we reached Chester. From there we seemed to run out of the storm and the rest of the trip was lovely. This place is really awfully pretty — great mountains surrounding it on all sides and the houses are quaint and attractive . . . but oh! how I do long for my blue nest at Harlakenden and I find myself listening for a dear footstep in the hall, or the sound of a vibrant tone that finds its echo in my heart . . .

If I wrote all night, my precious Woodrow, I could not tell you of the perfect happiness of these past weeks or thank you for the infinite tenderness and thought I felt you always surrounded me with. So, I leave it to your unfailing intuition, and comprehension; and only tell you that I love you with all my heart and that I am with you now and always. Goodnight my wonderful sweetheart.

Your own
Edith

W.W. TO E.B.G.

Cornish, N.H.
3 August 1915
Tuesday, 7:15 A.M.

My own Darling,

What a thrill it gave me to hear your dear voice over the telephone last night and what a struggle I had with myself to hold back from pouring out to you in words the love that was in my heart! I had made the day go well enough till lunch time, — so far as steadiness of spirits was concerned, — but the afternoon had been a fight in which I cannot claim to have altogether won, — and the whole world hereabouts was so desolately empty and devoid of beauty! I went to work immediately after your motor disappeared round the turn in the driveway — immediately after that lovely hand, waving its farewell, had been withdrawn the second time. The regular work of correspondence was done by 12 o'clock, as I had foreseen it would be, but I managed to eke out work enough to last till 1 by attacking the great pile of commissions and other papers they had sent up from Washington for my signature, some two or three hundred of them.

The time between lunch and 4, while Helen and Jessie and I went for a ride, was the critical period in my fight for self mastery because there was nothing in particular to do. I was even reduced to playing pool by myself and trying to put more balls in for you (the alternate shots) than for myself! While we were out driving Mac and Nell [McAdoo] arrived. They had come in their own motor from Boston. The baby has been perfectly well now for four or five days and Mac prevailed upon my dear Nell to come with him. She is radiantly well, just her own vital and delightful self, and it was a joy to see her and hold her in my arms again. Miss [Clare] Batten, Margaret's friend, had also arrived and we had quite a lively circle in the morning room after dinner. Four girls (and Frank on the arm by Jessie) sat on the lounge, and I sat in the desk chair.

I took Nell into the music room after a while and told her of the great happiness that had come to us, my precious one, and I know you would have been touched and delighted if you could have seen and heard how she took it, — with unaffected joy that I should have found escape from my loneliness and comfort and support now and in the days to come, and even the little she had seen of you had given her an impression of you that made her glad that it was you she was to welcome. Isn't it wonderful how they all three understand and how their sweet love for me interprets the whole thing to them perfectly? I *knew* Nell would receive the news as she did. If anything could have made me love these dear girls more than ever, this experience of their power to comprehend and sympathize has done it — bless their hearts! And when, in the sweet months and years to come, they have a chance to know you in the intimacy of family life they will love and trust you and admire you in a way that will complete our happiness, my Darling . . .

This afternoon Sister Annie, "little" Annie, the baby Josephine, and George Howe arrive and the circle in the morning room will be changed altogether . . .[1]

And so, my precious one, you are posted to date about all that has been happening to the Wilsons at your home at Harlakenden. In public business nothing of new consequence has turned up. I am putting in another envelope one or two letters and messages which explain themselves. The most interesting and unexpected piece of news is that that unconscionable old scoundrel [Victoriano Huerta], who is in the steady clutches of the six-foot-four Scots Presbyterian elder down in the Lone Star State, has appealed to the Imperial German government to protect him and his followers [in Mexico] against us! Lansing sent me a confidential letter from Bernstorff to him enclosing a copy of Huerta's message to him (B). The old fool seems still to look upon himself as a sovereign government and appeals to the German government to represent him at Washington — that's what it comes to. Did you ever hear of anything more amazing? I've no doubt Bernstorff would have been delighted, but didn't dare . . .

9 P.M.

I have stolen away to the study, my precious One, to have a few minutes with you. Sister and the rest are in the morning room, but I could not stand it there without you, — particularly

---

[1] This reference is to Wilson's sister, Annie Josephine, Mrs. George Howe, of Columbia, South Carolina. Her daughter, Annie Cothran, twenty-four, wife of Perrin Chiles Cothran of Greenwood, South Carolina, was the mother of a small daughter, Josephine. George Howe was Annie Howe's son. He was thirty-nine and was a particularly close friend of Wilson's, having lived with the Wilson family when he was a student at Princeton in the class of 1897. He was a classics scholar and taught for many years at the University of North Carolina at Chapel Hill.

now that I have that blessed love letter you wrote last night in Manchester at my heart and the hour has come when we used to shut out the world (the curtains are down close in the morning room now and the fire is lighted!) and look into our own hearts alone. How full the room seems of you! You said in your sweet note that you would be in Troy tonight, but Margaret and I have just called up *all* the hotels in Troy and have been told that you are not registered in any of them, so I suppose Mr. Rose changed his plans again and I shall have to deny myself even the sound of your dear voice tonight . . .

My heart aches because you are not here, but it rejoices and is full of joy and pride because you love me and have given me that supreme gift of love, your own dear, wonderful, delightful, adorable self, the noblest, most satisfying, most lovable woman in the world. I love you, I *love* you, and *you love me.* What can touch me now? My thoughts will follow you every hour till we meet again, with, oh, such deep and yearning tenderness. My hopes are all in your keeping — and I know them to be safe there. I am full of strength and confidence because our lives are united and my Darling is happy, as I am, in their union. These weeks have been infinitely happy and have given me what my heart desired. My Darling has blessed me, and I love her with all my heart. I am always and altogether hers!

Your own
Woodrow

Mrs. Galt continued to report on her progress toward Geneva, the next letter containing a paragraph on something that amused her:

E.B.G. TO W.W.

Schenectady, N.Y.
August 3, 1915
6 P.M.

Dearest —

. . . I must tell you something Mrs. Rose said to me last night in speaking of you and the girls. She said you all seemed so devoted to each other that she wondered if you should marry again if it would make the girls unhappy, adding that you were so charming and attractive she knew women would fall in love with you — but adding, in a comforted tone, that of course "with all he has on his mind he can't give his thoughts to any women . . ."

Edith

It was on August 4 that Mrs. Galt began her first letter from Geneva:

10 Park Place,
Geneva, N.Y.
August 4, 1915

Dearest and best beloved —

I have missed, and wanted you so today that I know you have felt it. And I can hardly wait until tomorrow to get your blessed letter telling me of yourself and

August 5, 10 A.M.

My precious one —

I began writing this last night as you see but could not finish it on account of one of those rare, but awful headaches I have. I had to stop and go to bed — and so before anything prevents this morning am going to have a much-needed talk with my "other self."

I am quite well again this morning and think the headache was really neuralgia as it has been so damp and rainy for days but this morning is perfect, with floods of sunshine — and I am by a big window with my purple writing case beside me and everything to make me happy *but, one great lack.*

How I did long for your tender fingers last night to rub away the pain in my eyes. After all I wondered if it was all physical pain — or if the longing at my heart increased it ten fold. It was *our* anniversary of May 4th and that made the distance between us seem greater.

Just here the postman came — and I have just finished reading your beloved letter covering Tuesday and Wednesday — and also the enclosure in the other envelope. You were sweet to send me such a long messenger when you had so many

On October 9, 1915—two days after their engagement was announced—the President and Mrs. Galt went to Philadelphia where they attended a World Series baseball game between the Phillies and the Boston Red Sox. (*Courtesy of the Library of Congress*)

President Wilson making a Flag Day address on the steps of the Treasury Department building on June 14, 1915, only a few weeks after he met Mrs. Galt. She referred to the speech in a letter dated the day before. (*Courtesy of the Library of Congress*)

A widely circulated newspaper composite picture of the President and Mrs. Galt released at the time of the announcement of their engagement in October 1915. (*Courtesy of the Library of Congress*)

Helen Woodrow Bones. (*Courtesy of the Library of Congress*)

Edith Bolling Galt in a photograph taken by Arnold Genthe in 1915, the official picture used in connection with the announcement of her engagement to President Wilson. It was the most widely used of all her photographs and was considered her favorite. *(Courtesy of the Library of Congress)*

President Wilson autographed this photograph for the crew of the U.S.S. *George Washington* on which he went to Paris for the peace conference in 1918–1919. *(National Archives)*

The President and Mrs. Wilson leaving a meeting of the Daughters of the American Revolution in Washington a few months after their marriage. *(Courtesy of the Library of Congress)*

The President and Mrs. Wilson. From a photograph in the Wilson room at the Library of Congress. (*Courtesy of the Library of Congress*)

The President and Mrs. Wilson during a visit to Princeton University. Dr. Cary T. Grayson is on the right. (*National Archives*)

Harlakenden House at Cornish, New Hampshire. It was the Summer White House in 1915. (*Brown Brothers Photograph*)

Col. Edward M. House. (*Courtesy of the Library of Congress*)

The President and Secretary of State Bryan photographed together in 1913. (*Courtesy of the Library of Congress*)

A newspaper photograph of Mrs. Galt's house at 1308 Twentieth Street made at the time of its demolition in 1960. She had sold it many years before. (*Washington Evening Star*)

The President and Mrs. Wilson at the opening of the first air mail service, between Washington and New York, on May 15, 1918. *(Courtesy of the Library of Congress)*

With tender love to the loveliest lady in the world.
W.
The President

18 Dec. '15

This card was enclosed in the President's gift to Mrs. Galt on their wedding day. *(Courtesy of the Library of Congress)* guests and things to claim you and every word has brought me happiness . . .

This is just the time we used to work, and I am wondering if you still take your work out on the porch, or if you sit in the study — or your room. I am always with you, and love the way you put one dear hand on mine, while with the other you turn the pages of history . . .

As always

E

At this moment the war news was particularly bad: Warsaw, the third largest city in the Russian empire, was captured by the Germans, the most serious loss yet for the Allies. Exultant German officials quoted in dispatches from Berlin predicted the end of the war before winter.

In San Antonio, Texas, a man named F. W. Juergens was arrested for sending threatening letters to the President demanding that this country stop selling munitions to the Allies.

W.W. TO E.B.G.

[Mailed from Cornish to Geneva, N.Y.]

4 August 1915

Wednesday Afternoon

My precious Darling,

Your dear letter from Schenectady has just come and has filled my heart with such a deep flood of joy (as that from Manchester did) and such a sweet abundance of content, that I must put everything else aside, close the door, take you in my arms, cover you with kisses, and tell you how full to overflowing my thoughts are with love for you, my wonderful Sweetheart . . .

5 August 1915

Thursday morning

Business has gone on in a sort of routine, my precious Sweetheart, since you left, and has been *most* uninteresting because you were not here to share it. The critical matter just now is Haiti, and the complications of that we have not yet mastered. We are holding Port-au-Prince until we fully know what they are and get some key to them. It's a pretty mess! A long note from Germany about the sinking of the *Frye* (long ago) gets us no where and affords additional proof of how insincere and impossible they are.[1] I am sending you, in a big envelope, Page's last letter, just received.[2] Keep it, Dearest, if it is not in your way, till we get back to Washington, unless you had rather return it and get rid of it.

Margaret and I labored last night for about a quarter of an hour with Central to try to get a telephone connection with 10 Park Place, to see if you had reached there and were told that Mr. Rose did not have a Bell telephone? Is that true? I did not believe it, but had to accept it, since I could not go out and find out for myself . . .

The Carters arrived yesterday afternoon [from Williamstown, Massachusetts]. Jessie and Frank got back from York Harbor (where they had left Helen well and happy to be with her friends again) about 5 and we had a most talkative evening. Mrs. Carter is very lively and attractive and is really great fun, and it was delightful, while she talked, to think of *you,* my charming, entrancing Darling, and of all that the sweet secret between us means.

It does not make me proud to think of myself as the (temporarily) beloved President of 100 million people of a great Nation, but it does make me proud to think of myself as the

---

[1] The American ship *William F. Frye* was sunk by a German auxiliary cruiser in the south Atlantic in January. It was carrying a cargo of wheat to England, a cargo Germany considered contraband. Berlin refused to concede that the sinking was a violation of United States' rights under a Prussian-American treaty of 1828 or under international law. She would pay for the ship but that did not satisfy Washington, which considered payment as settlement of damages only and was demanding assurances of the rights of its nationals to be safeguarded. The controversy over German recognition of these rights continued throughout the rest of the year in repeated German and American notes.

[2] Walter Hines Page, Ambassador to England, kept up his steady advocacy of United States' intervention in the war. When Wilson was trying to establish a law practice in Atlanta in the mid-1880s he met Page and they remained friends. Page became editor of several magazines, including *The Forum* and *The Atlantic Monthly,* and was a partner in the New York publishing house of Doubleday, Page and Company. His letters from England during the war were published later and were widely read.

accepted and trusted lover of the sweet lady whom I adore. While Margaret and I were sitting here in the study last night working over the telephone connections with Geneva, Sweetheart, she told me of a conversation she had had with Nell about us, and said that Nell was evidently deeply and sincerely happy about it all. Then we fell to talking about you and I think it would have made you very happy to hear with what warm admiration and affection she spoke of you. I did not lead her on to it or invite it. It came with evident spontaneity and the tones of her voice meant more than the words themselves. You are going to be the idol of your household, my precious One, and will have to accept the fealty and worship of us, but I hope you will wish it chiefly from

Your own
Woodrow

Now that Mrs. Galt had reached Geneva, the President wrote to her every day and sometimes more than once a day. On August 5 he told her that he had ridden over to Springfield, Vermont, for the sole purpose of seeing a hotel where she had lunched on the day she left Harlakenden. He appended to the letter a story about a dream he'd had that night:

W.W. TO E.B.G.

[Cornish, N.H.]
6 August 1915
Friday morning 6:30

I am just up, my precious One, and had such a strange experience in the night. At five minutes after 2 (I lighted the candle by my bedside and looked at my watch) I suddenly waked up with, oh, such a pang at my heart because *I could not find you.* I found myself exclaiming "Edith, my Darling, *where are you?*" It was as if you had been at my side but a moment before and had gone utterly away both in person and in thought. The desolation and loneliness of it was unspeakable. I had to get up and wake myself thoroughly to recover myself and see things right again.

I wonder if it at all corresponds with any dream or experience of my Darling's? I hope not. I would not like to have her suffer so. And it was so strange, coming as it did, in the midst of calm happiness! Perhaps it was only because no letter from my precious one reached me yesterday and I felt specially lonely. I can easily imagine how that happened because I have been finding out about the mails between here and northern New York and they are slow and roundabout . . .

I think of you every moment of the day. And the love is combined with so many vivid and delightful things which I am sure I should feel whether I loved you or not, with a deep admiration, with the consciousness of *greatness* of character in you, a greatness not only of faculty and feeling but also of personality which your extraordinary vitality and charm render irresistible.

I so deeply *enjoy* every thought of what you are and so rejoice to have the stimulation of it and the sense of beauty and sweetness, besides — of a wonderful woman, as trustworthy and capable and fit for counsel as any man, but quick with a power of love, of sympathy, of inspiration which no man could possess. I never feel so proud or so strong as when I know that I am

Your own
Woodrow

E.B.G. TO W.W.

Geneva
August 5, 1915
Midnight

My precious One —

Will you forgive a pencil tonight? For I am in bed where I cannot use ink without endangering some very lovely linen things in the way of sheets and pillow cases — and I must talk to you a little while before I put my light out.

Shall I give you a picture of my abode that you may better visualize me. Well, this is a big square room with high old-fashioned mantelpiece between two big windows. The latter have white curtains with blue borders and the walls are blue and white. All the furniture is big and massive, and by one window is a writing desk where you can sit and talk to loved ones or gaze out over a big green yard full of big apple trees and on into a vegetable garden beyond. But — to come back to the room — in the center of the side wall is a wide, old-timey bed with big pillows piled high and just now, in the center of them, rests a lonely lady who loves you very deeply and while she writes is almost deafened by claps of thunder and torrents of rain that roar and clash without. Just overhead is an electric light which makes even the vivid lightning less disturbing than it would be . . .

Mrs. Rose asked me in such a naïve way this morning when I said I wanted to write to Margaret and Helen to thank them for all their sweet courtesy to me, "Oh, but you won't have to write the President too, will you?" that I almost laughed but managed to say, "Well, I hardly suppose it is necessary but I might send him just a line." Then tonight when your telegram came, Mrs. R. answered the phone and then called me and said it was a telegram and she was afraid someone was sick. So, of course, I told her it was just a message from Margaret saying she hoped we had all arrived safely, when she said, "Oh, of course, they have read of all these dreadful rains and have heard nothing from you since you phoned the night you left. So they may have been uneasy."

I almost had to bite my tongue to keep from saying, "Oh, yes I have written every day except yesterday," but fortunately I caught myself in time and, instead, said, "Yes, I suppose they have and it was like Margaret to think of sending us a line of greeting."

Oh, Sweetheart I almost die of internal combustion when the Roses tell their friends of you and your charm and other people ask questions and say how wonderful they think you are. I want to go and hug them for appreciating you and then stagger them by saying you love me and how perfectly I worship you. But of course I can't do either of these things and just keep quiet for fear if I do speak I will say too much . . .

Your own
Edith

W.W. TO E.B.G.

My precious Darling,

It was a great comfort to get your letter today from Geneva and know that you were really safely there. There seems to be something strange and inaccessible about 10 Park Place! I've told you how we tried to telephone you the night you arrived, Wednesday, and were told that Mr. Rose had no Bell telephone connection. Well, last night, Thursday, Margaret tried to telegraph you, early in the evening "Hope you all arrived safe and well. Love from us all" and not only got no reply but was unable this morning to obtain any assurance from Western Union that the telegram had been delivered. Is Mr. Rose at outs with the telephone and telegraph companies?

I have no idea of the house or of the household at No. 10 apart from Mr. R's love of the motor and of golf and his passion for bridge in the evening, and find myself at a loss to follow my Darling with my thoughts through the day because I cannot picture what she does. Please give me a sample day or two and tell me something to think about concerning the people you meet and an idea of what your room is like, won't you, my precious dear One? I don't like to lose you in strange places. It is part of my happiness to be able to follow you very definitely in my thoughts . . .

I think it is likely that I shall be off to Washington by Sunday afternoon. Do you know that I am beginning to think of Washington with a liking that I never had before, and I think it is altogether because it has been *your* home, you like it, and I found you there! I can now think of it and feel about it otherwise than as merely the center of politics and personal intrigue . . .

I am more happy every day to be your own

Woodrow

[Mailed to Geneva from Cornish]
7 August 1915
Saturday evening

My precious, lovely Sweetheart,

Today's post brought me that sweet, sweet letter written in bed Thursday night and finished yesterday morning, and my heart is aglow with its love and tenderness and with the sense it conveys of your dear self. How ardently my love goes out to meet it, and what unspeakable delight it gives me to receive such adorable outpourings of my Darling's heart!

"Forgive a pencil," indeed! What difference does it — can it — make to me what my precious Sweetheart writes *with* when I read in every line evidence of the love that is the breath of life to me? You sweet thing! I fancy I can see you (you would not mind, would you?) propped in the old-timey bed in that stately spare room, writing to your lover, with a heavenly light in your sweet eyes! And how dear it was in you to divine that I would want to know what your room was like, and what one can see from the windows. You always read what is in my thought, and always will, I am sure; for love is a wonderful wizard in such things, and my Darling's love is of the sort that makes divination easy. You manage too, my sweet One, to get the *atmosphere* of love into your letters — how I do not quite make out — I suppose by the same magic by which you put your personality into everything you do and say. You succeed in thrilling me by everything you do and say. Your letters *make* the day for me.

Today has been uneventful, except for your letter. The mail has for the rest been quite barren of anything of interest. I had a long letter from Lansing in reply to one of mine about the reply he has just prepared to Austria's protest about the selling of arms and ammunition to the Allies; but you know the points in that controversy and there is nothing vital or critical in it anyhow. I am trying to see if there is anything workable in Page's suggestion to Sir Edward about a rescinding of the Order in Council of March 11th, in view of the declaration of cotton as contraband — and House is in communication with both Sir Edward and Spring Rice.[1]

I fear there may be a little irregularity, my Darling, about your receipt of my letters (although you may be sure that one will be dispatched every day) because these contemptible spies the newspapermen are curious about every special visit either the doctor or I or anyone in the family makes to the P.O. and I do not like to send my letters by messenger that carries the others from the house at regular intervals; and the big envelopes that contain the things I forward to you will not often come by the same post that brings me letters because they (the big envelopes) go out with the regular official mail which Tum [Secretary Joseph P. Tumulty] carries down every afternoon at 4, just as we are starting out for a drive. By the way, do not trouble to return any of the documents I send, Sweetheart, unless I specifically indicate that I should like to have them back at once . . .

How jolly, my Sweetheart, that you are taking golf lessons (and how I envy the teacher — you will be adorable as a pupil!) Of course, we shall have many and many a game together — as many as I can persuade you to play . . . Remember "Ye must take a fir-r-m hold on yoor cloob, but ye mustna sput on your hands." If you'll give yourself as free a swing in hitting the ball as you give yourself in walking, you'll beat me all to pieces. What jolly times we'll have together, you and the open fields and a good game all put together are surely all that a man's heart could desire when play time comes, as you and a good book or you and an interesting piece of work, or you and a good long talk are all that a man's heart could desire when the hours come when one must take up the things of the mind and the tasks of business.[2]

---

[1] Sir Edward Grey, British Foreign Secretary, and Sir Cecil Spring Rice, British Ambassador in Washington.

[2] Wilson played golf primarily because Dr. Grayson insisted that it was good for his health. His scores were never impressive, but he enjoyed the camaraderie of the game and loved making jokes about it. He had a favorite description of the game: "An ineffectual attempt to put an elusive ball into an obscure hole with implements ill-adapted for the purpose." Also, he loved golf stories, and one he told over and over again concerned President Grant: One of Grant's friends insisted on the President's coming out with him to

I can't get that fascinating picture of you in the midst of the pillows of the "big, low, old-timey bed" out of my head, or the longing out of my heart to stoop over you there and take you in my arms and cover you with kisses. Do the words of love I write make your heart glow, Edith, my precious Darling, and give you the deepest happiness? It must be because *something* of the *passion* of love that is in my heart as I write them — and all the other times of the day and night, too — gets into them, pale and inadequate as they seem to me as I write them. They are very poor coinage of my heart. I've never yet made "image and superscription" of my sovereign queen on them when I wanted them to be, or what my heart conceived . . .

I am in every thought of my heart

Your own
Woodrow

A domestic crisis arose this summer in Mrs. Galt's family. Her niece, Elizabeth Bolling, daughter of Mr. and Mrs. Rolfe Bolling, who were living in Panama where he was a banker, announced her intention to marry a Panamanian, Jorge Eduardo Boyd. Her parents strongly disapproved. The plight of the lovers attracted Mrs. Galt's sympathy, and the President fell heartily into the dilemma and tried to be of help, as the next few letters show. Despite the near-frantic efforts of her family to stop her, Elizabeth married Boyd on August 18. He was twenty-nine, a lawyer, and diplomat. He had received a law degree from the University of Pennsylvania and had served as secretary and chargé d'affaires in Panamanian legations in London, Paris, Brussels, and The Hague and as chief counselor at the Legation in Washington. He later was an associate justice of the Supreme Court of Panama and was Ambassador to the United States in 1940.

see him play the game, then new to this country. The friend was nervous over the presence of the President, and after teeing the ball, he struck the ground and the ball merely rolled from the tee. This made him more nervous and the next time he missed the ball entirely. The grave-faced Grant remarked: "It does seem to be good exercise, but what is the ball for?"

E.B.G. TO W.W.

[Geneva]
August 7 1915
Saturday 9:45

My own Precious One —
I need and want you today. I have had such disturbing news
from Panama . . . and I am heartsick for the dearest, tenderest
Sweetheart in the world. If your letter of Thursday and early
yesterday morning had not come by the same mail to comfort
and bless me, I don't know what I should do — but I have it
here close beside me and I am getting the calm help that your
presence always brings.
I am so sorry you were so unhappy in the night Thursday.
It came from no cause I can ascribe, for I was with you and
had not even gone to sleep after finishing the pencilled letter
I wrote you after midnight. And I have been with you all the
time. I am so glad you are playing golf and taking rides. It
will do you lots of good and I want you to be so well and so
happy . . .
The news from Panama is from my brother's wife and she
writes that Rolfe is on the verge of a collapse mental and
physical and that she is waked at night by his sobbing, and
thinks if Elizabeth does carry out her plans, it will kill him.
Still she tells me nothing about the man or why it is so awful
and that she had telegraphed her brother, who is a doctor
(and a jackass, I think) to come down and thinks if his influence avails nothing she will have him give the girl something
to make her unconscious and put her on a boat for home,
though first he is to *threaten* the man.[1] Did you ever hear of
such a dime-novel plot? She is keeping this from Rolfe as she
thinks he would go mad if he should have further anxiety.
She has also written another man friend of E's to come and
she has taken the Edwards into her confidence and Gen. Edwards' suggestion is as mad as hers.[2] It is to have Rolfe pretend

---

[1] Dr. George Litchfield, Jr., of Abingdon, Va.
[2] Brigadier General Clarence R. Edwards, United States Army, com-
manding general in the Canal Zone, and his wife.

to collapse in the bank, be carried to a hospital and have her told doctors think him in a hopeless state unless she gives up her plan, that this could easily be carried out for he looks so terribly that even Elizabeth wrote him a letter telling him how dreadfully she felt to see him so distressed and that she would do anything or give up anything *but* the man to try to restore him.

Forgive me for writing you so much stuff — but I know you agree with me that they are all crazy and there is nothing to appeal to in such a state . . .

All my love to you my precious Woodrow.

Always your own
Edith

E.B.G. TO W.W.

[Geneva]
August 7
Saturday 1:40 P.M.

My own Dearest —

. . . I am afraid my letter this morning was rather depressed but I have got myself in hand now and given up worrying over the Panama situation. I wrote Elizabeth this afternoon and told her that I was utterly in the dark as to why her parents objected to the man and only knew of the deep unhappiness that had come to them all, so I would reserve my judgment until I knew and hoped she would write me frankly and fully with the assurance that I would be loyal to her if I felt I possibly could, that by cutting herself off from those who loved her she was cheating herself and making what should be the happiest thing in her life a perfect tragedy — that, if Mr. Boyd was what she thought him, he would love and admire her for following her father's wishes long enough to prove to them by waiting; that he, Boyd, was worthy of her — or something along those lines. But I am afraid it will do no good and I really feel anxious about Rolfe's health . . .

Yours now and always
Edith

The President's Cottage
Cornish, N.H.
8 August 1915
Sunday evening, 9:30

My precious Darling,

It grieves me past all expression that you should have received such news from Panama and I not beside you to comfort you and counsel with you! It is *so* bad, so incredible, that I cannot believe that such mad counsels *can* prevail for long together. I *must* believe that they will all "come to" and see that they are making things worse, not better, and that General Edwards should join in the madness, caps the climax. Apparently, however, my brains will not work upon the matter any better than theirs will for I must admit that I am utterly at a loss to suggest *anything* that can be done. Perhaps a letter of deep *sympathy* from you, combined with calm advice, would serve to calm and soothe your brother a little; and it may be that, since she has written to you and taken you into her confidence, a letter of warning from you to Mrs. Bolling as to the danger and folly of her course might cause her at least to pause and consider. You may use my name if you choose, since she happens to think so much of me. *Any* means of impressing her could be justified in the extraordinary and alarming circumstances, and I hope you will not hesitate to act upon this suggestion. God knows it's little enough! My heart *aches* to think of my Darling's sore distress and perplexity and my inability to help, even with serviceable counsel. To think of her lying stark awake all by herself with not so much as a hand to touch while she thinks her distresses out, while all the time my heart is full of her and everything in me that is fine yearns to do her service and help her to happiness and peace of mind and heart, while I would give anything in the world to go to her and give my life to her — is almost too much to bear in addition to *my* need of *her*.

We are certainly being tested out, little girl! There is at least this solace in this letter of yours that tells of your increasing distress, that it shows that my love *does* help you, and that

you feel it in hours of unhappiness as something that sustains
you, — something that you can absolutely depend on. Indeed
you can, my precious One! Your days of loneliness are over.
All that I am is yours. And I have come to you for that very
purpose, — to *help!* If only I *could* help — if only *anybody*
could help in this blind, mad business. All that I can give is
my unbounded love and sympathy — my whole heart. I have
thought about the dear people in Panama almost as much and
as anxiously as you have, I venture to say, but alas! to no
practical purpose. I can only give them what you give them,
my deep sympathy, and such counsel as you may be able and
willing to convey for me. I wish with all my heart that they
had some friend down there with more sense than that fool
Edwards . . .

9 August 1915
Monday 6:30 A.M.
Last night, my Darling, I had a message from Lansing saying that he thought it was probably best for me not to come
down to Washington just now, for fear the newspapers might
give the impression that there was some sort of a crisis in the
Mexican conference. Always the newspapers! They make the
normal and thorough conduct of public business impossible.
I feel that I *ought* to be down there: there are so many critical
pieces of business, like that in Haiti, for example, the *small*
guiding threads of which — the threads which really define
the pattern of the whole transaction — I do not see clearly or
at all, and I feel that I am rather blindly following the lead
of the Secretary of State. I wonder what lead *he* is following?
The A.B.C. conference has adjourned to New York for convenience and on account of the great heat in Washington. It
will convene again on Wednesday. Its deliberations have been
most harmonious and it is acting, Lansing says, with enthusiasm because of being consulted at all. But I will send you
Lansing's letter about it. It is very interesting. If they do not
get lost in the jungle of abstractions, they may make the journey we wish them to make. Lansing has been sensible on the
selection of his committee to formulate a plan. They will

probably report something concrete and definite — I hope also workable.

Yes, Sweetheart, Page's last letter does throw a good deal of light, it seems to me, not so much on the situation as on the state of mind in England and among the Allies. And, after all, it is the state of mind that we must be guided by, if we cannot change it. They are ready to believe anything, evidently, — particularly the incredible. It would look as if Europe had finally determined to commit suicide, as Carlyle thought it had at the time of the French revolution, — and the only way we can help to save it is by changing the current of its thoughts. That's the only reason it's worthwhile to write notes to Germany or to England or to anybody else. They alter no facts; they change no plans or purposes; they accomplish nothing immediate; they *may* convey some thoughts that will, if only unconsciously, affect opinion, and set up a counter current. At least such is my hope; and it is also the hope for these distressed English . . .

My thought turns again to Panama this morning, my precious One, and the longing for you in my heart is, if possible, greater than ever. I still think that what your brother needs is, not counsel, not suggestions plots and plans and escapes, but just deep, loving human sympathy *in the presence of the inevitable,* and especially an outpouring of it from the dear Sister he loves and trusts and depends upon so. Does his foolish wife think that if by any trick they get Elizabeth away from the Isthmus, Boyd cannot and will not *follow* her at once; and does she not see that that would hasten the marriage, for he would certainly marry her the minute he found her? Indeed there is a sense in which he *ought* to, if he has a speck of spunk and gallantry in him. *I* would if I were in his place in such circumstances. And that will be the first thing that will occur to her also. Is Edwards going to arrange to have *him* kidnapped and start another Panama revolution? . . .

All the dear ones send their love. I send more than any letter or any messenger could carry, for I am altogether and in everything

Your own
Woodrow

W.W. TO E.B.G.

The President's Cottage
Cornish, N.H.
9 August 1915
Monday evening

My precious Darling,

Your letters fill me with a delight to which I do not know how to give expression! They breathe the very spirit of intimate love and give me the sort of deep-seated exaltation and joy that came to me during those last evenings we spent together here, when our hearts seemed absolutely opened to one another without need of interpretation, and the satisfying delight came to us in full flood of complete comprehension and acceptance of the great love that revealed itself to us, like a blessing without stint and out of heaven itself . . .

There is not a moment of the day when I am not consciously with you in thought, and with every thought there goes the yearning that can be quieted only when you are in my arms or holding lovingly onto my hand or sitting close beside me and sharing everything that I think or do. Just now, after dinner, I was sitting with Jessie and the doctor in the morning room. I was in the deep chair that stands between the writing desk and the fireplace. As I looked at that dear lounge, the curtains closely drawn behind it, tears came into my eyes — very happy tears, for there my darling had wholly surrendered her dear heart to me and endowed me with a love that makes me sure of every sweet and sacred and precious thing that my heart can desire, but tears of real pain too, because she was not there but hundreds of miles away, longing for me as I long for her, and yet kept away because those who do not and cannot understand command our lives and not we ourselves — and we must wait, for that which alone can make our lives complete! . . .

I think you wrote the right, wise, and sweet thing to Elizabeth, my Darling. You always *think a thing straight,* — and I cannot help hoping that what you have written her will make the deep impression on E. it ought to make. It may be that her distress about her father will do not a little to open her heart to advice. She knows that she has always got the truth

from you, and she knows it comes in love and not in reproof —
and it comes not from the heated air of Panama, but from a
cool distance where people can keep their heads. How sweet and
fine you are about it all, my splendid Darling! I am so much
obliged to you for telling me about it — and I am so proud
that such a lady loves and trusts me!

E.B.G. TO W.W.

Dansville, N.Y.
Jackson Health Resort
August 9, 1915

My precious One —
I was oh! so glad to get your two blessed letters this morning
before we started for here and could hardly wait to read them
but beyond just a hurried peep to see if you were still at
Cornish tomorrow long enough to get my letter, I had to wait
until this afternoon to really read them. Then I sat at my
window here overlooking the most wonderful view of smiling
valleys full of ripe grain and green hills beyond, and read and
reread your wonderful words of love and my heart was just
so full of love and yearning for you I felt you must feel it . . .
Tomorrow we are leaving here about 8:30 to go on to Letch-
worth Park which everyone says is entrancingly lovely. It is a
large tract of land owned by the state of New York, I think,
and containing wonderful trees and a waterfall . . . We expect
to get back to Geneva tomorrow night, where my heart will be
made glad by your letters of today.
I am so glad, you sweet thing, that you are beginning to
love Washington. Nearly half of my life has been spent there
and, while I would follow you wherever you went, I would
always be a little hurt if you hated Washington, and if you
can love it because I do and because you found me there, it
will make me proud and happy and I will do all I can to make
it from now on seem really like home . . .
Have you tried, my dear Lord, to write our story? Or have
you had time and heart to? Your letters are such love poems
that I feel selfish to keep them just to myself although it would
hurt to share them with anyone but you. So, someday I am
going to read them aloud to you to let you share the real joy

I have in them. I am so sorry you were so alone Saturday
night. My how I wish I could have stolen into the billiard
room and before you knew I was there put my hands over
those dear eyes and made you guess who? . . .
Good night — a real lovers' kiss — your own

E.

*An accumulation of things in Washington led the President
to decide on August 10 to cut short his vacation and go back
to the Capital. He left on the next day and arrived on August 12.*

*The Mexican situation had grown worse. Mexico City had
been under three different governments in 24 hours of street
fighting. Carranza, leader of a faction we were later to recognize, had now rejected the efforts of the United States and
the Latin American Conference countries to try to bring some
order out of the chaos. The day Wilson reached Washington
the newspapers that were on his desk said that the "Carnival
of massacre and loot in Mexico City is worse than the outer
world feared" and the "capital was ravaged by six successive
bandits with title of president leaving a trail of blood and
famine with American lives in daily peril."*

W.W. TO E.B.G.

The President's Cottage
Cornish, N.H.
10 August 1915
Tuesday evening.

My own Darling,
    I know that you understand why I am returning to Wash-
ington tomorrow afternoon notwithstanding the fact that I
have not been summoned and there is no *special* piece of
business that I am going back to handle in person, for your
mind acts as mine does in such matters of duty, and I instinctively feel you think, as I do, that I *ought* to go.
    Today, for example, I authorized the sending of the Atlantic
fleet to Veracruz on Lansing's judgment that the moral effect
would be good, — since it is said that the Carranza authorities
there are countenancing mob violence against foreigners. No

doubt he is right, but I do not know enough about the details upon which he has formed his judgment to be sure that he is, and the consequences of the presence of the fleet there are a bit incalculable. I ought to be at headquarters to guide the whole thing.

And so of other matters, in Haiti and elsewhere: I am depending too much on other persons' judgments. I was at the White Sulphur, I can't help recalling, when the Tampico incident occurred which led eventually to the occupation of Veracruz. I shall be in Washington in time to direct matters after the arrival of the fleet at Fool Carranza's capital. Just because he is a fool a delicate situation which will have to be carefully watched and safeguarded . . .

There is a story in the papers this morning which, I need hardly tell you, is chiefly not so. Yesterday, after the storm, as we were driving along the river road between Windsor and Ascutneyville we came upon a little group of three or four automobiles which had stopped near a machine which had turned turtle over the bank at the side of the road, a bank not more than three feet high. The people who had been in the machine — two women and a man — were already safely out and quite unhurt. We stopped and made inquiries, of course, and made certain that nothing could be done until the wreckers came from the garage in Windsor to which another passing motorist was just starting to carry word, and I left the Secret Service men and their car to take the women into Windsor and render any other service they could — that was all. There was no rescue or heroics of any kind, any more than there was when we found that car tipped against the sapling at Echo Lake one day. It was so commonplace an incident that I had forgotten all about it when I wrote you of our ride in my last letter . . .[1]

Wednesday morning 6:45
I must confess that I leave with a heavy heart. There is nothing but work down in Washington and the fussing and scheming and palavering of many minds — and that bare and

---

[1] Newspaper accounts of the President's role were considerably more dramatic. They reported that he found three badly bruised people trapped under the automobile and personally helped to pull them out of the wreckage.

empty house with its ghostly furniture is not a home-like place to go to. It will seem emptier than ever now. But I'm game for it. It is plainly my duty to go and stay long enough to get hold of things very thoroughly — it may be until *next* summer; and I shall get adjusted to it within 24 hours after I get there. Moreover, I shall be happier there than I've been for many and many a long day — for many and many a long *year*, if time were reckoned by events and anxieties. I shall have a peace of mind that will make me proof against all "the slings and arrows of outrageous fortune," for I shall rest secure in our perfect love, with thoughts of my adorable Darling, my own Edith, that will fortify me against everything but longing for her sweet presence, the sound of her voice and the touch of her lips. I'm secure against unhappiness now, whatever else loneliness and yearning may bring upon me . . .

Goodbye, Sweetheart; I must go to work. I shall try to write at least a few lines from the train, so that you may not go a day without a love message from

Your own
Woodrow

The next letter, which Wilson wrote on the train en route to Washington that night, is the first he wrote to Mrs. Galt on his typewriter. He used it constantly in his office, drafting many state papers on it. It was a 1913 Hammond multiplex portable. After his departure from office the machine was disposed of as surplus property during the Harding administration. Later it was acquired by members of the family of Dr. Grayson, and they gave it to the White House in 1962.

W.W. TO E.B.G.

En route (Cornish to Washington)
11 August 1915
Wednesday evening

My precious Darling,

I hate to write to you on the typewriter, but I simply cannot manage my pen at all on the train, and I do not want you to go a single day without a love message from me . . .

We left Windsor this afternoon at 3 and are now passing Hartford, Connecticut. After doing all the work in sight this morning after breakfast, I took a drive with the two girls and Sister Annie, and a rather interesting thing happened. We were on a quiet, out-of-the-way road that we have been on only once before this summer, as far as I can remember, the road from Plainfield to Cornish Flat, when we met another machine. The road was so narrow that we stopped to let it pass. It was driven by a gentleman who looked very hard at me as he approached. When he got abreast of us he stopped and, rising in his machine, said, "Mr. President, I have here a little bunch of thirteen four-leaf clovers for you. I hoped I should have a chance to see you, and now a happy accident has thrown me in your path. I twice had the pleasure of giving similar bunches of clover to Mr. Cleveland while he was President, and take great satisfaction in finding you to give these. There is also in the bunch a clover with seven leaves. I doubt if you have often seen one."

I stood up in our machine, as he did in his, and thanked him very heartily. I was so taken by surprise by the whole thing that he had finished his little presentation and gone on his way before I realized that I had forgotten to ask his name, and know only that he looked a thorough gentleman, and a very pleasant one at that, and was accompanied by a lady with a face full of sweet good nature and quite unusually quick intelligence. Wasn't that an interesting little encounter; and was it not odd that our ride should have taken us on that particular road today? I am genuinely sorry that I did not identify him. I liked his looks so much . . .

I shall mail this immediately on our arrival, and it will carry with it the whole heart of

Your own
Woodrow

I would like to keep on indefinitely, but the swaying of the train makes me a bit dizzy.

Arrived safe and well. Devoted love

W

10 Park Place, Geneva.
August 11, 1915
9:45 A.M.

Welcome home, my precious one, and oh! if I were only really there to throw my arms 'round you and make you *know* how welcome you really are — always . . .

I believe, in a way, you will be happier in Washington and certainly more content that you are in direct touch with things that are so vital . . .

Thank you again for all your sweet sympathy about Panama and your permission to use your dear name. I have not written to either Rolfe or his wife again because I did not want any other letter to get there at the same time mine did to Elizabeth for fear she would think they had asked me to write. I told her if she wanted to get away where she could think things over quietly for a while, to come to me — but not to let Mr. Boyd follow her — for that would defeat what she wanted — and I could not help her. Another letter from Rolfe said the uncle was to arrive the next day so I am holding my breath to see what happens. I am sorry you have really worried over it but please don't do any more for we have done all we can.

Now I must go. I will write tomorrow. My tender love and a welcoming kiss from your own

Edith

Geneva, N.Y.
August 11, 1915

My precious One —

The town clock is just striking midnight — and, while I lie here in my big bed with the windows wide open to the cool night air I am picturing you on a hot, dusty train rushing through the darkness and I will stop to whisper a little prayer for your protection and safe arrival in the place that has been home to me for so many years.

I have thought of you all through the day and pictured your leaving and all the longing in my heart has been rushing out to meet you. I do hope the faithful Mr. Hoover will have things ready for you tomorrow with flowers everywhere and the house with an air to bid you welcome.

I sent my letter to Mr. Hoover today and trust you will get it promptly. I am so afraid you are going to find it terribly hot in Washington, so please, Dearest, be careful.

After I finished my letter to you at noon I went down on the porch with Mr. Rose. He is really deeply distressed over the death of his brother and seems to dread being alone. We got maps and tried to work out the best route to Ocean City [N.J.] — for they have definitely decided to take me thence in their car and will remain a week before they come home and Mother, Bertha and I go back to Washington.

After lunch Mr. R. went to play golf and I wrote a lot of letters — among which was an answer to Nell's dear note to me. About four I got sleepy and took a little nap before reading the papers. We three went to the country club for dinner and as it (the club house) is beautifully situated on a point looking out into the lake it is very lovely there. And there was a beautiful sunset. We got back a little after 8 and Mr. Wheat came to play cards. We had an interesting game and did not stop until 11. Three other people came to call so we got started very late. I have had invitations for every afternoon and evening but as the Roses are not going anywhere I have been able to decline and I am enjoying the freedom of doing as I please.

Have you heard from Helen? I wrote her as soon as I got to Geneva but have heard nothing from her and do hope she is not sick, but just taking a good rest.

I saw an account in three papers of your going to the rescue of the motorists in distress — and, allowing for newspaper exaggeration — I suppose there must really have been a "human interest" story this time. How your description of the little Otter Creek Tea House brought back our happy afternoons there — and after reading your dear letter I fell asleep and dreamed it all over again just as it really happened. Just in the midst of the dream Mr. Rose called me to give me a telephone message and I thought for one happy moment that it was you who had called me — and, not until I was fully awake, could I convince myself that you were far away. You seemed here — in the room — and I could not let you go.

I will finish this in the morning after I get the mail. Goodnight my precious one. And a happy awakening when we get home!

Thursday — 12.

The mail came a half hour ago (just as your train was due in Washington) and I hope you are not tired out and can get adjusted to the change of climate before you have to plunge into work.

Your dear letter seems sad as though you felt the weight of things more acutely than you admit — even to me. I know it was hard to leave Cornish and all the dear ones there and feel that your real holiday may be over for months — but, I believe, (as I wrote you yesterday) you will worry less in Washington because you will have everything under your own control.

Bless your precious heart! How I wish I could really be the help you say I am. Never before did I long for the wisdom of a well-informed mind half so much for then I could be a staff for you to lean on — but if a keen sympathy and comprehension can lift the burden even a little bit, then I am a help to the wisest and dearest person in the world . . .

As to the other letter about that *Traitor*, my blood boils when I think of him — and I am afraid if he were left in my hands by an inscrutable Fate, I would put him where the world would never be troubled with him or his "peace" *sheep-clothing* again. Oh, but I would love to publish this letter in every paper in the land. And add to it what I think of him. Thank you for the picture and the cartoon. That is so absurd it doesn't hurt — but this other thing is so low words can't reach it. You will think me a firebrand if I don't stop — so I will change the subject and tell you that I am ashamed of these drably written sheets after reading your letters where even the clear, legible writing bespeaks perfection. But on the other hand, the two letters are characteristic of our personalities and there is no use my trying to impress you with even a pretense of law and order. I am what I am and as you love me you forgive the blots and overlook the faults and make me happy by your tender comprehension. Goodbye for today dear, tired little boy. Remember how I love you and that I am yours with all my heart.

Edith

The White House
Washington
12 August 1915
Thursday evening, 8 o'clock

My precious Darling,

Your sweet, sweet little letter of yesterday, though the last part of it was not written till noon, reached me, to my great delight, a little before noon today. Hoover walked into the study here, where I sat alone working, and handed it to me in his most sober and formal manner, but with an evident effort to make it seem as if it were a perfectly simple and routine thing for him to receive letters for me in that way. He's a brick! I respect him — his real tact and natural dignity — as much as I like and value him. He is going to be one of our best and truest friends. And what an exquisitely sweet letter it was he handed me!

Ah, my Darling, there is no adequate way in which to tell you what these precious letters of yours mean to me, with their tender intimate love, except to hold you close in my arms and cover you with kisses and whisper into your lips all the most endearing names that lovers ever invented to give their hearts ease. You *were* at the train at Windsor, Sweetheart, you were with me on the journey; and you were here to welcome me. You are every where for me, and the consciousness of you transforms all those familiar places, makes these empty rooms feel like home — a home merely waiting for you, its mistress and glory, to come. And I can almost *touch* you when I read those dear, dear letters. It is almost as if you were speaking them in soft whispers in my ear and your breath was on my cheek. I thrill with the sense of your nearness and your exquisite charm and loveliness almost as vividly as if I actually held you close to my heart and were soothed and quickened by your sweet caresses.

No, Sweetheart, I do not wear myself out or let any worry

upset my spirits. I am not keeping a calm face or "playing the game" to keep anxiety or distress away from you. I am well and do not chafe under the burden of the day. If you did not love me as you do, — as you have loved me since those blessed days of revelation at Harlakenden, when our spirits sprang together in a union which nothing can ever sever or disturb, — if you did not give me the wonderful tender love spoken so sweetly in those letters which are like your very own self, — I think that worry would find me out and wear me out. But there seems nothing to distress myself about since you gave yourself to me.

I think intensely about the intricate and difficult matters that press upon me so insistently and seem to afford no way out of perplexity; I give the best that I have of intelligence and of labor and of my conscience to them, and they tug mightily at my heart strings as well as at my mind; the day's work is always intense and sometimes exhausting; but it touches no vital part of me. I breathe an atmosphere now so sweet and tonic that nothing can really hurt me or impair my vitality. It was not so only a few weeks ago . . .

But I must not forget to tell you an amusing thing about Cornish. At the Discussion Club last Tuesday (this is a group brought in by the doctor from the Shipmans' — no one from Harlakenden attended) the subject was "Feminism: Is It a Menace?" and Mrs. Churchill read a paper on "Love" which went on and on for the better part of two hours! She paid no attention to interruptions or comments. Twice Mrs. [Herbert] Adams, in a sweet, gentle voice said, "May I ask a question?", but not the slightest notice was taken of her either by Mrs. Churchill or anybody else; and, when the paper seemed at last to be concluded, Mrs. Shipman said that without meaning to imply the least criticism of what Mrs. Churchill had said, she would very much like to know just what the point was that Mrs. Churchill had been trying to make? But Mrs. Churchill paid no attention to the question and neither Mrs. Shipman nor anybody else, as far as she could learn by pointed inquiry, ever did find out. I was dying to find out what Mrs. Churchill's idea of love is, and whether she thinks it works or not — but I could not — apparently because she herself could not tell. And whether feminism is a menace or not they seem to have forgotten to determine. What would I not have given to have had your account of Mrs. Adams' spiritual assessment of the workman's task . . .

That was a lovely letter you wrote Elizabeth, My Darling, — just like you in generous thoughtfulness and practical good sense. I wish that she might, under its influence, have a lucid interval, accept the invitation and come. Great a burden as it would entail upon you, that would be easier to bear than your present anxiety and perplexity about your brother. I, too, hold my breath for fear what we shall next hear from that uncle . . . The A.B.C. (and B.U.G. — Bolivia, Uruguay and Guatamala) conference adjourned after their meeting yesterday until they could hear from the factional leaders whom they had addressed in their appeal (I send you a printed copy of it today for your convenience, should you wish to refer to it). There was nothing further to discuss until they did. I do not expect much from the conference except a certain very valuable moral effect on Latin America as a whole, and, indirectly, on Mexico itself, because of what it so clearly indicates as to the *spirit* in which we are trying to act — not playing a role of selfish aggression, not even playing Big Brother to the hemisphere too arrogantly. And yet it may have some practical effects, too. I shall not give up hope for them until the whole program is worked out and I can see just how far we can make them go along with us . . .

Friday, 7 A.M.
13 August 1915

There is to be no Cabinet meeting today. There is nothing in shape to be formally discussed or finally decided, and I am never anxious to hear the opinions of my dear colleagues of the Discussion Club. I see those who are acting on the things that need action — and when I see them every word said means business. That's what I like. That's what I get satisfaction out of. Except for *seeing* people, there is very little more regular business each day here than there was at Cornish, but the exception is a huge one. All sorts of demands for interviews will come crowding in now. The town is beginning to fill up with men of the restless, meddling sort. Some of them are Southern Congressmen with wild schemes, propositions and impossible schemes to valorize cotton and help the cotton planters out of the Reserve Banks or out of the national Treasury or out of anything, if only they can make themselves solid with their constituents and seem to be on the job. Hoke Smith is one of these; Bob Henry of Texas is another.[1] The difference between these two in character is very great, however. Bob Henry is a fool, but he is honest — I need not complete the antithesis! I am going to send you today, in the big envelope, a letter from House which contains an interesting (!) item about Hoke Smith. Spring Rice intimated the same thing about him to House in a recent talk with him. If it's true, I hope they can prove it — and the sooner the better, for he is making a great deal of mischief . . .

Your own
Woodrow

W.W. TO E.B.G.

The White House
Washington
Friday 8 P.M.
13 August 1915

My precious Darling,

The doctor and I played golf on the Chevy Chase course this afternoon, and, as we were driving back, my thoughts full, as always, of you, I could not help thinking aloud when we reached the point on Connecticut Avenue just above Dupont Circle. "This is the place," I said, "where I first saw Mrs. Galt." "Yes," he said, "and you asked me who she was." We recalled that you were wearing a red rose that afternoon. And then we fell to talking of you, — how could I resist it? The doctor had said this morning that probably no one ever had in a lifetime more than one such friend as Colonel House, if he were fortunate enough to have one, and so, when we fell to speaking of you, I said that you were another such friend as

---

[1] Senator Hoke Smith of Georgia and Representative Robert Lee Henry of Texas were two leaders in the Congressional fight to get relief for the Southern cotton growers who were caught in England's embargo against the shipment of cotton to Central Europe. Senator Smith was pressing for a Congressional investigation into British interference with American trade.

Colonel House and he agreed very heartily. And it was no mere piece of sentiment on my part, Sweetheart, any more than it was on his. That is my deliberate judgment. I feel about your character and the disinterested loyalty of your friendship just as I have so often told you I felt about House.

If I did not love you I would still utterly trust you and cling to you and value your clear-sighted counsel, in which you would be thinking for *me* as House does, as I would value that of no one else in the world, not even his. You are talking nonsense, dear little girl when you speak of wishing that you had "the wisdom of a well-informed mind" in order that you might be a "staff for me to lean on." I have plenty of well-informed minds about me. I can get all the wisdom of information I can make use of. That is not what I need. What I need is what you give me, — not only a keen sympathy and comprehension, that you speak of yourself and know that you give me, but an insight into the very needs of my heart that nothing but your sweet love could supply, and the support of *a great character,* in love with reality, vivid with life, rich in all the qualities that inspire and delight. And the *capacity* of your mind is as great and satisfactory as that of any man I know. I have not loved you blindly, and I will not let even you depreciate the wonderful lady whom I love with my mind as well as with my heart. I have dealt with many sorts of persons about many sorts of things, things intellectual and things practical, and I know my equals when I meet them. I know what I say when I say that you are fit to be *any* man's helpmate, the partner of his mind as well as of his heart, and I include men who are far and away my superiors in gifts and capacity and character!

I don't think that you realize what pleasure, what delight, you give to every faculty of appreciation I have. You have faults, of course, — though I cannot for the life of me remember what they are, — but I do not "forgive" them: I love you so that I do not see them, — and I love you for cause, because you satisfy everything that is in me and call out all that is best in me. I could not love or admire a blue-stocking or endure a woman politician. So, please, Ma'am, don't try to alter yourself! It's *you* I love and admire and enjoy. It's you who completes me with what she gives of tender love and instant comprehension and frank counsel and companionship that fills *all* the needs of my thoughts and my affections. And, oh, Sweetheart, these dear letters that you are writing! They contain something that your letters never contained before, — something that makes my heart sing . . . I do not wonder that invitations pour in on you for morning, noon, afternoon, and evening. Who that has seen you and has been with you would not want you to be their sweet guest? But I like your declining them all. It shows your instinctive loyalty and characteristic good taste. My, how I *like* you, Edith, my incomparable Darling. And how you can *hate*, too. Whew! I fancy this very sheet lying before me on which you have written about Mr. Bryan is hot under my hand.[1] Isn't it rather risky to use mere paper when you commit such heat to writing? And yet, Sweetheart, I must add, that in my secret heart (which is never secret from you) I love you for that too. For he *is* a traitor, though I can say so, as yet, only to you . . .

My hand is very tired and shaky tonight — I've been writing for nearly two hours — and I must stop. It's hard to stop. These are the most precious and most delightful hours of the day for me, these hours when I can sit here, night and morning, un-interrupted, and talk with you, letting my love have sway and my thoughts dwell wholly on you, whom I love with all my heart, purely, passionately, ideally, — as only such a woman *could* be loved. Goodnight. A lover's kiss and love unutterable sent to you through the night to find you as you lie alone in the stately room and make you dream of your lover, who in every thought and purpose is yours. *My* Darling!

Your own
Woodrow

E.B.G. TO W.W.

Geneva, N.Y.
August 13, 1915
Friday 11:30 P.M.

My own Dearest —

I am afraid this has been another wretchedly busy day for you — for I know from the manifold things I found in my big

---

[1] See E.B.G. to W.W. August 11.

envelope today — how thoroughly you are going into things. You are a dear person to take the time to write little sentences on each of the papers you send me. It adds so much to the interest and gives them just the personal touch that would vitalize any subject for me and seems almost as though we had read them together. Just as the mail came I was reading the *New York Times* account of the A.B.C. matter and the letters that had passed between the Mexican heads and I was so glad to know the original note was to go as it was first drafted. Thank you my loved Lord for keeping me in close touch with these things that are claiming you and all your efforts.

It seems to me if Col. H has read the cipher message from our representative in Berlin he would advise a change of air for him as more necessary than to Mr. Page.

I could get little out of his message — as it seems to me he was not quite clear about it himself. What about Mr. Hoke Smith's speech in regard to cotton, etc., which, the papers state, caused the forwarding of a letter to you to ask for the convening of Congress — though stating that the men from whom the request came stood back of you? [1]

Also, is it true that you have asked the Secretaries of War and Navy to give you suggestions for preparedness for war — and that you are planning how to finance the increase in war preparedness? Everyone here says this is a splendid move on your part and I wonder if they knew and if you really are doing this. You know I do not mean this for inquisitiveness but just because I know you don't mind telling me, and I am so keen to know of everything you are doing.

I felt so queer this afternoon reading all these reports from the different theaters of war, sitting here in my quiet room, away from everything, in a tiny little town beside a calm lake. *I* — an unknown person — one who had lived a sheltered, inconspicuous existence now having all the threads in the tangled fabric of the world's history laid in my hands — for a few minutes — while the stronger hand that guides the

---

[1] Senator Smith in a speech in New York on August 11 urged that Wilson proceed as vigorously against British violations of neutral rights as he had against German violations.

shuttle stops long enough in its work to press my fingers in token of the great love and trust with which you crown and bless my life.

Always your own
Edith

W.W. TO E.B.G.

The White House
Washington
14 August 1915
Saturday, 8 P.M.

My own Darling,

You will be astonished to receive, by parcel post, a box of white and black silk stockings! It is one of four boxes sent by grateful Belgian women to the President of the United States and his family. There is, in addition, one box of silk socks. I fear that they will prove to be miles too big for you, the size being *á la Belgique*. If they are, send them back and I will compare them in size with the rest (I *think* I know how) and see if there are not some that are smaller. If there are not, we shall not know what to do with them, for you are as tall as any member of the family — though both Jessie and Nellie have bigger feet, I am sure. It will be jolly if they fit and you like them, for there are three boxes more of them.

I am all by my lone this evening. I dined, as my Darling has so often done at 1308, in lonely state. Tumulty has gone to spend the weekend with his family on the Jersey coast; Fitz William [Woodrow] has gone to Atlantic City at the summons of his new chief [Charles] McChord of the Interstate Commerce Commission, who is there; and the doctor is with Miss Gordon, I am glad to say, who leaves for the West tomorrow afternoon. He was with her last evening, too, till quite late (after 11), but he seemed grim and out of sorts this morning when we were playing golf — and played carelessly and very badly. He says nothing to me of how his intimate affairs are going, so I can judge and conjecture from external signs and symptoms only. Poor chap! . . .

I took a drive, too, all by myself this afternoon, from 3 to half past 5. My route was Potomac–Rockville–the Seventh

Street Pike . . . Ah, Sweetheart, my precious Edith, what memories crowded every foot of the way! If it had been evening and moonlight, I do not know that I could have stood the sweet pain of it all and when we (Murphy, Burlasque and I) got to the ford I could hardly keep from uttering out loud the longing that was in my heart.[1] I took the ride because of its memories and associations — and they were exquisite — *any*thing associated with you is exquisite . . .

I got back to the house before the band concert on the South Lawn was over and heard, I fancy, the greater part of the program as I sat writing at my desk. At the end, when they played "The Star-Spangled Banner," I stood up all alone here by my table at attention and had unutterable thoughts about my custody of the traditions and the present honor of that banner. I could hardly hold the tears back! And *then,* the loneliness! The loneliness of the responsibility because of the loneliness of the power, which no one *can* share. But in the midst of it I knew that there was one who *did* share — *everything* — a lovely lady who has given herself to me, who is my own, who is part of me, who makes anxieties light and responsibilities stimulating, not daunting, by her love and comprehension and exquisite sympathy . . . the whole divine partnership transforming everything, the Constitution of the United States itself included — and I thank God and took courage! . . .

Your own
Woodrow

W.W. TO E.B.G.

The White House
Washington
August 15, 1915
Sunday, 8:15 P.M.

I beg your pardon for not having told you about the preparedness business; and, please, dear little girl, don't speak of "inquisitiveness" in asking about it, — or about anything else. There can be no such thing on your part, so far as anything I know or am dealing with is concerned. Whatever is mine is

---

[1] James Burlasque, chauffeur for Presidential Secretary Tumulty.

yours, knowledge of affairs of state not excepted, — and that without reserve, except that, as you know, there may be a few things that it would not be wise or prudent to commit to writing . . .

It has been understood among us in the Cabinet for some time that I was, of course, to have a program [for preparedness] to propose to Congress in December and just before I went up to Cornish last time I told the Secretaries of War and Navy that I would like their full advice on the matter, made ready with the assistance of the best experts of their Departments, as soon after my return to Washington as possible. The War Department's report is now on my table, though I have not yet had time to read it even, much less study and digest it and form my own judgment about it (it came only yesterday) and [Secretary of the Navy] Daniels will have his in a very short time. He has outlined it to me orally already and I know the main lines and items of it. What the newspapers seem to have said (you know I do not read them!) is all their own invention. I have not yet got to that. That will have to be a part of the general revenue and taxation (or borrowing) problem of the next session, induced by the general circumstances of the war and the very great falling off in revenue caused by the immense inevitable decrease in dutiable imports.

You may be sure that I will pay precious little attention to anything else those excited (and stimulated) gentlemen from the South suggest. The last thing I shall think of doing, — the very last — would be to call Congress together in special session to debate the wild schemes of such men as Hoke Smith and Bob Henry. There will be folly enough released and rampant when the regular session of Congress comes in December. I would, as I am sure you will agree, be doing the country a great disservice to bring it on before it is inevitable. In the meantime, it is devoutly to be hoped that some of those troublemakers will have been exposed or will have hanged themselves by their own voluntary and voluble display of fatuous thinking!

There is one other matter I have not told you about which is new. It happens that we are just now necessarily in armed control in Haiti, the present congress and president of the dusky little republic depending entirely on our mercies to keep peace and maintain them in control; and the congress expires by limitation next Tuesday, the 17th. We have just rushed a treaty down (within the last 24 hours, by cable) for ratification by the congress which will, if ratified, give us practically complete control of the finances of the Haitian government (the only prize fought for by the many leaders of "revolution" there, and therefore the key to the whole political situation). To ask for its ratification now, when it can scarcely be refused, is nothing less than high-handed, and nothing but the extraordinary circumstances of the time could conceivably justify us in doing any such thing. But the circumstances are unprecedented; the necessity for exercising control down there is immediate, urgent, imperative; it is earnestly and sincerely desired by the best and most responsible Haitians; and our object, of course, is not to subordinate them, but to help them in the most practical and feasible way possible. I do not like the argument that the end justifies the means, but we should not stand on ceremony now unless we wish this country, as well as Haiti itself, to be seriously and perhaps fatally embarrassed. There is no analogy here to the Mexican case. The "revolutions" of Haiti have no political object and no popular aims; they are for plunder purely. Not to interfere and amicably take charge would be to leave them down there a prey to the most sordid chaos. And the effect on Latin America of our course down there will not, we think, be serious, because, being negroes, they are not regarded as of the fraternity! The whole thing will presently be known. I shall be curious to hear the public comments . . .

Have you seen the articles in the *World* about the German propaganda in this country?[1] The first one appeared this morn-

---

[1] This is the way the articles in *The New York World* came about: An attaché of the German Embassy in Washington left a briefcase on a streetcar in New York with papers in it concerning German activities in this country: subsidizing newspapers and motion pictures and lecture tours, bribing labor leaders to stir up strikes in munitions plants, and agitating for an arms embargo. Every detail was set down. The papers were found by a Secret Service man and turned over to the *World*, which started publishing articles based on them. There were banner headlines such as this one: "Germany's Secret Intrigues Involve U.S. in Great War and Stir Discord

ing. I hope you will get them and read them. It was to these revelations that House referred when he speculated that the publication might lead to war (I don't go with him there). This is all so private a matter that I hesitate to write it down. Suffice it to say that I know the sources from which the *World* got the material and they are absolutely reliable . . .

Your own
Woodrow

E.B.G TO W.W.

Geneva, N.Y.
[16 August 1915]
Monday 10:30 A.M.

You precious Sweetheart,

What a wonderful mail you had ready for me this morning. Your letter satisfied all the longing in my heart — I mean all the longing that can be satisfied without your very self — and then the two big envelopes full of interesting things — besides this marvelous box from Belgium. What a royal giver you are, a dozen pairs of such lovely stockings. When I saw them I made up my mind that I would have to wear them even if I had to take a tuck in the feet. But they are just the right size and I am so pleased to have them . . . They are beautifully done up, aren't they? the box and even the pathetic initial and decoration — it makes me sad — and yet proudly glad that it is a tribute to you and what you mean to the world. Even people across the sea whose hearts have been kept from breaking perhaps by the knowledge that there was still in the world such a man and that if anything can be done for them and other sufferers you can and will do it . . .

Goodbye my Darling — and thank you for being well and happy and for loving your devoted

Edith

Here by Press Campaigns Costing Many Millions Revealed by Original Documents in Vast Conspiracy."

There had been rumors since the beginning of the war about German spies, and this apparently documented series of stories confirmed them in many minds.

W.W. TO E.B.G.

[The White House]
16 August 1915
Monday, 8:30 P.M.

My precious, precious Darling,
... I am so glad that you are going to tell your mother and sister and your brother Randolph about "our wonderful secret." I not only approve it: it is what I have long wanted and hoped you would do. I particularly want your dear mother to know. I hope, — oh, how I do hope! — it will make her happy. I feel cheated that I have not known her before. After you have told her I shall feel free to go to her and try to make her love me. She knows her sweet daughter to be worthy of any man: I doubt if she thinks any man worthy of her sweet daughter. *I* certainly do not think *this* man worthy of her, — for she is incomparable and altogether lovely; and I shall be abashed and probably not at all at my best when I first present myself to Mother. But I shall try hard to make her love me and to overlook my faults because of my great love for you...
The doctor saw Mr. Clapham today. He (Mr. C.) has been making inquiries about Mr. Boyd (who, by the way, was once for a short time connected with the Panamanian legation here) and finds nothing at all against him. He is very handsome, well educated, of an excellent family which is not very popular because considered aristocratic; is one of five brothers; and is a lawyer in good standing... Mr. Clapham had just received a letter from your brother Rolfe which was perfectly cheerful and natural. In it he said nothing at all about his domestic troubles and spoke with a good deal of pride and enthusiasm of recent still further remarkable increases in the deposits and business of the bank. Don't you think we can take a good deal of reassurance and encouragement from that? I think about the dear people down there a great deal. I can't believe they are not already *my* folks, — I know they are ours...

Your own
Woodrow

[The White House]
18 August 1915
Wednesday, 8:15 P.M.

My adorable Sweetheart,

... This is the last letter I shall send to Geneva; and, unless you wait for the mail on Friday morning, I fear it will not catch you. I shall be anxious about you while you are on the road. Mr. Rose will have under his care my very happiness itself! It thrills me to think that the machine will be headed this way, bringing you every hour *nearer* to me at least; and at the end of the journey you will be in my old jurisdiction. No part of New Jersey ever gave those who had to administer the laws more trouble and anxiety than did Atlantic City and the resorts that flank it, north and south, upon that much resorted to coast. They are not communities at all, made up of responsible citizens, but merely places where people who have laid aside their usual steadying occupations, and who are for the time being idle, are catered to. You may imagine what some of them want — dissipation and distraction of the most exciting kinds; and no sort of law is respected in giving that kind what they are looking for and are willing to pay for.

I have had many anxious conferences about Atlantic City and have made many radical speeches there, in audience rooms opening off the boardwalk. It will please my fancy to think of my dear one in those, to me, familiar scenes, and where once her lover was responsible for the all-but-impossible processes of government. I have a very soft place in my heart for New Jersey. She has done me great honor, and done it very generously ...

Thank you, dear love, for the letter from Rolfe. It tallies in a way with the letter I told you Mr. Clapham had received from him. It even seems to me to have in it a certain degree of resignation and willingness to wait and see. Don't you think so? At any rate the hectic excitement of the earlier letters has gone out of it, and it sounds *rational*, even if not hopeful. I suppose the "George" mentioned is Mrs. Bolling's brother who was expected. Heaven send "George" may not lead them into wild courses and get them all in a mad fever again!

Your own
Woodrow

E.B.G TO W.W.

Geneva, N.Y.
August 18, 1915
11:30 P.M.

My precious Lord —

... I am afraid my letter of this morning was so hurried it was not presentable, but I could not do any better and I was awfully worried about the news from Panama.[1]

I don't wonder that Rolfe was so beside himself and wish with all my heart that I could have really helped them. Thank you again, my dearest one, for all you did to help them and me and for all your ever-ready sympathy. But I will not fill my letter with that for there is nothing to be done — and I am thankful George Litchfield got away without doing anything violent.

Today at noon I had the sweetest letter from Margaret and she surely knows the way to my heart when she says such exquisitely sweet things about you. I am going to send it for you to read and get you to send it back to me for I appreciate all she says so deeply — and think she has been so wonderful in her attitude toward me. From the very first she has made me feel she was glad — and I can't help feeling that her attitude, had it been the reverse of what it is — could not only have made both of us unhappy but would naturally, and unconsciously have influenced the younger girls. And so I not only love and appreciate her but I admire her very thoroughly and will always do anything in the world that I can for her happiness.

The more I see and know of these three "little women" the more I realize their superiority and fineness — and I only hope I can make them know how I love them and feel that I never

---

[1] Apparently this was a report (probably in a letter from Rolfe Bolling) that contained some things the Bollings considered derogatory about Boyd's family. It was not kept in this correspondence.

want to come between them and you — but rather to cement the bond that is already so strong between you. When you have the opportunity to impress this fact upon the girls, will you, Dearest, for they have all been so big in their welcome to me. I want them to know that they can count on me and my anxiety to be one with them in my love for you, but never to usurp a place or claim from them . . .

Always your own
Edith

The President's next letter — dated August 19 — mentions a new crisis in the German submarine war. The British White Star liner Arabic was sunk in the Irish channel with the loss of forty-four men, two of them Americans. The ship was bound for New York and was, therefore, carrying no contraband. President Wilson was greatly upset. The German Ambassador was in despair; he wrote later: "My laboriously constructed diplomatic edifice came tumbling about my ears, and things looked blacker than ever." The alternatives before Wilson were these: He could break diplomatic relations immediately, summon Congress, and lay the facts before it, or he could tell Bernstorff that this time it was a choice between a complete back-down and war. Colonel House confided in his Diary that he was surprised at the lengths the President would go to at this point just to keep the peace.

The sinking of the Arabic, startling as it was in the scare headlines, revealed one surprising thing: The Germans had already decided in secret to moderate their policy of submarine warfare. It became known that they had in June issued orders against ruthless sinkings. In spite of this, Wilson was still doubtful, and he determined to demand satisfaction in this case. On August 27 Secretary Lansing told Bernstorff that the time for debating submarine warfare had passed and that unless Berlin openly declared that there would be no more sinkings, the United States would declare war. Bernstorff reported that this was the most serious situation that had yet arisen and the German Foreign Office was able to persuade the Kaiser to overrule the Admiralty and to change its tactics. On September 1 Bernstorff wrote Lansing: "Liners will not be sunk by our

*submarines without warning and without safety to the lives of
noncombatants, provided the liners do not try to escape or offer
resistance . . ."*

The United States had forced Germany to give up an important war weapon, but Wilson was still not satisfied and kept pressing for an explicit disavowal of the attack on the Arabic. Germany was willing to concede that the commander of the submarine in the case had acted beyond his instructions, and agreed to reprove him and indemnify the United States, but Wilson held out for a more precise disavowal and did not hesitate to use the threat of a declaration of war. Finally, on October 5, Bernstorff wrote Lansing that the Kaiser's orders to submarine commanders were now *"so stringent that the occurrence of incidents similar to the Arabic case is considered out of the question . . . The Imperial Government regrets and disavows this act . . ."*

Thus Wilson fought the Admiralty to a standstill. It was considered a diplomatic triumph for him. Bernstorff thought at the time that it had eased anti-German feelings in this country, but he was, of course, wrong.

w.w. to e.b.g.

[Sent to Ocean City, N.J.]
[The White House]
19 August, 1915
Thursday, 3:15 p.m.

My sweet, my precious Darling,

My heart aches with sympathy for you. If I could only take you in my arms and tell you so, it would all be so much easier for both of us! I have just read Rolfe's letter about the Boyds, — and would have known, if your letter had not shown me, what effect it must have had on you, to whom everything in the record is of course especially abhorrent. There is nothing to do, as you say, but to hope that he will prove better than his kind, and, then, if the apparently inevitable happens to poor Elizabeth in the future, of utter disillusionment and unhappiness, to go to her aid to the utmost in whatever way the circumstances may permit. Neither we nor her parents can think for a moment of abandoning her to her fate and if, too late, (i.e., after her marriage) she comes to herself and will *let* us help her, we must go to her, with love and forgiveness, and do for her what we would do for our own.

Ah, my Sweetheart, how plainly your pain and mortification are written in those few lines of your letter which are so restrained and reticent as to be better evidence of your wound and its kind than any outpouring could have been; and my heart is full of it all, as if it were happening to my very own — as indeed it is. When *you* suffer the suffering is doubled for me, for the one thing that is most distressing to me is that you should be given pain. And I know how keen this pain is, because I know your nature so well, — its purity, its quiet, instinctive revulsion against anything unclean or debased, its aloofness from anything that could demean. I honor you so, and quiver as you do under anything that might make you feel that you or yours had been touched with any sort of dishonor. The whole thing is simply tragical; but, my Darling, my noble Darling, it is just in the presence of tragedy that we must show our strength. Nothing can touch us that we do not do ourselves, and our duty is always love and sympathy and tender pity. It is touching how Rolfe turns to you in loving admiration and dependence, as his tower of strength, who will understand and of course *help*. I can understand his feeling and his confidence there, — for I do the same. You are now my help-mate, God be praised! I have strength to give as well as to ask, my Darling, I hope and believe, and I am particularly happy that I have been sent to you to help at this very time, when love and comprehension is the very help you need. You have given me *everything* that I need, and it is a sweet privilege to be able to give you what you need. There is a sense, my precious Edith, in which I am glad that, if such things must happen to you, they should happen at this time, when I can have the joy of sharing them, and the *pride,* — for I am proud to be partner with you. And, Sweetheart, don't let the thing look to you more tragical than it is. After all, what really matters is what sort of man this particular Boyd turns out to be. If he proves himself straight and honorable and makes Elizabeth happy, I, for my part, think that the rest is a matter we can almost forget. It is *her* fortunes we are interested in; and

I cannot help conjecturing that what Rolfe says of the man's antecedents and connections rests largely upon rumor and may come from hostile, or, to say the least, unsympathetic sources. It would be bad enough at best to have anyone we love to marry into any Central American family, because there is the presumption that the blood is not unmixed; but *proof* of that seems to be lacking in this case, as I read and interpret Rolfe's letter; and, even if it be so, we must not turn away from and abandon the girl, who is of *our* blood. That is the fixed rule of love, as I read life; and there may be a great many ways in which we can help. It is hard, — it is almost intolerably hard, — to be separated from you at moments when you are disturbed and unhappy. You *need* me, that's enough to make it almost impossible for me to stay away from you. It would be such a happiness to take some of the strain off my Darling's heart by making her feel, as I hold her close, so close, to my heart, that *nothing* hurt *too* much that we could share and go through and think out *together*. I think that at such times, when I realize your need, I also realize my love for you as I do not and cannot at other times. *Then* I know how truly and entirely you have become a part of me, your interests my interests, your feelings mine, all the little shades of your thought mine too, and my heart utterly yours, with a love that escapes all measure. There is a sense in which a special *happiness* comes to me: for nothing makes me so happy as a sense of *union with you!* Ah, my Beloved, how complete, how sweet, how satisfying and happy it all is! I am only sad that I must write it instead of speaking it in tones that would really interpret it, into your own dear ears and sweet lips.

— 6:05 P.M. —

. . . I am starting an automobile trip tomorrow morning. I am going to motor over to Philadelphia and back, to pay my promised visit to [Dr. George Edward] de Schweintz, my oculist. The doctor [Grayson] and of course my keepers will go with me . . .

8 P.M.

Apparently the Haitian Congress did *not* adjourn on the 17th. If it did, we have had no news of the adjournment. The new president of the republic — a man chosen with our approval and therefore in a sense, our man, — said when the text of the proposed treaty was presented to him that he would expedite its ratification as much as possible, and that is the last we have heard . . . That no report of the proposal of the treaty has come to newspapers from Port-au-Prince would seem to be a convincing indication that the attention of the world is so engrossed with other things that what happens in Haiti may pass without comment, even if reported at all.

This afternoon brought the news of the torpedoing of the White Star liner *Arabic* on her way *out* from Liverpool by a German submarine, without warning, and her sinking within 10 or 11 minutes. There are said to have been Americans on board and it seems that not all on board were saved; — but the facts will all be known and printed long before this reaches you, so I need not even speculate as to whether any of the American passengers were lost or not, — and, after all, that may not prove to be an essential detail in any case. If they were on board and no opportunity was given for them to escape before the torpedo was fired at the vessel, this would appear to be what we told Germany we should regard as "a deliberately unfriendly act," knowing the significance of the words we used. You may easily imagine, therefore, my precious One, my sweet Counsellor, what sober forebodings are in my mind tonight. As always, I am holding my mind off from decisions until I can know what actually happened, but meantime the news plainly means something very serious for this dear country we love . . .

Certainly the Germans are blood mad. You notice the *Arabic* was bound *out* from Liverpool. There can be no plea of destroying arms and ammunition that were intended to be used against sacred German lives. It is just an act of wanton disregard of international law and of brutal defiance of the opinion and power of the United States . . . As the stress and the responsibility increase, with the seriousness of the situation in Europe and the world, your love and sympathy and counsel become more and more sweet and satisfying and vital to me. By "vital" I mean necessary to my *life* . . .

20 August 1915
Friday 8:10 P.M.

Our motor trip came off, but not exactly as planned. Burlasque, the only driver here now, is a feather-headed person (not that Robinson would be much more *intelligent*) and had not taken the least pains to study out the way *through* Baltimore and the other big places we had to pass through, and Murphy's attempts to direct him only made matters worse, so that we took an hour and a half longer to reach Philadelphia than we ought to have taken. I wanted very much to be back here not later than 8 o'clock; we therefore changed our plans and came back by train, reaching here at 6:40. But the *way* we did everything out of the ordinary, very much annoyed the Secret Service men and constituted the day quite a spree. The oculist pronounced my good eye as in splendid condition and its powers of vision were above normal, and said that the bad eye was successfully holding its own; so that you need give yourself no anxiety on the score of my eyes, my precious One.

After my consultation with him we went to lunch on the roof of the Bellevue Stratford too late, alas! to mix with many people (it was quite 2 o'clock), but not too late to see a good many of them and to have escaped from my sacred isolation. The roof of the Bellevue Stratford is a delightful place on a warm afternoon, and the lunch we had was very good indeed. Meanwhile, while I was with Dr. de Schweintz, Dr. Grayson had, at my request, gone down and secured accommodations for us on the ordinary parlor car attached to the 3:30 train to Washington, — a drawing room, and chairs for the Secret Service men, — just what I have wanted to do again and again instead of taking a stupid, lonely trip on one of those tiresome special cars and paying the railway company an iniquitous price for the privilege.

We finished lunch in time to take a walk down Walnut Street and up Chestnut Street before our train was to start. That was not a very pleasant move, as it turned out, for practically everybody on both streets that looked at us recognized me, and before we reached the railway station we were being followed by several hundred people and escorted by a mounted policeman. The doctor overheard a very funny conversation.

"What's all this?" asked a big Irishman of some one who was following in our wake. "It's the President," he was told. "The President of what?" "Of the United States, you damned fool." "Oh, the hell you say, is *that* so!"

The journey back was comfortable and I felt more normal and more like myself, the real W.W. than I've felt on any journey since the 4th of March 1913. [Presidents were inaugurated on March 4 until 1937.]

When we reached Washington there was no car waiting for us, of course, as we had left both the laudalette and the Secret Service car in Philadelphia to find their way back as they went. So we took a taxi with glee and completed a day of freedom as it should have been completed! Our cars will get back sometime between 10 and 11 tonight, I dare say. I am tired, but not too tired to enjoy a chat with you. Shall I ever be too tired for that?

All day long, my precious Sweetheart, my thoughts have dwelt on you and on the *Arabic,* even on you even when they were most concentrated on the *Arabic, —* for I think of all public questions — and of all others, too, — now with my hand on yours, as we used to sit on the West Porch at Harlakenden, and seem always to be thinking *with* you, so that you are always present and I am conscious of your sympathy and help whatever my thoughts may be doing. You may imagine, therefore, how blank I felt when I found that no letter had come from you today, — not even a belated one! The faithful Hoover, whom I shall always love and value as a personal friend, went down to the Post Office after all the deliveries had been made, but there was nothing there. He is going down again, bless him, and will report again about 10 o'clock tonight whether the 9:30 mail from New York has brought me what my heart waits for. It is the first time I have had to go without a letter from my generous Darling, and I must admit I am very blue. It was a most inopportune day for such a disappointment (though I know it cannot have been your fault or neglect, my dear little Girl) for it has been a day of special anxiety, of course, in the presence of the apparently "deliberately unfriendly act" of Germany, in sending the *Arabic* to the bottom, and the likelihood that that act has brought us to the final parting of the ways. It was as if I had taken my hand from yours for a moment, to turn a page — a page with the shadow of war upon it — and that when I had sought it again and looked to get the reassurance in your dear eyes you were not there! Besides, — and this disturbs me deeply, — the letter I got yesterday closed hastily and with the shadow of that letter from Panama on it and I cannot but fear that my Darling hesitated to write while the depression of that was upon her, for fear of conveying the pain of it to me! No, no! that cannot be it! She would know how that would hurt me, — holding me away when she most needed me. The letter will come! This is the very time when I most belong to you, my darling Edith. I never before felt quite so intimately identified with you, or more happy in the identification, — more thankful that you had come to me in season to let me share and help. We shall work something out of this sorrow that will make us know and love each other better still. The only thing that could make it a tragedy for us would be *not* to share it! And you will have something happy to tell your dear mother and sister as well as this sad story of Elizabeth's tragical blunder! I am *so* glad about that.

Your hand is in mine again now; your dear eyes have cleared and have loving counsel and intimate comradeship in them, and I return to talk of the *Arabic* again. I spoke just now of the shadow of fear being on the page I was turning, but I must reassure you. This is not *necessarily* so. There are intermediate courses to pursue if the course is left to our choosing. We can recall Gerard [Ambassador to Germany] and give Bernstorff his passport, and note the effect of such a breaking off on all dealings with Germany before we go further. In that case *Germany* might declare war and the guidance of our policy be taken out of our hands. Bernstorff will probably, quite apart from this affair, have to be asked for an explanation of these matters which have been appearing in the *World*, and they may lead to our requesting that he be withdrawn. After breaking off diplomatic relations, if we wished to go further, probably the next step would be to call a conference of neutrals ... to consider the present treatment of neutrals by *both* sides in the war and concert some action, to be taken either severally or jointly, calculated to make neutral rights more secure. The one thing that is clear, or, rather, the two things that are clear are that the people of this country rely upon me to keep them out of war and that the worst thing that could possibly happen *to the world* would be for the United States to be drawn actively into this contest, — to become one of the belligerents and lose all chance of moderating the results of the war by her counsel as an outsider.

Your own
Woodrow

E.B.G. TO W.W.

August 19, 1915
Thursday, 11:30 P.M.

My precious One —

This is my last letter from Geneva . . . You have been in my thoughts so constantly today and tonight when I read of the sinking of another ship [the *Arabic*] I knew how worried and upset you are . . .

I read most carefully the report of the Secretary of War and while it is interesting and practical as far as the necessity for greater increase [of the Army] goes, it offers no plan and gives no working basis for cost, etc. As you say, it seems intended for publication and carefully avoids intimate details of what you need and want but which, of course, could not be given to the public. It is just about what I expected though, that you would have to do all the work . . .

Goodnight
Edith

W.W. TO E.B.G.

[Sent to Ocean City, N.J.]
[The White House]
22 August 1915
Sunday 6 P.M.

My darling Sweetheart,

You see I am getting in the habit of sitting down at any and all hours — whenever I get a chance — to talk to you. I have just come in from a three-hour ride with the doctor and

Fitz, out to Marlboro [Md.] and around by T.B. [another town in nearby Maryland] and there is a full hour before dinner for a little chat.

I think that you said you had read Stephens' *Demi-Gods.* Do you remember the lines I have just copied on my typewriter and will slip in with this? [1] They made me think so of your own dear, vital beauty that I thought I would adopt them as a description of your own lovely poise and beauty, — all but the "consciousness" of it. You seem altogether unconscious of it, though you must have a mirror! But you have never seen yourself move . . .

The opinions you quote from an Albany paper about the loss of Americans on the *Arabic* are rank Bryanism. The Germans have admitted all along that they had no right to sink any ship carrying our flag without first making themselves responsible for the safety of the lives of those on board, — as they did in the case of the *Frye,* — even though she carried contraband consigned to England. The case we based our protest on was that of the *Lusitania,* chiefly, — a British ship, and the case of the *Arabic* is the same in principle and worse in fact. It was your friend W.J.B. who took the ground that we must let Americans understand that they took passage on British ships, or any ships owned by belligerents, at their own risk and peril. Beware of heresies! It may very well be that this Bryan and Albany doctrine is the more reasonable and practical one, my precious Sweetheart, but it is not the doctrine of international law, and we must base our claims of right on the undoubted practice of nations, — for which Germany is show-

---

[1] Enclosure — from James Stephens's *The Demi-Gods:*

> She walked carelessly as the wind walks, proudly as a young queen trained in grandeur. She could run as a deer runs, and pause at full flight like a carven statue. Each movement of hers was complete and lovely in itself; when she lifted a hand to her hair the free attitude was a marvel of composure; it might never have begun, and might never cease, it was solitary and perfect. She was so conscious of her loveliness that she could afford to forget it and so careless that she had never yet used it as a weapon or a plea.

Stephens (1882–1950) was an Irish poet and fiction writer. His whimsical tales frequently dealt with the supernatural. *The Demi-Gods* was published in 1914.

ing such crass and brutal contempt. The road is hard to travel, but it lies plain before us. She has no right whatever to deal with ships owned by *belligerents* as she has dealt with the *Lusitania* and the *Arabic,* and the *Falaba* before them, and when our own people are on board we must tell her so. It was another *Lusitania* [that] we told her we should regard as "deliberately unfriendly . . ."

No news of consequence or new significance has come in today, though I shall have a few "flimsies" for the big envelope which will be mailed to you tomorrow. I must admit I am thankful when nothing new comes in. There has been no *good* news on public matters that I can remember for a year past now. Everything new seems simply to add to the confusion and increase the darkness amidst which we are left to thread our way through the confusion.

There seems to be no relieving particular in the *Arabic* incident, such as Lansing thought there might be when he wrote the letter to me which I sent to you the other day; and, since it is just a clear and simple case of insolently ignoring the protest and warning of our three notes, there seems to be nothing for it but to go forward and do the things I have already outlined to you. I suppose we shall be expected first to send Gerard to the Foreign Office in Berlin to ask [Foreign Minister] von Jagow whether he has anything to say about the case or not; but I do not see what he *could* say to alter the significance of it. I will take it for granted that he will neither offer an apology nor disavow the action of the commander of the submarine, — and these formalities, gone through with only to satisfy ourselves that *we* omitted nothing that might conceivably alter the result, will do little more than delay for a few days the announcement of our decision.

You understand, of course, my Darling, that the withdrawal of Gerard and the dismissal of Bernstorff will not necessarily lead to *war*. *We* will not declare it (*I* cannot; only Congress can), but Germany may (I doubt it — but the hope may be father to the doubt), and if she does, we are at last caught in the maelstrom and our independence of action is lost; I must call Congress together and we are in for the whole terrible business. If she does not, we can call the conference of neutral nations of which I spoke and it is *possible* that what issues from its deliberations may affect the whole course and the ultimate results of the war. It is our judgment (Lansing's and mine) that it should be asked to meet, not on the other side of the water, but in Washington, and I take it for granted that I should myself be obliged to take an active part (if I did not preside) in the deliberations.

These are very solemn thoughts, my precious One, my little partner, and they seem somehow to draw me nearer to you than ever. As things thicken about me I more and more realize what you mean to me and more and more feel my dependence upon you to keep the *darkness* off, hold the lamp of love for me to walk by, keep the loneliness at bay by your loving, intimate companionship, make me free from everything that could weaken or dismay my heart. With your hand in mine, your head close at my shoulder, your eyes beaming with confidence and reassurance, your lips ready always to speak love and counsel and give the kisses that mean our absolute union, I am fit for anything and can fare through any trial! . . .

Your own
Woodrow

W.W. TO E.B.G.

[Sent to Ocean City, N.J.]
The White House
24 August 1915
Tuesday, 8 : 10 P.M.

My precious One,

. . . I did not realize until yesterday and today when the great heat returned how great a strain this *Arabic* affair had put upon me, — because, no doubt, of the conviction, which I could not escape, that the (perhaps all along inevitable) break with Germany had come, and that yet this "deliberately unfriendly" act notwithstanding, the people of the country were still demanding of me that I take no risk of war. There is a *little* rift of hope in the telegram from Bernstorff which I enclose, though I so thoroughly distrust him that I suspect some maneuver for delay (until the Balkan states have been forced to a decision?); but I cannot see how the German government can deny or explain away the facts and it is not likely that they will apologize and reprimand the commander of the submarine. You can imagine how the hot days have made me realize the drain this anxious matter has been on my vitality . . .

Don't fancy, Sweetheart, that there is anything to be anxious about so far as my health is concerned. There is not. I am perfectly well . . . I am simply and only more tired than usual when the day's work is over, — and am taking better care of myself than usual. This forenoon, for example, when I found that I *could* run away, I sent for the car and took a ride all round the park, all by myself, dozing comfortably almost the whole time I was out . . .

I was thinking today, my precious One, that perhaps I had not set the *Arabic* matter in its full light before you, to enable you to see just what questions are involved and just what facts we are seeking to clear up. Before we act we ought to be sure that the German authorities admit the act as the act of one of their submarines. The people on the *Arabic* saw no submarine, though many of them claim to have seen the torpedo approaching through the water. The *Dunslea,* the vessel seen sinking from the *Arabic,* was, it seems, being *shelled* from some quarter and her captain says it was by a submarine which was concealed behind his vessel from those on the *Arabic,* and he says the submarine passed around his vessel to get clear of her and launch a torpedo at the *Arabic.* What account the Germans will give of the whole matter I cannot conjecture, but Bernstorff's message must mean that their account of it will be different. While it seems clear (and this is the second point) that the *Arabic* was not under convoy at the time she was attacked and sunk, it is not entirely clear that she did not leave the Mersey under convoy. If she did, the German commander may say with some color that he naturally assumed that her convoy was still at hand, and that a convoy rendered her a public vessel (as distinguished from a merchantman) and made it legitimate to attack her and destroy her in any way she could (which is good international law). A third point, is, did she (the *Arabic*) give the German commander any reason to think she was coming to the assistance of the *Dunslea?* One of her passengers said she had put about and was heading for the

Dunslea. Her captain seems to say that she was not. These are points of varying importance of course but they are all points upon which the Germans are entitled to be heard, *if they wish to be.*

The papers have stated that we have asked the German Foreign Office for an explanation; but we did nothing of the kind. We merely instructed Gerard to call on von Jagow, as I told you the other day, and ask whether he had received an official report on the incident, and so give him a chance to say anything he may wish to say. No doubt all these points have been clear enough to you from the first, my Darling, but the newspapers confuse the whole matter with so much that is irrelevant and so much that is false, that I have set them down here for your convenience in keeping step with me day to day and interpreting the flimsies I send you. The big envelope you receive today will contain an extraordinary and alarming dispatch from our consul in Moscow; but I must believe he is under the influence of rumor and panic.[1] It's a bolt out of the blue, so far as I am concerned. I have not heard anything like this from any other quarters. According to him, the Russian defense has gone to pieces and the Russian government itself is thinking of taking refuge in Siberia . . .

Wednesday, 7:10 A.M.

Having gone to bed happy with thoughts of you, my Darling, and having had a fine sleep, I feel as fit as a fiddle this morning. The air grew lighter toward bedtime and sleeping was easy and refreshing . . .

I was offered a job the other day, to be undertaken when my present job is over by the statute of limitations! A man who must have thought me a very easy mark, Mr. Howland of *The Independent* came, on behalf of a syndicate of magazines and papers, to ask me to be the editor of a history of the present war, to be written by the generals on both sides who have taken part in it![2] I said him Nay with such emphasis that I

[1] The consul was J. H. Snodgrass. His report said 10 million refugees were moving across Russia in advance of retreating armies and that people there expected St. Petersburg and Moscow to fall before the end of the year.

[2] Harold J. Howland was associate editor of *The Independent* magazine from 1913 to 1920.

think he was a little jarred, and told him Roosevelt was the man he wanted, not W.W. He made a wry face and went away. Think of spending precious working days fighting this wretched war all over again when everybody ought to be engaged in the healing work of setting up honorable peace and civilization again! And the main idea, of course, was that my name would be a good commercial asset, and enable them, besides, to get more participants to contribute to the volumes. He did not know what contempt he bred in me. And, like all the others of his kind, he had sought the interview with me on the ground that his errand (unstated, of course) was of pressing and immediate importance . . .

Your own
Woodrow

E.B.G TO W.W.

Hotel Normandie-by-the-Sea
Ocean City, N.J.
August 24, 1915
[Tuesday] 9:45 P.M.

My own precious One —

There is so much I want to tell you — and answer — in those dear letters I found waiting for me and the one that has just come that I hardly know where to begin . . .

Along with the sweetness of your letters came the bitterness of the account of Elizabeth's marriage . . . I have only a line from Rolfe saying they would not go to the ceremony and that their hearts were broken. Poor fellow, I can't get him out of my mind. But all your love and sympathy ease the pain in my own heart and I know would help him if he only knew our secret and I could send him a copy of what you say about him . . . Of course I can't do this, but I love to rest on your strength and comfort my distress with the splendid knowledge of your love . . .

I have not yet had a chance to talk to Mother for we did not get here yesterday until lunch time and we all were together for the afternoon and evening.

The Roses and Mother were tired so we came home and Bertha and I walked two miles up the boardwalk in the moonlight and talked over many things — not cabbages, but kings — she asked me if I minded telling her if I was engaged to you. And I told her I did not *mind* telling her anything but I wanted to talk to Mother first. Then she said she *knew* and that she was sorry she asked but she just could not help it. But that she thought you were perfectly delightful and that after she met you she felt it was a foregone conclusion, that if it meant my happiness she was happy and that she realized so what her life had missed that no one could more fully appreciate the glory of such a love than she. I know as soon as I can talk to Mother they will both write you. I can never make them understand how proud, how splendidly proud, I am of you, of your love for me or make them know what you are — that must wait until the blessed opportunity comes to them to know you for themselves and comprehend you as no one can through description, even though the description comes from one who adores you . . .

Mr. and Mrs. Rose are going home by way of New York and are crazy for me to go with them and stay one or two days and they will go early Monday the 30th. If I did that I would get home Wednesday or Thursday . . .

Always your own
Edith

W.W. TO E.B.G.

[The White House]
25 August, 1915
Wednesday evening

My own precious Darling,

My but it was hard to write and advise you to go to New York with Mr. and Mrs. Rose — turn in the opposite direction again — when you had seemed actually on your way here at last! . . . But it was clearly the right decision. It would worry me to have you in an empty house, without even Susie to look out for you — and I cut off; and I knew that you will have a good time and you *need* some real diversion now that the dear folks in Panama have seen their fears realized.[1] I don't wonder

---

[1] Susan Booth, maid and personal attendant to Mrs. Galt for twenty years, first at 1308 Twentieth Street and later in the White House.

the Roses are crazy to have you go to New York with them! There they will try to induce you to go back to Geneva with them. They will not give you up to me until they have to. And in my heart I don't blame them. Who would ever willingly give you up that had ever spent a day with you? But I envy them desperately. You are mine, not theirs; and yet you cannot come to me and can stay with them. How the gods play with us and make sport of us and laugh at the game! Have a good time, my Sweetheart, a light-hearted, jolly time, for my sake, because even in the midst of our loneliness for each other, it will make me happy to think of you at the theater and going about the gay city as a care-free looker on, merely waiting till you can go to your lover. And I have something up my sleeve. We *can* see one another *just as soon as you get back.* So don't be later in arriving than Susie herself. You are hereby bidden to dinner on the evening of the Fourth [of September,] note the date and the coincidence. On a certain Fourth of the month four months earlier you were bidden to dinner here: I want to continue the conversation begun that evening! . . .

You know how I feel about being allowed to share your anxieties about the dear ones in Panama; and I hope with all my heart that there will be some practical way in which you and I can be of service to Elizabeth. Would it not be delightful if we might some day be instrumental in reuniting her to her parents? They are sore now — and a bit hard — as we often are when deeply wounded, but their hearts will melt within them before long when they think of their daughter, whom they have so tenderly loved. Maybe, some of these days before *they* are ready to do it, we can have Elizabeth and her husband come to us, and then induce Rolfe and his wife to come too. Sorry as I am about the marriage, tragical a mistake as it seems, I cannot help feeling a great relief that it was not prevented in any of the outrageous, melodramatic ways that old fool Edwards had suggested and we had feared the doctor might try to carry out . . . I can't help hoping against all probabilities, that she will be happy in this willful marriage, after all. Your own heart, I know, is harboring the same hope . . .

I find I am getting more and more to transfer what I have

to say about affairs, my dear Love, to the little slips I attach to the papers I put in the big envelopes, because I think you will like to read my comments and explanations along with the documents themselves. But there is one item about Bernstorff that ought to be added as very interesting (though I am not yet clear as to what he is up to). He telephoned [Oswald Garrison] Villard of the *New York Evening Post* that he was disappointed that the papers had not "played up" his message to Lansing about suspending judgment [on the *Arabic* sinking] in a more emphatic way, that it was intended as a disavowal of the act of the submarine commander. And a newspaperman who manages to keep quite intimate with Bernstorff and to get from him most of what is in his mind, telephoned Lansing today that he might expect an official disavowal of the act through von B. at their interview tomorrow morning. But such tips seldom prove to be worth serious attention, and von B. may be "stuffing" both Villard and his other newspaper friend (a man named O'Laughlin).[1] What *is* clear, however, is that von B. and his superiors in Berlin are seriously disturbed over the possibility of a breach with us, and have determined, at this 11th hour, to prevent it if they can. The disavowal must be very explicit and must involve a virtual promise that these barbarities will stop . . .

Your own
Woodrow

W.W. TO E.B.G.

[The White House]
26 August 1915
Thursday evening

My own Darling,

. . . I must beg you, my sweet Darling, not to attach too much importance to Washington gossip [of their romance], or to what anyone is saying. If we keep within bounds, as we shall, and give them no proofs that they can make use of, we

---

[1] John Callan O'Laughlin.

can and should ignore them. And there are some very big reasons why we should ignore them, within the limits we, of course, mean to observe. Our happiness is not an ordinary matter of young lovers; it is, for me a matter of *efficiency*. I hate to argue the matter in my own interest, but I know you are thinking of that side of it, too, and will, in your generosity, forgive my speaking of it. I can of course practice self-denial to any extent — spend any proportion of my energy upon it that is required — so far as it is a mere question of strength and resolute self-control; but it costs me more than anyone but you and I can know, and I doubt if it is my duty to use myself up in that way any more than is unavoidable. I am absolutely dependent on intimate love for the right and free and most effective use of my powers and I know by experience — by the experience of the past four weeks — what it costs my *work* to do without it to the extent involved in entire separation from you. And so we are justified in taking risks.

If during this dreadful week that has just gone by — the most anxious week of my whole term as President, when loneliness sat upon me like a pall — I could have had you actually at my side, if only once or twice a week, I would have *laughed* at the strain and carried it with a light heart . . .

Friday, 6:40 A.M.

Good morning, my precious One! I love you with all my heart, and it is sweet to be closeted here again alone with my thoughts of you, the sweetest, most delightful thoughts a man's heart could desire . . .

I am worried about the small amount of rest and sleep you take. I wish with all my heart it were much more. I wonder if I can teach you better habits? Ah, if I could only steal in and sit by your bedside and watch you as you sleep and throw loving thoughts about you to make sleep sweeter, as I used to do in the half light by the davenport in the morning room! I would not touch you: that would startle you, for you would not be expecting me. I would only sit and watch that lovely face . . .

Woodrow

E.B.G TO W.W.

Hotel Normandie-by-the-Sea
Ocean City, N.J.
August 26, 1915
9:20 A.M.

My own precious Sweetheart —

...I was so boiling mad when I read the account of that villain's speech about you (I mean T.R.) at Plattsburg that I could hardly eat my breakfast.[1] Did you stoop to read it? I just wish for a few minutes I was a man as big as old Ollie James.[2] I would go and make him eat his words or his disgusting teeth one. Perhaps both. For someone ought to thrash him for the honor of the men in America. But you will tell me again that I am an incendiary if I don't hush...

I hope if Colonel House comes to Washington, which he implies in the letter you sent me, I will see him. I know I am wrong but I couldn't help feeling he is not a very *strong* character. I suppose it is in comparison with you — for really every other man seems like a dwarf when I put them by you in my thoughts. I know what a comfort and staff Colonel House is to you, precious One, and that your judgment about him is correct but he does look like a weak vessel and I think he writes like one very often. This is perfectly unnecessary for me to tell you this but it is such fun to shock you and you are so sweet in your judgments of people and I am so radical. Never mind, I always acknowledge my mistakes and take a secret joy in finding you right and stronger than I am in every way...

Keep a stout heart, my precious Woodrow, and remember how I love — love — love you

Edith

---

[1] Former President Roosevelt had been making speeches that were extremely critical of Wilson's policies.

[2] Democratic United States Senator from Kentucky.

E.B.G. TO W.W.

Hotel Normandie-by-the-Sea
Ocean City, N.J.
August 27, 1915
10 A.M.

My precious One —

  ... Yesterday just after we all came from a walk on the board-walk I found a good opportunity to tell Mother and Bertha together of the great happiness you had brought into my life and Mother, in her own quiet way was (as she has always been) full of sweet interest and thought for me. I think she was quite unprepared for an announcement so definite and said, if it was for my happiness she was happy — but that, of course, she did not know you save by reputation and certainly nothing could be finer than that is and she would welcome you more than anyone else but she could not help a feeling of sadness. I told her that was only because she did not know you, that if she did, her sadness would turn to joy and thanksgiving for you were the most splendid person in the whole world and she would be so proud to know you loved me as tenderly and strongly as I love you.

  Did I tell you, Precious One, that Mother is as shy as a girl of sixteen and can never express what she feels? When you meet her you will understand better than I can explain her peculiar suppression of all emotions. It has always been so and if I did not know and completely understand her I would often feel almost hurt. But she is pure gold and would give her life to help any of us.

  You will find her hard to know, at first, and don't try to discuss intimate things with her for she simply can't do it. If you feel like writing to her, do it, and in that way you will reach her better than by speech. I am afraid this is a sort of formidable picture I have drawn but she is the least formidable person I know — only very reticent and easily embarrassed. You can say anything you want to in writing — sure of her understanding receptiveness and on any subject but personalities you will find her responsive and eager to talk to you . . .[1]

Another letter from Rolfe last night said E. was married on the 18th but instead of the ceremony being at 5 a.m. as they had expected Mr. Boyd was too ill to come to the church until 4 p.m. and was too ill to go on the trip so they were with his people there and Rolfe knew nothing more about them. Annie, E's mother, "could not desert her so went to the church with her and stood by her during the ceremony but did not speak to him or his family."

I think Annie was right to stand by her and am sorry Rolfe did not do the same . . .

Goodbye, I love you
Edith

W.W. TO E.B.G.

The White House
28 August 1915
Saturday evening

My own Darling,

I was *so* glad to learn that you had told your dear mother of our great happiness, and it was sweet and thoughtful of you to tell me of her great shyness, so that I might understand her as you do. And a great deal of your own singular power to understand and interpret those you love came out in the explanation. You are singularly frank and just and discriminating. Your mind sees clearly and yet your heart interprets tenderly . . . I feel that I know the dear lady whom I already regard as my own mother as you yourself know her, and I am ready to love her as much as she will let me. I have only this uneasiness about her first impression of me after I meet her; I, too, am intensely shy with shy people. If they are not demonstrative, I cannot be. If they do not put their feelings into words, and suppress their emotions, I follow suit, almost in-

---

[1] Mrs. Galt described her mother, Sallie White Bolling, in *My Memoir* as "the purest spirit I have ever known . . . no one ever heard her say an unkind thing." After bringing up nine children (two died in infancy) in a large house in Virginia, she came to Washington several years after her husband's death in 1899 and lived in a small apartment with her daughter Bertha. She died in Washington in 1925 at the age of 82.

evitably. You must coach me in my dealings with her, for it would make me very unhappy if I did not win her love and succeed in making her think of me as really her son . . .

You *are* a little hard on some of my friends, you Dear — House and Tumulty, for example; but I understand and am able to see them, I think with your mind as well as with my own. Besides you do not know them and have not been faithfully served by them, and therefore your heart is not involved in the judgment as mine is. Take Tumulty. You know that he was not brought up as we were; you feel his lack of our breeding; and you do not like to have me represented by any one less fine than you conceive me to be. You think that my Secretary, the man who must speak for me in most of the dealings and transactions of my office, ought to be a gentleman in the same sense that I am one, with tastes and manners that will commend him to the finer sort of people that come to see me. To your fastidious taste and nice instinct for what is refined, he is common. And all of that is true. I share your judgment up to a certain point, and *feel* it as perfectly as if it were my own — though there are fine natural instincts in Tumulty and nice perceptions, which you have not yet had a chance to observe. *But* the majority, the great majority of the people who come to the office are not of our kind, and our sort of gentleman would not understand them or know how to handle them, — neither are the majority — or even a considerable minority — of the men at the Capitol, in either House; neither, I need hardly add, are a majority of the voters of the country. Tumulty does understand them and know how to deal with them, — much better than I would, and I need the assistance of just such a man. He is absolutely devoted and loyal to me, — of that I have abundant evidence every day. He hates what is crooked just as heartily as you and I do, and ferrets it out much more quickly and shrewdly than we could. He tells me with almost unfailing accuracy what the man on the street, — the men on all streets, — are thinking (for example about T.R.). In this particular job of serving the country through political action to which we are just now devoted a great diversity of talents is indispensable, and the greatest possible variety of breeding. An administration — an office — manned exclusively by "gentlemen" could not make the thing go for a twelve-month. The only thing we can afford to have uniform in the administration of the affairs of a democracy, the only uniform requirement for office we can wisely insist on, is morals — a sound character and enlightened principles, and Tumulty has these. Moreover, he is only technically common, not essentially. Wait until you know him and like him, as you will.

And, then, dear House. About him, again, you are no doubt partly right. You have too keen an insight and too discerning a judgment to be wholly wrong, even in a snap judgment of a man you do not know. House *has* a strong character, — if to be disinterested and unafraid and incorruptible is to be strong. He has a noble and lovely character, too, for he is capable of utter self-forgetfulness and loyalty and devotion. And he is wise. He can give prudent and far-seeing counsel. He can find out what many men of diverse kinds are thinking about, and how they can be made to work together for a common purpose. He wins the confidence of all sorts of men, and wins it at once, — by deserving it. But you are right in thinking that intellectually he is not a great man. His mind is not of the first class. He is a counsellor, not a statesman. And he has the faults of his qualities. His very devotion to me, his ardent desire that I should play the part in the field of international politics that he has desired and foreseen for me, makes him take sometimes the short and personal view when he ought to be taking the big and impersonal one — thinking, not of my reputation for the day, but of what is fundamentally and eternally right, no matter who is for the time being hurt by it. We cannot require of every man that he should be everything. You are going to love House some day, — if only because he loves me and would give, I believe, his life for me, — and because he loves the country and seeks its real benefit and glory. I'm not afraid of the ultimate impression he will make on you, — because I know you and your instinctive love and admiration for whatever is true and genuine. You must remember, dear little critic, that Sweetness and *power* do not often happen together. You are apt to exact too much of others because of what you are yourself and mistakenly suppose it easy and common to be.

About T.R., now, we are entirely and enthusiastically in accord! But what's the use of wasting good serviceable indignation on him? He is too common a nuisance to bother our minds about and the best way to vanquish him is to take no notice of him whatever . . . I am *so* glad Elizabeth's mother went with her to the church and stood by her at the wedding, and I wish, with you, that Rolfe had done the same. Poor Elizabeth. Being myself by nature an insurgent, I find myself more and more inclined to judge her not at all. And wasn't it pitiful that Mr. Boyd should be ill and spoil, or at least mar, the little happiness that it had been possible for them to plan that day, the trip, etc. By the way, I understand that Mr. Boyd has $40,000 in his own name in (I believe) Rolfe's bank. He can evidently afford to support Elizabeth as she ought to be supported. How my heart dwells on these dear folks! . . .

Your own
Woodrow

E.B.G TO W.W.

[Ocean City, N.J.]
August 28, 1915
Saturday 9:30 A.M.

My own precious, wonderful Sweetheart,
 . . . I am almost sorry I wrote you what I did yesterday about Colonel House, but I can no more keep things from you than I can stop loving you, and so you must forgive me. I know he is fine and true, but I don't think him vigorous and strong. Am I wrong? . . .

Yes, my precious One, I do understand that we will have to stand gossip and try to be callous to it and do not mean to make your burden heavier by useless heed to such stuff, but I thought right now, when the country thinks you are giving every thought to the complications of Government, it might be particularly bad to have you discussed. But I know you would not suggest anything that would not be dignified, so I will live in radiance of the thought that we will be together a week from today. It seems a long time, but, in comparison with these past four long weeks, it will be short . . .

I am, my Dearest, all your own

Edith

E.B.G. TO W.W.

Hotel Algonquin
Manhattan
August 31, 1915

My precious One:

When you read this I shall probably be at *home*. Think of it, really in Washington again!! I have just decided to take the midnight train and should be there by 7. I am going up to the Cordova to breakfast with Mother and afterwards to my own nest.[1] I wonder if I can wait until Saturday to see you — but, at least, I will know you are near . . .

They are waiting for me, so goodbye my precious One. Hurrah — no more letters for I am coming!

Edith

W.W. TO E.B.G.

(29)   The White House
31 August 1915
Tuesday evening

My precious Darling,

. . . Do you know what that figure in parenthesis at the top of the page means? It means that this is the 29th day since my Darling drove away from Harlakenden with the Roses, and seemed to take the very light of the day with her . . .

I have *tried* to fill the day so as to keep off impatience but I have been aware all the while that I am merely marking time. I had one really vital conversation, with General Hugh Scott, the Chief of Staff, who has just come back from the Mexican border, with very definite impressions which he was

---

[1] The Cordova was an apartment house at Twentieth Street and Florida Avenue, N.W., a few blocks from Mrs. Galt's house on Twentieth Street, and her mother and sister lived there for many years. The address is 1908 Florida Avenue, N.W., and the name of the building now is the President Madison.

stating to me in his laconic, soldierly way, and to whom I could state (because I have known him a long time and knew him to be utterly loyal and trustworthy) what I wanted from the War Department by way of a program of preparedness, much more satisfactorily and with much greater assurance that I would be entirely understood and entirely and intelligently obeyed than I could to that self-opinionated politician, the Secretary of War, who is a very able person but who concentrates his entire attention on his own opinions and does not listen to mine, and who is, if plain truth must be spoken, a solemn conceited ass! . . .

Senator [James A.] Kern [of Indiana], the leader of the majority in the Senate, was in, too, and I discussed with him the advisability of calling an extra session of the Senate alone, to convene in October and discuss executive business. It is imperative that the Senate's rules of procedure which, as they stand, permit the minority and indeed any individual Senator, to block action on any matter indefinitely, should be altered before the regular session begins in December, so that at that session something definite in the way of legislation may be accomplished . . . There are some treaties, too, notably the one with Colombia, that ought to be pushed to ratification. I can call the Senate into extra session without the House for the consideration of matters in which the House has no part and when Congress adjourned in the Spring I had a sort of understanding with some of the leading Senators that I would do so. But the acute difficulties with Germany which have developed since then and the likelihood that some mischief makers like Hoke Smith of Georgia would add to the delicacy and difficulty of the situation by intemperate speeches and ill-considered proposals . . . and the thought that probably my hands had better be left absolutely free (which is devoutly to be wished) had made all of us hold back a little on the plan . . .

I am putting up a bluff, Sweetheart. I am *writing* about preparedness and information concerning the Mexican border and arguments for and against calling the Senate in extraordinary session, but I am not *thinking* about them. I am *thinking* about you . . .

I am *so* delighted, my Darling, that your mother (would

you feel that I was going too fast if I simply said "Mother" — it would be very delightful to me if I might, at least in speaking to you?) and Bertha were pleased with my letters to them ...

Wednesday 7:05 A.M.

... my heart beats so I can hardly keep my pen steady! You *are* in *Washington!* Hoover has just handed me your little note ...

Your own
Woodrow

SEPTEMBER 1915

By the time they were both back in town, the engagement of the President and Mrs. Galt was almost official. Certainly it was no secret. Their families had been informed and the romance had been so thoroughly rehashed in Washington gossip that the subject would have been dropped if it had involved anyone less than the Chief Executive himself. Colonel House wrote in his Diary that the President was so much occupied with courting that he was doing little else. Chief Usher Hoover wrote later: "He was simply obsessed . . . he put aside practically everything . . . important state matters were held in abeyance while he wrote to the lady of his choice."

The letters now were shorter, however; after all, 1308 Twentieth Street was only ten blocks from the White House and, also, the direct telephone line from the White House was available.

War news blotted out almost everything else. The French were losing ground on the Western Front. Zeppelin raiders continued to hurl bombs on London. A series of Russian gains had failed to stop the Teutonic army. On September 2 the President read this headline in the Washington Post:

NO PEACE UNTIL BRITAIN IS DEFEATED,
SAYS GERMAN PRESS

American intervention was the big question. It was still considered likely in the end, but occasionally a bit of good news seemed to brighten the outlook: For instance, Germany had officially altered its submarine policy to meet United States' objections, but it was generally said by the wisest men that it did *so for fear that we might declare war. Certainly we were going ahead with preparations to strengthen our armed forces and to help the Allies: The Navy announced that its new shore station for submarines would be in New London, Connecticut, and Wall Street financiers were lending $500 million more to England and France.*

Hopes for peace were turning more and more on the President of the United States. He saw himself in the role of a possible peacemaker, and Colonel House kept his bags packed to go anywhere at any time to talk about disarmament or anything else, even — in Wilson's wildest dreams — some kind of league of nations. On a single day in September 20,000 peace telegrams were received at the White House. Cardinal Gibbons came over from Baltimore to bring a message that Pope Benedict XV suggested that Wilson renew his offer to act as a mediator. Henry Ford came from Detroit to tell him about his own private peace plan (which ended up as a fiasco). King George V, in a toast at a dinner at Windsor Castle, said: "It will be an everlasting testimony to the wisdom and good will of the American people that in most trying and difficult circumstances well nigh impossible to conceive, they stood loyally behind President Wilson."

Mrs. Galt dined at the White House on the evening of the day of her return to Washington, and the next day the President wrote to her twice before lunch:

W.W. TO E.B.G.

[The White House]
2 September 1915
Thursday morning 6:30

My own Darling,

These are the papers I forgot to bring you last night.

May I just smuggle this line in to say that I love you with all my heart; that it is a great comfort to have you near; that I am well; and that I do not know what to do with myself this morning?

With all the devotion of a full heart.

Your own
Woodrow

W.W. TO E.B.G.

Thursday 10:40 A.M.

My precious Sweetheart,

I could not talk to you as freely last night as if we had been alone. I was sorely puzzled by your decision that we ought not to exchange letters on the days when we cannot see one another. That would be giving up our *only* inconspicuous means of keeping in touch with one another because we would have to avoid frequent use of the conspicuous ways. But I loyally accepted your decision, as I am bound and most willing to accept any decision that will relieve you of distress — whatever distress it may cause me.

I am breaking your rule now only because I found I could not bear to be *more* cut off from you on this day of apparent triumph than I was when you were hundreds of miles away and were every day helping me to bear days of deep strain and anxiety . . . Nothing means anything to me unless you share it with me. I do not care for it a moment unless you care. My heart is full of you — and of nothing else, and I am, though for the moment disobedient

Your own
Woodrow

Apparently Mrs. Galt had no intention of following her own decision that there should be fewer letters between the two, for she wrote on the same day:

E.B.G. TO W.W.

1308 Twentieth Street
September 2, 1915
Thursday

How can I resist sending you just a tiny little note this morning when I have just gotten that perfectly blessed letter you sent me to New York. Could anyone ever write a more perfect symphony of love? And to think that I have seen you again, Sweetheart, and you are *really-truly* more wonderful than I remembered and yet you love me! I was so excited last night for fear you would not like me as well as you thought you did, that perhaps your memory had played tricks and you pictured me more interesting and lovable than I am — and this letter (although it was written of course before you saw me) seems a sort of answer to my fears.

It is like a steady hand holding my nervous excited one and has the same effect that your dear presence had last night. When I was all aquiver at the things that had happened during the day — and after being with you, clasping your dear hands and feeling the protection of those tender arms fold 'round me, the troubles seemed to melt quickly away and I came home serene, secure, and happy.

I was afraid, my precious one, that you went away with a little ache in your heart, not only that you thought I was worried but — well, that I did not seem responsive. Am I right? If I am, I want to set it right and know you will understand. I just can't discuss intimate things before anyone else — even our dear loyal little Helen. It is not that I doubt her affection or interest, but I can't do it except to you and, even if the intervals and separation are far apart when it will be possible to see you just by ourselves, I would rather wait. Do you mind? I hope you don't and perhaps I will get used to a third party but just now I would rather talk of general things — than the precious ones that mean nothing to anyone but you and me.

5 P.M.

Dearest, Dearest — I had to stop here — and now I have just gotten your little note written at 10:40 this morning. Bless your heart for writing it and saying just what you did. Am I breaking my own rule? Surely I can't blame you for doing the same thing . . .

Please write to me — and pay no attention to what I said. Love me all you can.

Edith

W.W. TO E.B.G.

[The White House]
3 September 1915
Friday morning, 8.

Why, my Darling, my Darling! "Love you all I can?" Why I love you with the passion of my whole heart. There seems to be nothing in my heart — and no room for anything — but love,

love, love for *you*, the most precious, adorable woman in the world. I felt dumb Wednesday night, I was so excited, so *overcome* with the delight of finding you more wonderfully beautiful and sweet and adorable than I had remembered or even yet conceived. I just received your little letter of yesterday. It has so delighted and overjoyed me that I cannot make this pen go straight. I will write you a real letter later today when I can behave.

I love you past all thought

Your own
Woodrow

w.w. to e.b.g.

[The White House]
3 September 1915
Friday

My precious, incomparable Darling,

... Yesterday *was* a day of pain for me, my blessed Sweetheart, though I am ashamed to confess it, but *not* because I did not understand, only because you seemed to me upset and distressed Wednesday night, and not happy, and it had made you a little constrained and unresponsive while I was overcome with joy at seeing you. I knew that the slight constraint came from the most natural and sufficient causes, but I could not help being a little affected by it, and what gave me *pain,* then and all day yesterday, was nothing that you could help (Love interprets me perfectly to you now) but the *separation,* not withstanding your actual presence.

The presence of a third person, though it was our darling Helen, restrained me, too, and of course prevented my taking you in my arms and applying the only cure possible for our distresses — the pouring out in words and kisses of our perfect love and intimate confidence.

And then I had to *leave* you and endure a whole day and two nights without a chance to know what you were thinking or let you know what I was thinking! I wanted to tell you that when I saw you Wednesday night the whole wonderful glory of you came upon me with a new revelation . . .

We have both been two foolish persons, my precious Darling,

these last 36 hours. I am not ashamed of it — it makes me feel glad, rather — *especially* glad that you were as foolish as I was, for it shows how much, how delightfully deep, we are in love. We have both been unhappy with longing and because we could not completely reveal our feelings to each other. And does that not prove that the only way we can be sure of being sensible and keeping steady is by *writing* on the days on which we do not see one another? The mails, sent through the Post Office, tell no tales to gossips, and we've got to risk the gossips anyway, if we are not to long ourselves sick. Write as much or as little as we please, we can at least let each other know *every day* the state of our minds and hearts. It grieves me so that my precious Edith should have been unhappy yesterday because of me — because she feared she had put some sort of ache in my heart, when all my heart was overflowing with love for her . . .

I love you more and more every minute I live!

Your own
Woodrow

In the next letter the "triumph" the President refers to was the assurance the German Ambassador had given the United States on September 1 that "liners will not be sunk by our subs without warning and without safety to the lives of non-combatants, provided the liners do not try to escape or offer resistance." On September 4 an explosion shattered the British liner Hesperian *and eight were killed, but the one American on board was uninjured. Ship's officers thought it was torpedoed, but the German Foreign Office declared that there was no submarine in the area. After the war it was revealed that indeed it had been hit by a German U-boat, the crew of which thought it was an auxiliary cruiser.*

w.w. to e.b.g.

The White House
6 September 1915
Monday, 9:15 A.M.

Well, my precious Darling, the great "triumph" did not last long, did it? Apparently nothing can last long which depends on Germany's good faith. Of course we do not know all the

facts yet, and it is *possible* that the facts, when fully disclosed, will put a different face on the sinking of the *Hesperian*, but it seems to me a very slim possibility. And of course my first thoughts turn to you, my blessed Sweetheart, by means of whose love I am able to face *any*thing with a steady heart . . . Since Saturday night my heart has been singularly at peace. I have had two of the finest, sweetest nights' rest I have had in a long time — because all the while conscious of you! . . .
With a full heart in which you are all in all

Your own
Woodrow

W.W. TO E.B.G.

7 August [September] 1915
Tuesday, 9:45 A.M.

My own precious Darling,
. . . I came upon a little poem yesterday, Sweetness, that partly expressed what I tried to write you the other day:
Mine to the core of my heart, my beauty!
Mine, all mine, and for love, not duty:
Love given willingly, full and free,
Love for love's sake — as mine to thee.
Duty's a slave that keeps the keys,
But Love, the master, goes in and out
Of his goodly chambers with song and shout,
Just as he pleases — just as he pleases.[1]

Your own
Woodrow

E.B.G. TO W.W.

1308 Twentieth Street
September 7, 1915

My precious One —
I am so glad you went to the theater last night and had something to divert and cheer you.[1] We all enjoyed the tea party so

[1] From "Plighted" by Dinah Maria Mulock Craik (1826–1887).
[1] The bill at Keith's vaudeville theater on Fifteenth Street near the White House was headed by David Bispham, the noted American baritone.

yesterday and Mother is in love with you, said she did not feel the least bit embarrassed or formal with you, that, on the contrary, she felt she had known you always and knew she was going to love you . . . and Bertha was distressed that she had no opportunity to say all the sweet welcoming things she wanted to say to you. I was so proud of you, Sweetheart, and always expect to be.

It was right funny that after dinner last night Randolph said, "Let's all go to Keith's" and I said I was too tired to do it and came home at 9:30 and went to bed. I wonder if I would have felt braced enough to go if I had known you were there?

Always your

Very own
Edith

w.w. to e.b.g.

The White House
13 September 1915
Monday morning, 9:50

My precious Darling,

The weight of public matters rests rather grievously upon me this morning and I have been obliged to fill the morning with many important engagements, beginning with the Secretary of State in half an hour, but there is one resource for me always: I can turn to you (what would it not be worth to me if I could *go* to you) and all the burden will fall away with the realization of your love and vital, comprehending sympathy.

The Secretary and I will be obliged this morning, I fear, to make some decisions that *may* affect the history of the country more than any decisions a President and Secretary of State ever made before and it gives me such a steadiness and added *balance* in my thinking that you have come to my side and put your hand in mine and given your splendid life to sustain mine . . .

I did not sleep last night; but in the middle of the night I got the first volume of Morley's *Life of Gladstone* and the tonic of sound thinking and acting I found there helped to take my thoughts off what was annoying me not only but brought the iron back into my blood. I had a most unexpected attack of pain (in my digestive organs) in the midst of my wakefulness, as has so often happened to me as the result of anxiety, and was in dire need of a loving visit from my Darling. The mere sight of her would have cured me, but I pulled through all right despite the loneliness and feel tolerably fit this morning . . .

Your own
Woodrow

E.B.G. TO W.W.

1308 Twentieth Street
September 13, 1915

Dearest —

You left me last night with the feeling that you sternly disapproved of me and thought me willful. I am so sorry.

I did not take the ride!

This is the day that you said would be full of grave anxiety for you and that a word from me would help lighten the burden . . . I want to dispel any disappointment or disapproval I caused last night. Please don't worry about me in any way, Dearest One. I am well and strong and love you so that I will try to give up my nocturnal rides if they cause you any anxious moment . . .

Your own
Edith

W.W. TO E.B.G.

[The White House]
13 September 1915
Monday, 3:30 P.M.

No, no, my precious Darling, not "stern disapproval" or any kind of disapproval that involved *blame:* I understand you too perfectly for that; but just loving anxiety, about your personal safety from danger or any kind of insult, and, now that you are, alas! so much under observation, from misconstruction of any kind; and the distress that you should ever find it easier to wander about at night instead of seeking sweet sleep that would preserve your bloom and your splendid vigor. I dread to think of my sweet one as so restless and unable to find peace and rest, with all the responsibilities she has to carry. I thought that that was what my love had brought her — peace and happy thoughts, and hoped she would no longer have to run away from herself or from shadows or from *anything*.

That was my whole thought, my own precious Sweetheart. There was no disapproval, bless your sweet heart, but only deep, loving, tender solicitude. It's all love, Edith my Darling. There's nothing else in my mind or heart for you. I am feeling all right this afternoon, though it seemed more prudent not to play golf in the intense heat. I've just been out buying you some golf sticks . . .

Your own
Woodrow

W.W. TO E.B.G.

[The White House]
14 September 1915
Tuesday, 7:40 A.M.

My precious Darling,

What a delight it was to see you and hear your voice last night! A tantalizing delight, of course, because I could not go to you in the theater, as I longed to do, and because I could not speak my heart out to you over the telephone, but a vast deal better than nothing. You looked so lovely and were such good chums with Randolph, whom I envied and yet for whose sake I was glad. What must it not mean to him to have such a sister! When you smiled, Sweetheart, it seemed to me to fill the whole atmosphere of the theater with sweetness, — for you were the only person in the room for me, — the only person I *could* think about or wished to look at . . . The play really did not make any difference, except that it was silly and vulgar, and I hated to have anything vulgar associated with you *even in space,* particularly when its vulgarity touched some of the most sacred and beautiful things in the world.[1] I did not have to think about the play, and did not think about it. I thought only of you, and the air of the place was pure . . .

The Browns came last night, Darling, and Tumulty is back,

---

[1] A musical comedy, *The Only Girl* by Henry Blossom and Victor Herbert, was playing at the Belasco Theater on Lafayette Square opposite the White House. Joe Weber was in it.

but I *beg* that you will come to dinner tonight.[2] I cannot see you alone, but we can make it one of the old *reading* evenings, if you would like that, and it will mean such a delight to me to have you here, part of the circle . . .

Your own
Woodrow

The President's happiness in his new love grew every day, but his associates were worried. Reports were coming to Washington that he was being criticized for neglecting his duty and devoting too much time to Mrs. Galt and that many people felt that instead of a strong, Lincolnesque figure in war-threatened Washington there was only a man acting like a college boy in love.

Derogatory remarks and vicious stories were circulated. Many people sincerely felt that there was a lack of propriety because of the comparatively recent death of the first Mrs. Wilson and that the President was not paying the proper respect to her memory.

Seriously, the possible effects on his re-election were being evaluated. It was known that Mrs. Galt had entertained such fears herself and that at one time she urged him to wait until after the 1916 election before they were married, but he said he could not wait and she now agreed.

It was at this point that the most incredible episode in the whole situation arose.

The President, aware that there was criticism (although the amount of it may well have been kept from him), asked Secretary McAdoo in his role as son-in-law to discuss with Colonel House and Secretary Lansing, and possibly others, the political effect they thought his marriage to Edith Galt might have. Apparently both Tumulty and Grayson also were alarmed over the possibilities of the courtship's hurting the President at the polls. They all joined in a round of apprehensive conferences and even wrote letters in code to each other on the subject. It

---

[2] The reference to the Browns is to Colonel E. T. Brown of Atlanta, Ellen Wilson's cousin, who had been a visitor at the White House on July 20, and his wife, who accompanied him this time.

was a matter of such delicacy and in the end it turned out to be so embarrassing, that what actually happened is still disputed; no one came out of it looking very good.

It involved a woman named Mary Allen Hulbert Peck. In 1907 Wilson had visited Bermuda and met her. She was forty-five, attractive, moved easily in social circles, was interested in what was going on in the world, and had a reputation as an original and lively conversationalist. Her first husband had died, and she was estranged from her second. She was known then as Mrs. Peck but by 1915 had resumed the name Hulbert. She and Wilson became friends and after his return to Princeton he wrote many letters to her, a correspondence that lasted for eight years.

She met all the members of Wilson's family and they became friends, too; she visited them in Princeton and later when he was Governor of New Jersey. The Wilson-Hulbert correspondence was a steady one; he usually wrote her every Sunday afternoon, letters in which he unburdened himself of his personal reactions to many things. He expressed himself in the strong language of affection that he used in letters to women all his life. (When the letters became a topic of comment, Colonel House said: "We Southerners like to write mush notes.")

There was gossip of a romance between Wilson and Mrs. Hulbert, and it almost became an issue in his first Presidential campaign.

Now in the fall of 1915, at the peak of the Wilson-Galt romance, the letters emerged again. Somewhere in the worried discussions of House and McAdoo and others about how to postpone the marriage, a plot was dreamed up. The President would be told that an anonymous letter had been received from Los Angeles (where Mrs. Hulbert was then living) saying that she was displaying "improper" letters from Wilson and that they revealed that he had given her money.

The details were ludicrous and unlikely to make much sense as read now, but Wilson fell into the net. He was upset over the idea of any scandal's coming out, fearing that it might embarrass Mrs. Galt. He asked to see her at once:

[The White House]
18 September 1915
Saturday afternoon

Dearest,

There is something, personal to myself, that I feel I must tell you about at once, and I am going to take the extraordinary liberty of asking if I may come to your house this evening at 8, instead of your coming here for dinner. You will understand when I have a chance to explain, and will, I believe, think even this extraordinary request justified in granting it. I love you with the full, pure passion of my whole heart and *because* I love you beg this supreme favor.

With a heart too full for words.

Your own
Woodrow

E.B.G. TO W.W.

1308 Twentieth Street
[September 18, 1915]

Dearest One —

Of course you can come to me — but what is the matter? I feel so worried that anything should trouble you. May I ask one thing, precious one — and that is that you ask Dr. Grayson to come up with you? I know he will have intuition enough not to stay and it will look better if anyone should see you — and it is also a protection to you . . .

Your own
Edith

Apparently, Wilson went to her house and the two talked — in what words and for how long will, presumably, never be known. It is evident from the letters that follow, however, that she did not give him immediately the complete reassurance he wanted, and when he left her she'd said only that she would think it over. Before he knew her answer, he wrote this letter:

[The White House]
19 September 1915
Sunday, 7:20 A.M.

My noble, incomparable Edith,

I do not know how to express or analyze the conflicting emotions that have surged like a storm through my heart all night long. I only know that first and foremost in my thoughts has been the glorious confirmation you gave me last night — without effort, unconsciously, as of course — of all I have ever thought of your mind and heart. You have the greatest soul, the noblest nature, the sweetest, most loving heart I have ever known, and my love, my reverence, my adoration for you, you have increased in one evening as I should have thought only a life-time of intimate, loving association could have increased them. You are more wonderful and lovely in my eyes than you ever were before; and my pride and joy and gratitude that you should love with such a perfect love are beyond all expression, except in the great poem I cannot write. But I am equally conscious that it is anything but pride and joy and gratitude or happiness that the evening brought you: that it brought you, instead of a confirmation of your ideal of me, an utter contradiction of it, dismay rather than happiness, uneasiness in the place of confident hope, — the love that is solicitude and pity, not admiration and happy trust, — and that intolerable thought has robbed me of sleep. When it was the deepest, most passionate desire of my heart to bring you happiness and sweep away every shadow from your path, I have brought you, instead, mortification and thrown a new shadow about you. Surely no man was ever more deeply punished for a folly long ago loathed and repented of, — but the bitterness of it ought not to fall on you, in the prime of your glorious, radiant womanhood, when you embody in their perfection for all who know you the beauty of purity and grace and sweet friendship and gracious, unselfish counsel. I am the most undeservedly honored man in the world and your love, which I have least deserved, is the crowning honor of my life.

I have tried, ah, *how* I have tried to expiate folly by disin-

terested service and honorable, self-forgetful, devoted love, but
it has availed only to lead the loveliest, sweetest woman in all
the world, for whom I would joyfully give my life, to mortification and dismay. May God forgive me as freely as he has
punished me! *You* have forgiven me with a love that is divine,
and that redeems me from everything but the bitterness of
having disappointed you. For all but a little space I have tried
for a laborious life-time of duty done to be worthy of such
love; but the little space defeats the life-time and brings me
to you stained and unworthy.

I humbly sue leave to love you, as one who has no right to
sue, and yet I know all the time I am offering you a love as
pure, as deep, as void of selfishness and full of utter devotion
as any man ever offered any woman, worthy even of your
acceptance. I know I have no rights; but I also know that it
would break my heart and my life if I could not call you my
Darling and myself

Your own
Woodrow

*Within two hours after writing this letter, he received her
reply:*

E.B.G. TO W.W.

1308 Twentieth Street
September 19, 1915
[Sunday]
Dearest —

The dawn has come — and the hideous dark of the hour
before the dawn has been lost in the gracious gift of light.

I have been in the big chair by the window, where I have
fought out so many problems, and all the hurt, selfish feeling
has gone with the darkness. And now I see straight — straight
into the heart of things and am ready to follow the road "where
love leads."

How many times I have told you I wanted to help and now
when the first test has come I faltered. But the faltering was

for love — not lack of love. I am not afraid of any gossip or threat, with your love as my shield and even now this room echoes with your voice as you plead — "Stand by me" — "Don't desert me"!

This is my pledge, dearest one, I will stand by you — not for duty, not for pity, not for honor — but for love — trusting, protecting, comprehending love. And no matter whether the wine be bitter or sweet we will share it together and find happiness in the comradeship.

Forgive my unreasonableness tonight (I mean last night, for this is already Sunday morning) and be willing to trust me.

I have not thought out what course we will follow for the immediate present for I promised we would do that together. I am so tired I could put my head down on the desk and go to sleep — but nothing could bring me to rest until I had pledged you my love and my allegiance.

Your own
Edith

W.W. TO E.B.G.

[The White House]
[19 September 1915]
Sunday 9:10 A.M.

My precious Darling,

Thank God there is such a woman and such love in the world. Your note has just come and I could shout aloud for the joy and privilege of receiving such a pledge, conceived by such a heart. A nobler, more wonderful, more altogether lovely, loyal, adorable (woman) there could never be. I pray God may give me strength to love and serve you as you should be loved and served.

Your own
Woodrow

Thus this curious episode came to an end, an episode based on unfounded fears, but one that served to test the Wilson-Galt romance as effectively as if it had been genuine.

[The White House]
23 September 1915
Thursday, 7 A.M.

My precious Love,

I had a *fine* talk with House last night, which cleared things wonderfully, and I am so glad that I am to have a little while with you before lunch to tell you about it. It would be most unsatisfactory to write it, because it needs to be discussed. He is really a wonderful counsellor. His mind is like an excellent clearing house through which to put out ideas and get the right credits and balances. I am sure that the first real conversation you have with him, about something definite and of the stuff of judgment, you will lose entirely your impression that he lacks strength. It is a quiet, serene strength, but it is great and real. I am impatient to have you know him, — and still more impatient to tell you what he said last night, after I had purposely laid our problem before him in the baldest way, as if it were a question of business or of politics, and not of the heart at all. I wanted a perfectly cool-blooded judgment and I'm sure I got it.

How empty the day was without you, my precious Darling — how empty all days are without you, and how hard! And yet yesterday was full enough of interesting happenings. I had a call from Mr. Ford — *the* Mr. Ford — who is a friend of ours politically and who is going to help us study the motors in our submarines. I amused myself talking ideas to him — in the vein of that essay of Gardiner's on Bernhardi — and observing how ideas took no root in his head, which did not stir until you gave it a fact.[1] And then came W.J.B. (yclept "The Traitor," by a lovely lady I know and love — and love partly for the enemies she makes, for herself).

---

[1] *The War Lords* by Alfred George Gardiner was a book of essays on the origins, issues, and conduct of the war in the light of the personalities of its principal actors. In addition to the heads of state discussed (Wilson was among them) there was a chapter on General Friedrich von Bernhardi, who had written extensively from the German point of view in various newspapers and magazines and books. Gardiner saw in him a good example of "the strange mentality of the Prussians."

It was a most surprising interview. It seemed to have no definite object. He was perfectly natural and at ease, as I was too, for that matter. It was as if he was still in the Cabinet and, without having any particular piece of business to lay before me, had dropped in to tell me what he was thinking about and learn what I was thinking about. He had the air of one who feels himself at home and a member of the family. It was amusing and amazing. We spent a third of the time, I should say, telling stories and discussing matters which had no connection whatever with public affairs . . . He looked extraordinarily well and seemed quite happy. I cannot, I am glad to say, understand such a person . . .

Your own
Woodrow

E.B.G. TO W.W.

1308 Twentieth Street
September 24, 1915
Friday, 10:40 P.M.

Dearest One —

. . . I did have such a nice talk with Colonel House and he is just as nice and fine as you pictured him and his admiration for you is sufficient to establish my faith in his judgment and intellectual perceptions. I shall wait and tell you some of the things he said, and you will tell me honestly if he *liked* me. Helen said he said nice things about me but you will know if he meant them or if he was just trying to mean them for your sake . . .

Goodnight and my love and tender thoughts

Your own
Edith

The question of the announcement of the engagement of the President and Mrs. Galt was much on their minds as September ended. Apparently Mrs. Galt dreaded the publicity that would follow, but the President was eager to have his happiness made public. After discussing the matter on Wednesday night, September 29, he felt that his fiancée seemed unhappy

about something, and he wrote her this whimsical dialogue
between himself and an imp named Anxiety:

30 September 1915
Thursday, 7 A.M.

A Dialogue
Dramatis Personae: The Imp Anxiety.
                       W.W.
Scene: A dark bedroom
Time: 4 A.M.

Imp: (squatting on W.W.'s solar plexus) Did you notice
that half sad, half absent look on Edith's face when you came
out into the city's light last night?

W.W.:   Indeed I did. I could not have gone to sleep at all
last night for thinking of it if I had not been so tired that
exhaustion was stronger than my heart. There was the same
aloofness and a sort of gentle constraint in her manner when
she said good night. My heart ached from it, and aches still.

Imp: What caused it? What had you said to her?

W.W.:   There's the trouble. I don't know, and I *ought* to
know. My intuition is generally infallible in understanding
what is going on in her dear heart, but this time it was and is
at fault. My own heart was never more full of tenderness and
eager love. It is always a mistake for me to be with those I
love when I am worn out and discouraged; I suppose because
I am then most selfishly absorbed in myself. And yet it is just
then that I need them most. I ought to have been able to read
that love on Edith's face, but I was not. It was not quite like
any other expression I ever saw on it. It made her face exquisitely beautiful and yet it was as if the beauty were not
for me!

Imp: May it have come from something Helen had been
saying?

W.W.:   I tried to think so; but her slight constraint of
manner was with me, not with Helen, so far as I could per-
ceive and there was the same tone in her voice when she spoke
to me over the telephone a few minutes later.

Imp: What had you been talking about?

W.W.: Helen had been trying to persuade her to announce our engagement at once.

Imp: Didn't you see how she shivered at the idea of being conspicuous and being talked about? Had she not already generously promised that she would announce the engagement two weeks from now, and had you not already frightened her by talking about the articles that would have to appear in the papers?

W.W.: Yes, and I had no right to urge anything. Perhaps I should have taken her part against Helen in the argument — but really my heart's desire got the better of me and I could not help agreeing with Helen that Edith will be happier when the announcement is made and all possibility of *unpleasant* publicity past than she is now with everything under cover — under very uncertain cover.

Imp: Well, what are you going to do about it?

W.W.: I am going to tell her how my heart aches to have disturbed her and that my love for her seems to be the only thing my heart contains, seems to be the whole substance of my life.

Imp: And are you going to let her alone when you are tired and unfit to love her as she ought to be loved?

W.W.: You don't know her! That's the very time she *wants* to comfort and help. She is the sweetest lover in the world. But I have, I hope, at last learned a lesson — to love less selfishly and particularly to guard myself when I am tired and forlorn, wounded as at Princeton, worn to a frazzle as yesterday at Washington.

Curtain: 5 A.M.

E.B.G. TO W.W.

1308 Twentieth Street
September 30, 1915
Thursday — 11 A.M.

My precious One —

I am so sorry you were unhappy last night because of me and this "Dialogue with the Imp" is a perfect nightmare — and caused by your own weariness and depression. I don't mean that I had no responsibility about it for I know I suddenly grew silent and you felt the change — but, if you had been at par yourself you would not have troubled over it.

I was cross and half sick last night or my feelings would not have been hurt by your quickly agreeing with Helen that the Smiths' coming should settle the day of announcing things — regardless of me.[1] You first were eager to have it the 5th as Helen suggested. Then when she said, "Oh! the Smiths will then see it in the papers before you tell them," and you said — "Oh, yes, well, we will wait until they come, *whatever* day that is — and then announce it."

Without even a word to me — and frankly, it hurt my feelings and made me feel I was treated as a child.

Then at the door when I said to you impulsively, "Oh! I am so tired of having to ask people things — and now even have to get the Smiths' permission to announce our engagement . . ." YOU still did not seem to think it important or to comprehend my meaning.

I know it is better to tell you plainly how I felt — though it will worry you, which I never want to do. But it all comes from the fact that I have never had to ask permission to do things in my whole life. I have always just done them — and that ended it. And I have seldom even discussed what I was going to do.

Now, while I know it must be different, when things are discussed and consulted over I get impatient and restless, and if I did not love you, would be off with the bit in my teeth and showing a clean pair of heels to anyone who dared try to catch me. There — I feel better already just to have told you about it. And I won't sulk anymore.

Please go and play golf this afternoon — and clear away my own share in your depression and know that I still love you enough to walk up to the harness and put it on though I may kick it all to pieces if you don't know the trick of handling the ribbons so as to guide without my knowing it . . .

Always your own
Edith

---

[1] Lucy Marshall Smith and Mary Randolph Smith were New Orleans friends of the Wilson family.

OCTOBER 1915

The war news was bad. On the Western Front a great offensive by the French and the British to force the Germans to withdraw from northern France failed. In the second battle of Champagne, the French attacked on a front between Rheims and the Argonne, making use of an immense concentration of artillery as well as manpower. The Germans, however, held their own on the heights above Rheims so that after many weeks of desperate fighting the French had little to show. The British contribution to the offensive was around Artois. Greatly outnumbering the Germans, they managed to drive the enemy back toward Lens and Loos but then failed to follow through on this advantage by hesitating to use reserves. Thus, the situation in the West remained substantially what it had been a year earlier.

Washington was not convinced that the German pledge over the sinking of the Arabic *was one that could be counted on. Berlin had not sufficiently disavowed the sinking of the* Lusitania, *as a matter of fact, and that was the incident that lingered in the public's mind and caused resentment. Newspapers and magazines kept up a steady stream of articles on German intrigue and spying in this country, and while proof was sometimes lacking, enough evidence existed to convince even the President that there was a real danger. Secretary of State Lansing demanded the recall of two attachés in the German embassy in Washington for plots against American neutrality.*

The indefatigable Colonel House, firmly convinced that the triumph of German militarism in Europe would imperil future

American security, was still trying to start a movement for peace under Wilson's leadership. The President listened to him with sympathetic attention and prepared to send him back to Europe to keep trying.

More and more war talk was heard. Those who did not have to measure their words took it for granted that it was only a matter of time until this country would be drawn into the fighting. Wilson himself knew the decision could not be put off much longer. "My chief puzzle," he wrote to House on September 20, "is to determine when patience ceases to be a virtue."

The pressures on the President were steadily mounting — greater this month than any before — but his correspondence with Mrs. Galt hardly reflected them. It was concerned, on the other hand, with such things as the date of the official announcement of the engagement, an event which the President felt would free the couple to be together more:

W.W. TO E.B.G.

The White House
2 October 1915
Saturday, 7:40 A.M.

My lovely, adorable Sweetheart,
. . . What is my lady's verdict? Are we to have our freedom next week, or must we wait until the 15th?

Ah, my precious One, how full my heart is of you, and how hard it is to fill the hours with any sort of contentment that I must spend away from you! . . .

Your own
Woodrow

I am just starting out for golf.

W.W. TO E.B.G.

[The White House]
4 October, 1915
Monday, 7:30 A.M.

My own precious Darling,
Good morning! I hope you had a lovely, restful sleep and that you felt my arms about you, my heart close to yours. It is five months today, my Sweetheart since I told you of the great

love for you that had come into my heart and asked you to be my wife, — only five months, and yet I seem to have known and loved you always. I cannot think of happiness apart from you. You fill my thoughts and my life. My spirits rise and fall with yours. Your thoughts and your love govern the whole day for me. And, as these crowded months have gone by, filled with experiences that seemed to search our hearts to their very depths — to depths to which no plummet had ever reached before — how steadily we have struggled towards the light — with what joy we have seen it broaden about us, until now we stand, hand in hand, where it shines warm and life-giving in all its full and vital splendor. We have not lived lightly, my Darling. With a great price we have bought this supreme happiness. It has been tested by fire, and has come out refined and purged. We know ourselves and we know one another better than it would have been possible to learn them by the experience of any ordinary five years, or any commonplace lifetime; and we know that it was inevitable that we should love one another and utterly give our hearts up to one another. Out of the fire has come to me, little by little revealed and made perfect, the woman I perfectly love and adore, the lovely, lovely woman who, at each stage of the strange struggle, seemed to me to grow more lovely and more desirable. I loved you, my precious Edith, oh, how tenderly, and deeply, that May evening when I first opened my heart to you; but now I know that that was but the beginning of my love. It has grown like a great tide of life and joy, until now I know that my whole destiny is centered in you, my sweet, sweet Love, my incomparable Darling!

Your own
Woodrow

W.W. TO E.B.G.

The White House
5 October 1915
Tuesday, 1:30 P.M.

My precious Edith,

I slept late this morning and ever since I got up have been chased by tasks I could not elude, — so that this is the first moment I have had to send you a love message.

Ah, how *full* my heart is of love for my precious Darling ...
It makes me sad that she must go through the picture [taking]
business and all the rest that goes with it and that she dreads
and hates so; but I know she is a dead game sport, and it makes
me so proud that she is willing to go through it all for my
sake — for dear love's sake! And I am so eager (I must confess)
to have everybody know how wonderful and beautiful she is ...
Lansing came at noon to tell me that Bernstorff had come
to terms [on the *Arabic* sinking] and given perfectly satisfactory
assurances — so that my heart is light about that, too. And
now we are free to be gay and happy! ...

Your own
Woodrow

*On October 6 a two-line statement was handed to reporters
at the White House:*
*"The engagement was announced today of Mrs. Norman
Galt of this city and President Woodrow Wilson."*
*The announcement was for publication in the newspapers
of October 7. The White House, besieged by reporters with
questions, responded with this statement, written by the President on his own typewriter:*

*Mrs. Norman Galt is the widow of a well-known business man
of Washington who died some eight years ago. She has lived
in Washington since her marriage in 1896. She was Miss Edith
Bolling and was born in Wytheville, Virginia, where her girl-
hood was spent and where her father, the Honorable William
H. Bolling, a man of remarkable character and charm, won distinction as one of the ablest, most interesting and individual
lawyers of a State famous for its lawyers. In the circle of culti-
vated and interesting people who have had the privilege of knowing her Mrs. Galt has enjoyed an enviable distinction, not only
because of her unusual beauty and natural charm, but also
because of her very unusual character and gifts. She has always
been sought out as a delightful friend, and her thoughtfulness
and quick capacity for anything she chose to undertake have
made her friendship invaluable to those who were fortunate
enough to win it.*
*It was Miss Margaret Wilson and her cousin Miss Bones who
drew Mrs. Galt into the White House circle. They met her first*

in the early part of the present year, and were so much attracted
by her that they sought her out more and more frequently and
the friendship among them quickly ripened into an affectionate
intimacy. It was through this association with his daughter and
cousin that the President had the opportunity to meet Mrs. Galt,
who spent a month at Cornish this summer as Miss Wilson's
guest. It is, indeed, the most interesting circumstance connected
with the engagement just announced that the President's daugh-
ters should have picked Mrs. Galt out for their special admira-
tion and friendship before their father did.

The news was given out at exactly the hour when the Presi-
dent was entertaining his fiancée and members of her family
and of his at a dinner in the White House. Present were: The
President, Mrs. Galt, her mother, Mrs. Bolling, Bertha Bolling,
John Randolph Bolling, Helen Bones, the Secretary and Mrs.
McAdoo, the Misses Smith, Colonel Brown, and Dr. Grayson.

The Washington Post said the romance had been known for
"the last three months," but the news received large headlines in papers all over the country. Only two other Presidents
had ever been married while they were in office, John Tyler in
1844 and Grover Cleveland in 1886.

There was one irony in the announcement: On the same day
the White House issued a statement saying the President supported woman suffrage and would vote for it in the November
election in New Jersey. His position was that the matter was
one to be settled by the various states. His failure to take a
stand had been widely criticized by women's organizations, and
the fact that he chose the day of the announcement of his engagement to declare that he was now in favor of women voting
was not allowed to pass without sardonic comment.

The letter that follows was written by Mrs. Galt a few
hours before the engagement was made public:

E.B.G TO W.W.   [1308 Twentieth Street]
                                            October 6, 1915
                                                8 A.M.

My precious One —
I waked at 6 after a very restful night and have just come

for a little talk with you before going up to tell the rest of the family our secret.

It does give me a queer feeling to think that by this time tomorrow it will no longer be just our *own* secret but blazen to the world. And I confess it costs much to give it up.

But you are worth anything it could ever cost and I loved you more last night than ever before. But it was such a solemn, deep love that I seemed unlike myself.

But I came home and went straight to bed and read *The War Lords* until I felt sleepy and then I shut the light out and put my arms 'round your dear body and my head on your shoulder and went to sleep.

I think it was about 1 o'clock and I did not move until 6. So, you see, I am quite refreshed and ready for the day.

I hope so that you are and that the German conquest is only the happy beginning of good fortune. I am so proud of you, my precious Woodrow, and so proud that the world will know you through big situations, such as this, for only in big things can you find your true interpretation.

* * *

Just here your note has come and I feel so guilty, Dearest, to have caused you a sleepless night. I will kiss those splendid eyes tonight until they close in spite of themselves and make you dream instead of *think* of how I love you.

With all my love — always your own
Edith

W.W. TO E.B.G.

The White House
7 October, 1915
Thursday, 7:30 A.M.

My own precious Darling,

How my heart yearns for you this morning! What would I not give to be with you all through the day, to protect you from any kind of annoyance and to try to make you feel only the deep, deep happiness that is in my heart and the love for you that wells up inside like the tide of life itself, and the pride that I should have won your love and its sweet acknowledgment to the whole world. To feel that today and for the rest of our lives you are identified with me, — one who I know to be and all the world will presently know to be the loveliest and most adorable woman a man ever won, — with *me,* who had no claims except pure, unbounded love and my great need, — makes a new day for me, a day of strength and joy and confidence, and of zest in work and duty.

The old shadows are gone, the old loneliness banished, the new joy let in like a great healing light. I feel when I think of the wonderful happiness that your love has brought me, a faith in everything that is fine and full of hope, a new confidence God's in his Heaven and all's right with the world. Duty looks simple and the tasks of the day pleasant and easy. And with what unspeakable joy do my thoughts hover about the incomparable lady who has wrought this miracle by her love! It is so *delightful* to think about her, — and to know that she is mine is a sweet, sweet ecstasy! I love to think of her grace, her tenderness, her quick, comprehending sympathy, her wit, her instant grasp of whatever she is interested to know, her ineffable, unfailing, irresistible charm, her deep deep love tides . . .

Her own
Woodrow

E.B.G. TO W.W.

[1308 Twentieth Street]
October 7, 1915

My precious Woodrow,

How like you to be the first to send me a greeting on this day of days and what an infinitely tender message it is. I am keeping Mr. Hoover long enough to write a short answer because it is so much nicer to address it to you instead of even Helen. Thank you for all you put into those words that leave me so much for just my own interpretation and I still feel your presence here in this room and reach out to find you and long to kneel as I did before the fire last night and put my arms about you while I whisper I love you and trust you and will never again hurt you if I can help it.

I have seen the *Post* and everything is guided by that dear, strong hand I love and into whose keeping I have put my own in utter faith and trust.

Please be happy today, Dearest and let the sunshine of our love keep out all the clouds — and forget everything but the blessed fact that we belong to each other.

Your own
Edith

With the announcement of the engagement, Mrs. Galt became overnight the most talked-about woman in America. Presidents' wives usually move gradually into public notice with their husbands during years of officeholding. In Mrs. Galt's case there was no preparation: From a modest woman moving in a small circle of friends in private life, she became an instant celebrity whose every move was watched and reported fully in all the nation's newspapers.

She was a handsome woman and a gracious one, and she made a favorable impression. Thousands of letters were written to her. The White House handled the bulk of the mail, and a secretary was assigned to her, Miss Edith Benham, daughter of the late Admiral A. E. K. Benham and a young woman wise in the ways of social Washington, having worked for the wives of the British and Russian ambassadors. Miss Benham (later Mrs. James M. Helm) remained at the White House as social secretary and then, in later years, returned in the same role for Mrs. Franklin D. Roosevelt and Mrs. Harry S. Truman.

The President and Mrs. Galt appeared in public together on October 8, the day after their engagement was made public. They went to New York, where he visited Colonel House in his apartment at 115 East 53rd Street and she stayed at the St. Regis Hotel. While at House's apartment the President selected a diamond solitaire engagement ring from a number brought to him by a Fifth Avenue jeweler. That night they went to the Empire Theater to see Cyril Maude in Grumpy, a play by Horace Hodges and T. Wigney Percyval.

The next day the party went to Philadelphia for the second game in the baseball World Series, Philadelphia vs. Boston. This was Mrs. Galt's first appearance before a big crowd as the future First Lady, and she received a tremendous ovation, putting an end to the fears of some of Wilson's advisers that the public might resent her. The President threw out the first ball (this was the first time a President had ever attended a World Series game), and Boston won, 2 to 1.

The following day, Sunday, October 10, the couple went to Baltimore to spend the day with the President's brother, Joseph R. Wilson, and his family and to attend church services there. Then they returned to Washington, where the President dined that night with his fiancée at her house. Dismissing his automobile, he walked the few blocks back to the White House just before midnight, accompanied only by his Secret Service man.

The President was certainly appearing before the public in a new and more human light in these months. He delighted Washington by strolling out of the White House one day and walking into the nearby shopping district to buy a leather traveling bag. He accepted a bar of gold from the daughter of the owner of the oldest working gold mine in California to be made into a wedding band for the new Mrs. Wilson. He was pleased to be made an honorary member of the Bald Heads Club of America in a resolution that began, "Whereas all the world loves a lover . . ." When Mrs. Galt celebrated her forty-third birthday on October 15 he gave her a bracelet watch studded with diamonds.

No more letters dated in October appear in this collection. The couple were together daily. Their public appearances included a visit to the Belasco Theater to see a double bill of George Bernard Shaw's Androcles and the Lion *and Anatole France's* The Man Who Married a Dumb Wife *and several trips to Keith's Theater for vaudeville programs. On one occasion, they drove in the rain to Harpers Ferry, West Virginia, a distance of 72 miles, for a picnic outing. Another day it was to Point Lookout in southern Maryland. Several times a week the President went to Mrs. Galt's house for dinner to meet some of her relatives and friends he did not know. The sight of his Pierce Arrow parked in front of 1308 Twentieth Street became a familiar one in the neighborhood.*

NOVEMBER 1915

War news figured hardly at all in the letters for November;
they were concerned, rather, with preparations for the wedding.
All Washington seemed caught up in the event. Congress dis-
cussed the propriety of taking up a collection to buy a present.
While it argued, Vice President Thomas R. Marshall sent a
surprised Mrs. Galt his present, a Navajo Indian chief's blanket.
Mrs. Galt made an almost public project out of shopping for
her trousseau. Washington merchants (of whom she was one)
had been informed that she would buy most of her dresses in
the capital, but she also turned up in stores in Baltimore and
New York. As the month began she was in New York on a
buying trip, and the President addressed a letter to her at the
St. Regis Hotel:

w.w. to e.b.g.

Washington
1 November 1915
Monday evening

My precious Darling,

It is just a few minutes before dinner time. I will begin this
little epistle now and finish it after dinner, before I go to work
on a revision of the statement the Secretary of War wants to
publish about our preparation for national defense. Grayson
and I played 18 holes of golf at the Columbia [Country Club]
course. (I won.) I have had my bath and dressed . . . I feel
fine not a bit too tired. Grayson examined the "whelp" on my
back and makes nothing of it. The bone, he says, is absolutely

all right. One of the ligaments on one side of it seems to have slipped a little and can be felt over the vertebra but will come all right of itself. The back feels a little better every day and the inconvenience it gives me now is really negligible.

After Dinner

We had a little adventure on the golf course. Before we had got out of range from the seventh tee a fool drove off from it and his ball (fortunately at the end of its flight and when most of its force was spent) hit Grayson on the fleshy part of his leg. It gave him only a painful bruise, but the extraordinary conduct of the player who was responsible made me so angry that I walked back to the tee and told him (I do not know what his name was) what I thought of it . . .

I must stop and get this off. My whole heart goes with it.

Your own
Woodrow

E.B.G. TO W.W.

Hotel St. Regis
New York
November 1, 1915

My own precious One —

What a long day this has been without you, and yet how near you have been in my heart and thoughts. It is now a quarter of 8 and I am just picturing you in the study at work and long so to slip in and put my arms about you . . . How I did hate to leave you on the sidewalk this morning and sail away in your car . . .

Now I will begin where we left off and tell you all we have done. I found Helen and Dr. Grayson at the station . . . the trip was uneventful and Mr. Jervis most attentive. When we got off the train there were Colonel House and Mr. Malone and the car you ordered for us.[1] And Mr. Malone had got rid of a lot of reporters and apparently no one followed us. They

---

[1] Dudley Field Malone (1882–1950) was a New York lawyer internationally known in later years as an advocate of liberal political causes. He was active in Democratic politics when he was a young man and went to Washington in 1913 when Wilson appointed him third assistant Secretary of State.

[Malone and House] came to the hotel and Mr. Malone asked us for a theater party Wednesday night . . .[2] Here at the hotel we were welcomed with open arms and have such nice rooms with a little sitting room which is filled with flowers . . . We decided we would walk down Fifth Avenue and Mr. Jervis went with us. He said there were a number of newspapermen here but that they had promised not to do anything impertinent . . .

We went to three places for dresses and saw some lovely things but decided to look further before positively deciding . . .

Thank you precious, for the flowers, the car, Mr. Jervis and Helen — and remember that I love you with all my heart.

Always your own
Edith

I am sharing honors here with His Excellency the Governor of New York [Charles S. Whitman] and it is great fun seeing who creates the greatest excitement.

The President, remaining behind in Washington, was seeing various callers at the White House. One of them impressed him very much:

w.w. to e.b.g.

Washington
3 November 1915
Wednesday

My precious Darling,

. . . My most interesting interview today has been with Mr. Herbert Hoover, the chairman of the Belgian Relief Commission. I wish you could meet him. He is a real man, and came to me for a little help against a member of the committee in New York who is seeking to make trouble for him — help which I gladly gave. He is an American mining engineer living in London, one of the very ablest men we have sent over there, and has devoted his great organizing gifts and a large part of his fortune, too, to keep nine million people alive (at a cost of

---

2 The play at the Cort Theater was *The Princess Pat,* a comic opera by Victor Herbert, starring Eleanor Painter.

$10 million a day!) so that he has become a great international figure. Such men stir me deeply and make me in love with duty! . . .

Your own
Woodrow

On November 4 Wilson went to New York for an important speech at the Democratic Manhattan Club on the occasion of its 50th anniversary. It was on Preparedness. He had formulated his plans for a larger Army and Navy and he revealed them here. They led ultimately to an enlarged Army (220,000 men), integration of the National Guard into the national defense system, creation of an Officers Reserve Corps, the building of a large number of new battleships and cruisers for the Navy, an appropriation of $50 million for construction of new merchant ships, and the creation of a Council for National Defense to coordinate industries and resources. The President considered his program a moderate one, but nevertheless it set off one of his hardest political fights and occupied much of his time until its enactment in the summer of 1916.

After the speech, Wilson remained in New York overnight and returned to Washington on November 5 with Mrs. Galt.

On Saturday, November 27, the couple were back in New York for a visit. They saw the Army-Navy football game at the Polo Grounds in the afternoon (Army won 14 to 10), and that night they went to the Globe Theater to see a musical, Chin Chin, *where the audience laughed at these lines of the heroine:*

"It's the poor little widow who causes half of the trouble in the world."

They spent Sunday there too, Wilson as the guest of Colonel House and Mrs. Galt with Gertrude Gordon at 12 West Tenth Street. They attended services Sunday morning at the Fifth Avenue Presbyterian Church and then went for an automobile ride and later dinner at Miss Gordon's. Wilson left about midnight to return to Washington, but Mrs. Galt stayed in New York. She was being accompanied everywhere by a Secret Serice man, as threatening letters had been received. One man was taken into custody because of his persistence in trying to get her attention. (He explained that all he wanted was to get her help in marketing an invention he'd made, an egg carrier.)

W.W. TO E.B.G.

Washington
[November 29, 1915]
5:25 P.M.

My precious Darling,
  Just twenty-four hours ago you were sitting on the side of your bed in your wrapper writing the little note Murphy handed me this morning just as we were walking away from the train. My Darling, how incomparably sweet and lovely you are! The little piece of paper thrilled me when I took it from Murphy as if it had been a touch of your dear hand . . . That little piece of paper in my pocket, its contents in my heart, has made the whole day different. It has been as if my Darling were here — and the work has gone finely! . . .
  Politics has begun to boil. The Democrats of the Senate are here working on their organization for the Senate and men whom we will have to side-track are trying to get control. I've been interrupted twice since I began this note to give counsel as to what is to be done, and can see that things are from this time on going to grow hotter and hotter. But I am not made nervous by a fight — and I shall have you . . .
  I am in every thought and wish and purpose
Your own
Woodrow

E.B.G. TO W.W.

12 West Tenth Street — New York
November 30, 1915

My precious One,
  Now to give an account of myself . . . We went to M. Kurzman's Sons and saw some very lovely things and I got an afternoon dress . . . Then we went to A. Jaeckel and Co., the fur store and saw such really lovely furs and I was recklessly extravagant in your gift of a coat. They will make it to order for me of caracul and a border of Yukon (which is white fox)

colored and the price would be nearly a thousand dollars but they will make it for *me* for $475. Don't faint or think I have gone crazy but it was just so pretty I couldn't help it! although my conscience hurts me dreadfully and I want to come and sit in your lap and have you tell me you love me even if I am extravagant . . .

Your own
Edith

W.W. TO E.B.G.

Washington
30 November 1915
Tuesday

My precious Sweetheart,
　. . . I am *so* happy, Sweetheart, about the fur coat. It sounds like a great bargain, — but I would have been delighted to pay the full price. You are *not* extravagant — you are only doing what I begged you to do! It is delightful that you have found something *really* beautiful and satisfactory. So many of the fur garments they are making now seem freakish in shape and purpose both. Your success yesterday raises hopes for [her return] Wednesday night . . .

　I did not play golf today because there were so many little things to do, and the morning was full of the Cabinet and miscellaneous engagements. The town is filling up with members of Congress so fast that there are very few hours I can call my own. — The baby has another tooth. I believe that is the only real important piece of news. And the Message (to Congress) went to the printer this morning. But what fills all my thought is that you love me . . .

Your own
Woodrow

DECEMBER 1915

The last month of 1915 was a dark one for the Allies. In Western Europe the Central Powers had established a secure fortress; their communications and supply networks were working well. There had been two million casualties on the Western Front so far, but it was still in a stalemate. Russia had suffered her greatest casualties, two million killed and wounded and another million in German prison camps since August 1914. Submarines were still sinking Allied vessels.

At home Wilson walked a tightrope of neutrality and pushed ahead with plans to rearm the country. In a speech in St. Louis he said of the conflagration in Europe: "We must keep our resources and our strength and our thoughts untouched by that flame in order that we may be in a condition to serve the restoration of the world, the healing processes. The world will not endure, I believe, another struggle like that which is going on now."

Once again he decided to send Colonel House to Europe, this time to talk about his ideas for the future peace of the world: military and naval disarmament and a league of nations to suppress aggression and to maintain the freedom of the seas. The Colonel sailed on December 28.

The domestic political campaign of 1916 was coming up; the President was also the leader of his party and he had to keep an eye on that. Even if his renomination came off as expected, he faced a bitterly fought challenge by the Republicans who were already criticizing him severely.

There was a brighter side, however; preparations were going

on at the White House and at 1308 Twentieth Street for a wedding. The date remained a secret, but gifts were already pouring in: Every manufacturer, producer, and merchant wanted to send a sample of his wares. A man in Frederick, Maryland, sent a fruit cake that was fifty years old. Everything from alabaster lamps to barrels of sugared popcorn, from furniture to mineral water, from brooms and dusters to sixteenth-century Ming bowls, diamond and sapphire brooches to soap, bearskin rugs from the frozen North and lace tablecloths from Puerto Rico — all were taxing government storage space and creating problems otherwise. A policy was finally established that presents of appreciable value from people who were not known to either of the principals would be returned. Newspapers and letters brought all kinds of suggestions about the ceremony. A man from Philadelphia offered his trained canary to sing.

On December 10 the President went to Columbus, Ohio, to make a speech on preparedness before the Chamber of Commerce. Mrs. Galt wrote him a letter so that he would know she was thinking about him when he arrived there:

E.B.G. TO W.W.

Washington
December 9 [1915]

My own Precious One . . .

. . . I am sending this little message of inexpressible love to greet you tomorrow morning when you are so many miles away.

It can't be anything but just a message, for I had so much rather talk to you than to write. But nothing ever written or spoken can ever tell you how completely you make the world for me, or how I shall miss you these next two days.

I am so infinitely proud of you and feel so exalted above other women in having your love that I feel I must do some wonderful thing in the world to prove my wish to serve you.

Don't be blue, Precious. We are not *really* apart. And Saturday will soon be here. And then *no more journeys!*

With all my love
Your own
Edith

*On Thursday December 16 Chief Usher Hoover boarded a
streetcar in front of the White House and rode a few blocks
to the office of the clerk of the Supreme Court of the District
of Columbia, paid $1, and applied for marriage license No.
72225 for Woodrow Wilson, fifty-eight, of 1600 Pennsylvania
Avenue, and Edith Bolling Galt, forty-three, of 1308 Twentieth
Street.*

*Two days later they were married in a ceremony at Edith's
house on Twentieth Street, and there were "a few over" 50
guests present, all members of the families of the bride and
the bridegroom. Chief Usher Hoover had been given the job
of decorating the small house (it was only two rooms deep),
and he did it with relish. He took all the furniture out of the
front drawing room, turned its bay window into an altar, and
lined it with heather. He attached red roses and orchids to the
walls. From a perch on the third floor, an orchestra from the
Marine Band mingled "Hail to the Chief" with "Here Comes
the Bride."*

*The bridegroom arrived at 8 o'clock for the 8:30 ceremony,
and Hoover was on hand to see that everything went without
a hitch. The bride was dressed in black velvet, and her dashing
black hat was trimmed with a goura feather that swept her
cheek. She wore a diamond brooch, a gift from the bridegroom.
The President was in a cutaway coat. The ceremony was per-
formed by Mrs. Galt's pastor, Dr. Herbert Scott Smith of St.
Margaret's Episcopal church, and Wilson's pastor, Dr. James
H. Taylor of the Central Presbyterian church. When Dr. Smith
said, "Who gives this woman in marriage to this man?" her
mother, proud and beaming, stepped forward — a touching
moment for all the family present.*

*Although crowds gathered in the street outside the house,
the police kept them at a distance so that when the couple left
to go to their train for the honeymoon trip they had no trouble
in getting away. An elaborate scheme had been set up by
Hoover and the Secret Service to make reporters believe that
the President and his bride would leave from the Union Station, but instead their train left from there without them and
they drove to nearby Alexandria, Virginia, to board it. They
arrived before the train did (the President's punctuality never*

deserted him), and consequently they had to sit in the railroad yards in their limousine for 20 minutes until it finally arrived at 11:45.

The honeymoon destination — a secret — was Hot Springs, Virginia. The train had a private car for the Wilsons and ample accommodations for their large party of Secret Service men, communications officers, emergency office aides, and personal servants. It was an easy overnight ride to Hot Springs. Colonel Starling of the Secret Service recounted in his book that early the next morning, after the train reached its destination, he went into the Presidential car, walked down the corridor flanking the bedrooms, and "suddenly my ear caught the note of a familiar melody. Emerging into the sitting room I saw a figure in a top hat, tailcoat and gray morning trousers, standing with his back to me, hands in his pockets, happily dancing a jig. As I watched him he clicked his heels in the air, and from whistling the tune he changed into singing the words, 'Oh, you beautiful doll! You great big beautiful doll . . .!' "

At the Homestead Hotel the honeymooners devoted their days to golf (sometimes it was too snowy) and motor rides (snow didn't stop them, even when the mountain roads were treacherous). The President attended to only the most pressing business; some papers were brought to him from Washington and he was in daily touch with Secretary Lansing, but the next two weeks were pleasant, comparatively idle ones. Mrs. Wilson wrote letters and sorted messages of congratulation. They were in their own special section of the hotel and saw little of the other guests, but their presence was the most important fact in the hotel's holiday season. On Christmas day they had their turkey dinner in their own dining room, while back at the White House the efficient Hoover had seen to it that every employee received the customary gift of a turkey from the President in his absence. On December 28 Wilson celebrated his fifty-ninth birthday anniversary by cutting an almond sponge cake decorated with candy roses and tulips designed by his bride.

The days of snowy drives and happy birthdays were interrupted, however, before the time came to celebrate the New Year. On Thursday, December 30, a British passenger steamer, the Persia, bound from London to Bombay, was torpedoed and sunk in the Mediterranean with considerable loss of life. Some casualties, it was feared, were Americans. That news was still on the President's mind on Saturday, New Year's Day, when he and Mrs. Wilson went to the hotel's lounge for a reception for all the other guests and for people from the surrounding countryside.

The President decided the next day that he should cut short his vacation on account of the Persia, and on the morning of the 4th he and his bride returned to Washington; she went to the White House to take up her role as official hostess (she hated the title "First Lady"), a role that was to fill all her time and energies and to keep her steadily in the limelight for the next five years.

Three days later she and the President entertained at their first White House reception. The guests included the delegates to a Pan American Congress, and more than 3000 people were there. The new Mrs. Wilson was resplendent in a gown brocaded in silver, with white tulle draperies called "angel sleeves." She fell easily into her new role and recorded later in her biography what a thrill it was "to greet all the Cabinet in the Oval Room upstairs and then with the President to precede them down the long stairway with the naval and military aides forming an escort, the Marine playing 'Hail to the Chief' and the waiting mass of guests bowing a welcome as we passed." The Washington Star, whose writers were the most knowledgeable commentators on the social scene, said: "The President's bride made a wonderfully charming impression."

Weightier thoughts occupied the President's mind. The year 1915, which had brought him such personal happiness, was ending with few if any of the world's pressing problems any nearer solution. He knew that because of the war in Europe he still faced the most momentous decisions any President had faced, perhaps in our entire history. His efforts to keep the United States neutral seemed headed for failure. The notes of protest to Germany and the remonstrances to England were ineffectual in enforcing our neutral rights. He would not be rushed into war, but he was deeply aware of the possibility of war and of the need for the country to be prepared. Thus, his *major domestic efforts in the first months of 1916 were directed to his preparedness program.*

To complicate matters, since 1916 was an election year, distasteful as it was to him, Wilson had to get himself renominated and re-elected. There was no trouble about the nomination; it was his by acclamation at the convention in St. Louis. The election turned out to be a different matter. The campaign took more of his energy than he thought he should give it, and he was, also, apprehensive over the Democratic slogan: "He kept us out of war."

The new Mrs. Wilson was at his side in all his political travels. She was an asset not only in the party councils but on the stump as well, in some very unexpected ways: On one occasion, in Omaha, when he was speaking to a gathering of Indian voters, she was introduced to the crowd as a direct descendant of Pocahontas.

The election turned out to be a surprise. For many hours after the polls closed it appeared that Wilson had been defeated by the Republican candidate, Supreme Court Justice Charles Evans Hughes. It was not until two days later, when the returns were in from California, that he was declared the winner by 277 electoral votes to 254.

The election behind him, Wilson immediately renewed his appeals to the belligerents in Europe to stop the war. They had no effect; in fact, Germany resumed the ruthless submarine warfare it had modified the previous year after American protests. In the months of mounting troubles and tensions that followed, it was clear that all moves to keep the nation's honor and its interests intact were failing; and on April 2, 1917, Wilson asked Congress for a declaration of war. "The world must be made safe for democracy," he said, and it became a battle cry of irresistible force. In the next year and a half the United States put all its efforts into the war, and in an incredible burst of energy and dedication built up an army of four million men. Two million of them served overseas, and more than fifty thousand died in battle.

The war brought to Wilson the added role of spokesman for the Allies, and when it ended he was at the summit of world influence. Because he was the acknowledged leader of the victorious Allies his decision to violate tradition and go in person to the peace conference in Paris was accepted as necessary. With Mrs. Wilson at his side, he sailed for Europe in December 1918, and she shared in the ovations when adoring crowds in France and England and Italy hailed him as the savior of the world.

He returned to America in July 1919 after the signing of the Versailles peace treaty, and his subsequent losing battle in the Senate for the treaty and the League of Nations, whose purpose was to be nothing less than the outlawing of war forever, is one of the most dramatic stories in our history. The drama involved Mrs. Wilson directly when, after long months of work and strain, the President collapsed in Colorado in September, while on a speaking tour for the League, and returned to Washington a very ill man. It was then that she became a figure of the greatest controversy.

The President's seizure on the trip was followed quickly by a paralytic stroke on October 2 in the White House. He was confined to his bed after the stroke, and he still had a year and five months more in office. Whether he was able to discharge the powers and duties of the office as required by the Constitution was the question that was not answered then and probably never will be answered. Mrs. Wilson undertook the role in his life that led some historians to call her "the first woman President of the United States." She acted as intermediary between him and his associates so completely that they felt she was in charge. Direct information on his condition was lacking, and the ugliest rumors arose, rumors that even said he was insane. For the next six and a half months, from October 1919 to April 1920, he was out of direct touch with all his associates, even Cabinet members. His wife alone decided what matters should be brought before him, summarized them, and then took his decisions to the Cabinet. This aroused intense resentment. A Senate committee, acting under the guise of talking to him about something else, insisted on seeing him and went to the White House to find out if he was mentally competent, although suspicions did not disappear. Mrs. Wilson did not relax her watchfulness even when the President recovered enough the next spring to hold Cabinet meetings. She was there through the slow, closing months of his Presidency and until his departure from the White House on March 4, 1921, a broken and ill man. While historians are still divided on the extent of her participation, Mrs. Wilson defended her role to the end: "Woodrow Wilson was first my beloved husband whose life I was trying to save," she wrote in My Memoir, "fighting with my back to the wall, and after that he was the President of the United States."

The President bought and presented to his wife a handsome house at 2340 S Street, Northwest, in the Kalorama section of Washington, a section of embassies and mansions. He died there on February 3, 1924. Mrs. Wilson remained in the house for the rest of her life, years in which she took an active part in the social and political life of Washington and lost no opportunity to do anything to preserve Woodrow Wilson's place in history. Erect, white-haired, and clear-eyed, she was a figure of distinction, dressed always in the latest style, an orchid in place and a modish hat tilted at an angle. No Democratic social function had the proper éclat without her. In one of her last public appearances, at the Inauguration of John F. Kennedy in 1961, she received applause from the crowds and a kiss on the cheek from Harry S. Truman.

In that same year — on December 28th, Wilson's 105th birthday anniversary — a bridge across the Potomac River connecting Maryland and Virginia was dedicated to his memory. Mrs. Wilson was to have been present, but she was too ill to appear. That night she died. She was eighty-nine and had outlived her husband by thirty-seven years. She was buried in a crypt near his tomb in the Washington Cathedral.

Mrs. Wilson left the house on S Street to the National Trust for Historic Preservation as a permanent memorial to her husband. Everything remained exactly as it had been when he died; the books he was reading were on his bedside table — Milton's Poems, Lamb's Letters, and a now all-but-forgotten book that was popular when he was young, Ik Marvel's The Reveries of a Bachelor. The house is a large and formal one, but there are old and much-used pieces of her own family furniture that recall 1308 Twentieth Street, and here and there, an odd memento, casual and surely there by pure chance, to recall 1915, the year of their meeting and courtship: a framed card enrolling Wilson as an honorary member of the Bricklayers, Masons and Plasterers' International Union dated April 6, 1915, just before his correspondence with Edith Galt began, and a copy of his book Mere Literature, *autographed for Bertha Bolling on June 22 when he was reasonably sure that she would be his sister-in-law, and a silver loving cup inscribed to "Edith Bolling Galt from the Virginia Delegation in the 64th Congress" and dated December 18, 1915, the most important day in her life.*

LEE COUNTY LIBRARY
SANFORD, N. C.

Index

INDEX